Jezar Erkench
Dimotika
Tajardi
Makri
R. Maritza
Enos
Kishan
Ainajik
Rhodosto
Midiah
Eski Baba
Serai
Injighis
CONSTANTINOPLE
Pop. 500,000
Pera
Bosporus
Sakarieh
C. Baba
Eregli
Boli
MARMARA SEA
Xeros G.
Gallipoli
Erdek
Lamsaki
Muhalitch
Ulubad
Brusa
Olympus
Dardanells
Troy
Ru.
Tenedos
L. Manias
L. Abulionte
Susugherli
Mt. Ida
Adramyti
Kespit
Babikesri
R. Edrenos
Tashanli
Eski Shehr
R. Sakarieh
Saradi
Kestabeg
Sarila
Mitilini
Ayasma
A N A T O L I
Bergamo
Bogaditza
Singerli
Ru. of Azani
Kutayah
Sidi-Ghazi
Sevrihissar
Pop. 9000
Ak Dagh
Kirkagatch
Sandarli
Simaul
Ak Hissar
Chander
Alekiam
Hamza
Emir Dagh
Khio
Tumuli
Adala
Selendi
Ushak
Kodus
Manisa
Kasaba
Sart
Ext. Volcano
Koula
Ahat
Afiom Karahissar
Chesme
Smyrna
Pop. 130,000
Beinder
Tireh
Allah shehr
Sejikler
Sulimanli
Sandukli
Ishekli
Aineh
Scala Nuova
Samos
Ru. of Ephesus
Nazeli
Buladan
Dinair
L. Hoiran
Borlou
L. Eyerdir
Eyerdir
Yalobatch
Ru. of Antioch
Akshehr
Nikaria
Aidin
Inek
Eski Hissar
Pambuk
Chardak
Denizli
Isbarta
R. Meinder
Yerah
Ru. of Alabanda
Palatia
Ru.
Karaiouk
Buldour
Allahsoun
Ru. of Sagalassus
Mt. Taurus
Naxia
Patmos
Melasso
Eskihissar
Ru. of Selge
Ru. of Termessus
Lero
Boudroum
Moulah
L. Ghiul
Katra
Adalia
Amorgo
Kalimno
Kos
Marmar
Dolomon
M. Climax
Almali
Pop. 20,000
Tlos
Rashat
Ru. of Side
Menavgat
Stampalia
Nisyro
Symi
Makry
Avlan
Tekrova
Piscopi
Plaka
Karki
Rhodes
Seven Capes
Yanar
Ru. of Patara and Xanthus
Kastelorizo I.
Kakava
Myra
Phineka
Grambusa
Stazida
Scarpanto
C. Khelidonia
Caxo
C. Salmone
C. Xakro
Koupho
C. Epiphan
D I A

BRITAIN'S GREEK EMPIRE

BRITAIN'S GREEK EMPIRE

Reflections on the history of the Ionian Islands
from the fall of Byzantium

MICHAEL PRATT

PHOTOGRAPHS BY
PHILIP BOUCAS

REX COLLINGS LONDON 1978

First published in Great Britain by
Rex Collings Ltd, 69 Marylebone High Street
London, W1

ISBN 0860360253

Typesetting by Malvern Typesetting Services Ltd
Printed and bound in Great Britain by
The Westerham Press, Kent

Foreword

The Ionian Islands are of especial interest to the student of Hellenic History for, situated as they are off the extreme western coast of mainland Greece, they have stood apart from the rest of the country, and their fortunes and development have not always run parallel with that of Greece proper.

Even in Classical times they were still thought of as alien and mysterious, and Corcyra (Corfu), the most important of the group—although second in size to Cephalonia—was reputed to be Homer's mythical Scheria, the Isle of the Poseidon-favoured Phaeacians.

Because of their geographical position, the Ionian Islands have served as stepping-stones between Greece and Western Europe. While the mainland passed under the sway of an Eastern despotism, the Ottoman Empire, for over three and a half centuries after the Fall of Constantinople, these islands were subject to Venice and thus were never cut off from Western influences. This is still reflected in their culture, their customs, their language (the *patois* of the Ionian Islands retains Italian words—that of the rest of Greece, Turkish) and even their folk-music. Their characteristic love-songs or *Kantades* well exemplify the tendency towards western rather than eastern melodies.

The long Venetian domination, an enlightened one compared with Ottoman rule on the mainland, did not, however, particularly encourage local culture and literary traditions. This trend was completely reversed when the Seven Islands became an 'independent' State under the more liberal British Protectorate (1815–1864), and especially after the founding of the Ionian Academy in 1824 by the philhellene Frederick North, Fifth Earl of Guilford.

During the short space of sixty years which comprised and immediately followed this period, the 'Septinsular Republic' became the intellectual focus of a Greece which was then only just emerging from its long night of servitude. A wonderful flowering of talent suddenly took place, including such names as the poets Dionysios Solomos, Iakovos Polylas (who numbered several translations of Shakespeare among his works), Gerasimos Markoras, Andreas Kalvos, Aristotelis Valaoritis, Lavrentios Mavilis; the novelist Constantine Theotokis, and the historian Andreas Moustoxidis. With the exception of Solomos, none of these writers can, perhaps, be enrolled in the first rank of genius, but they all influenced the development of Modern Greek letters to a very marked extent.

The ratio of above average ability among the population of the islands was far greater than normal, repeating on a small scale those two great upsurges of human genius: the City-states of Ancient Greece and of Renaissance Italy.

This phenomenon, which appears to bear out the contention of certain classical philosophers that the population of an independent State ought not to exceed the number of ten thousand adult citizens should it wish to attain the highest intellectual level, greatly enhances the interest of Lord Michael Pratt's present book. Its contents will prove a valuable source of information not only to the historian, but also to all students of human psychology and of the effects of government upon man's nature and cultural development.

TH. P. STEPHANIDES

Contents

List of Photographs

Acknowledgements

So many people have been helpful and kind to me during the three and a half years I have spent writing this book that it would be impossible to mention them all. But to a number of friends in England, Greece and elsewhere I am particularly indebted:

Doctor Theodore Stephanides for writing the foreword and providing much sage advice for the text; Sir Steven Runciman for his hospitality and for allowing us to photograph his collection of paintings by Edward Lear; Robin Lane Fox for his shrewd and witty comments on my efforts to unravel the islands' classical past; and the late Mr Panaghis Vergottis for interesting me in the whole idea originally. My thanks also go to Mr Alexander Philon formerly at the Greek Embassy in London, to Professor Brian Pullan, to Mr Richard Brain of the Oxford University Press, Professor Douglas Dakin of Birkbeck College, London University, to Mr and Mrs John Frangos, Mr Nicos Vlassoupoulos and Mr Stelio Hourmouzios. My gratitude to the staff of the London Library for helping me with my erratic researches is incalculable as is my debt to Anne Hopetoun, who patiently helped me compile the index.

In Athens I am especially grateful to Mr John Phrantzes for his unfailing hospitality; to Mr Lambros Eftaxia for permitting us to photograph in the Benaki Museum and to Mrs Stathis, who took great trouble to research into Ionian history since 1864. Mr and Mrs Evangelis Averoff, Dr Prevelaikis of the Academy of Athens, Professor D. Zakythinos, Count Dionysios Romas and Professor M. Hadzidakis have also been more than kind. Moreover, but for the assistance of the officials of ELPA the Automobile Club of Greece, of the Greek National Tourist Office in Athens and Corfu, and of Ambassador Tsamados of the cultural department of the Foreign Ministry, I doubt that I should have ever got my trips organized.

More people in the Ionian Islands than I could possibly enumerate were helpful to me; from the nomarchs, who gave me their time, to the shepherd in Levkas who gave us yoghurt and bunches of grapes.

I must however mention Mrs E. M. Brooke-Tsatsopoulos, formerly H. M. Vice-Consul in Corfu, Dr P. Calligas, formerly Director of the Museum there and his successor Dr A. Choremis, Mr John Kollas, Miss Marie Aspioti, Mr Piero

Kourkoumelis and his mother Mrs Mary Kourkoumelis, Mr Nondas Stamatopoulos and Mr Mouhas who allowed me to use the Reading Room's splendid library. In Cephalonia Mr and Mrs Marinos Cosmetatos aided me unstintingly: so did Mrs Forresti; while in Zante Dr Nicholas Barbianis, Mr Charalambos Zoïs and Mrs Chronopoulos were kind and hospitable. In Kythera my thanks go to Mr Byron Dapontis, and to the long-suffering police force who drove me round and round the island in their jeep. Finally to Captain Frank Nash, who navigated his yacht around the islands for a fortnight to enable us to take all the photographs we needed.

In Venice I owe a great debt of gratitude to Madame Marietta Guetta Stern, who arranged for my research work there, undertaken initially by Mr Shaw and completed by her granddaughter, Sonia Pasquali; also to Sir Ashley Clarke, Professor Pertusi of the Fondazione Cini, Professor Manoussakas of the Instituto Ellenico and the late Mr Ronald Shaw-Kennedy. Last but by no means least there is Philip Boucas. Without him and his wife, Maria, and all their friendly advice and encouragement, I doubt I would ever have finished this book nor would I have the marvellous photographs which illustrate and supplement the text.

Introduction

'Ye isles beyond the Adriatic wave,
Whose classic shores Ionian waters lave!
Ye plains of Greece! The Muses' ancient pride,
Whose rising beauties crown the western tide.'

So wrote Waller Rodwell Wright, Consul-General in the Ionian Islands during the Napoleonic Wars. His enthusiasm was, alas, greater than his poetic talents. Yet he was one of a long line of visitors, before and since, who have been captivated by the charm of the islands. Their landscape is greener and gentler than most of mainland Greece, which is perhaps why Corfu has remained for so long a favourite with the British. Nor do they lack rugged, barren scenery, particularly in Cephalonia, where the dramatic grandeur of the mountains bears comparison with anything the Balkans have to offer. Nowadays they may seem to be little more than developing or already over-developed tourist areas. But the Ionians represent a cultural and historical synthesis unique in the Mediterranean.

My interest in the islands was first aroused when a friend suggested I should write a short history of one of them. On closer examination to consider one island in isolation from the other six appeared to me a folly. The Ionian heritage, a blend of Greek, Italian and English, with traces of Turkish, French, and Russian occupations, should not be judged by such parochial criteria. In classical times the islands stood on the western fringe of the Greek world, a meeting-point of Hellenic and Roman civilization; more recently they were the easternmost limit of Christian Europe, where the Ottoman Empire began on the other side of the narrow straits.

This book provides a study of them in the nineteenth century when, in under seventy years, they emerged from the Venetian sway, saw a change of as many as five foreign masters, and ultimately fulfilled their historic destiny of reunion with the rest of Greece. It would however be meaningless to attempt this without a substantial introduction, concentrating in particular on the centuries of Venetian rule, the most vital formative influence on Ionian history. And, in the hope that the reader will not have reached 1864 with unmitigated relief, an account of them in the last hundred years is included as well.

Historically the Ionian Islands represent a stage in our own imperial past, when the buccaneering spirit of eighteenth century mercantilism was giving way before the conscientious administrators of mid-Victorian England. Perhaps the British Protectorate with figures like Maitland, Napier and Guilford belonged to a more carefree age than that of the Indian Mutiny and 'the white man's burden'. It also affords an interesting comparison with Venetian colonial policy, both when 'the Queen of the Adriatic' was at the zenith of her power and in the last stages of decay.

The Ionian cultural heritage is remarkable too. After Crete fell to the Turks, the islands were the last haven of Byzantine tradition, the setting in which its painting gradually blended with Western art. The Ionian school is a peculiarly effective mixture of East and West, and deserves more general recognition. Similarly, the islanders' musical and literary talents were vigorous and original enough to promote a cultural resurgence in late nineteenth century Greece, while the graduates from the Ionian Academy provided most of the academics and civil servants in their newly independent mother-country, where even Athens lacked a university until 1837. The irony is that today the islands do not contain one institute of higher education.

As always, history has its limitations. A lack of material for some periods is balanced by a plethora for others. From the beginnings of Roman rule until about 1500, when all the islands except Levkas were reunited under the Lion Banner of St Mark, there are few sources specifically concerned with them, so their evolution must be viewed in a wider context. In recent times, when the Ionians constitute a small proportion of their native race, the same fact applies.

The subject has been treated chronologically, as to do so island by island would involve endless duplication, and would of necessity concentrate the bulk of the material on Corfu. Inevitably on so broad a canvas, some of it is superficial. No proper catalogue of the Venetian archives exists, nor have all the documents in the islands been thoroughly sorted yet. As far as the British Protectorate is concerned, all the papers are readily available, but there is far too much to be fitted into a volume of this size. Finally, I hope the text will not be found too confusing. An attempt to keep to the same names and spellings throughout has been difficult. Corcyra was known as such from classical times to the Middle Ages, and thereafter as Corfu, while it is Kerkira to the modern Greeks; Zakynthos and Kythera were called Zante and Cerigo by the Venetians, in the first case I prefer the Italian, in the second the Greek form.

Levkas was usually described as Santa Maura by the Venetians, a name hardly ever used today. Grappling with Greek and Italian nomenclature is no easy job, and my spelling may not always appeal to the reader.

A general map should prove a useful aid to understanding the geographical setting of the islands and their relationship to the mainland nearby. The book includes many photographs to portray the beauties, natural, architectural and artistic of the Ionian Islands. Most were taken especially to illustrate this book, although a few are older, showing towns, buildings or scenes before the catastrophic earthquake of 1953 devastated Cephalonia, Zante and Ithaca.

This brief introduction will, I trust, serve to show why the Ionian Islands (Corfu, Paxos, Levkas, Cephalonia, Ithaca, Zante and Kythera with their appendages) occupy a unique place in the culture and history of the Mediterranean, indeed of all Europe. Surely no author needs a better apologia than that?

In memory of my beloved mother

Chapter I

BACKGROUND

Burckhardt once remarked that history is the one field of study where it is impossible to begin at the beginning. This is a truism for any book about the Ionian Islands, which have traces of human settlement as old as any in Europe, where fact and fable blend almost indistinguishably and the legends of the Argonauts and of the Odyssey are a vital part of the Ionian past. It is, however, indisputable that the Corinthians founded a colony on Corfu, or Corcyra as it was known in the Ancient World, in the late eighth century B.C. This colony flourished and grew powerful; the rivalry with its erstwhile mother city culminated some three centuries later in a quarrel, which was to rank as one of the prime causes of the Peloponnesian War.

Amid the decay of Classical Greece the islands still seemed a desirable possession to a diversity of conquerors, Macedonian, Sicilian, and Epirote. Ultimately Corfu, with its mainland dependencies and neighbouring Paxos, became the first Roman Protectorate in Greece, although the whole country was soon engulfed in the spread of empire. The Ionians witnessed the struggle between Pompey and Julius Caesar, and that between Mark Antony and Octavian. Indeed, the battle of Actium, which decided the destiny of the then known world, was fought off the promontory facing Levkas.

The centuries of Roman and Byzantine rule saw a procession of distinguished visitors, the resurgence and the eventual decline of trade, while Christianity arrived early in the islands and took deep root. The Ionians endured their fair share of barbarian raids, and of the endless civil wars which afflicted the Eastern Empire during the Dark Ages. They were mostly incorporated in the Cephalonian Theme, one of the last to be created, in 800 A.D. By about 1000 A.D. stability had returned, and the islands were reckoned as one of the more prosperous parts of the Byzantine dominions. Most vestiges of their early history were, however, destined to disappear, thanks to earthquakes, piracy, vandalism, and subsequent looting by Venetian, French, and British collectors. But if the Ionian classical remains are scanty, the heritage they retained was sufficient to keep alive the spirit of their race and culture, their Greek national identity in essence, during the centuries of rule by alien overlords that lay ahead.

It had been the islands' fortune, good and bad, to serve as the stepping stones from west to east and vice versa. So in the late eleventh century, the Normans, who had recently established themselves in southern Italy, used them for their invasion of the Eastern Empire. Under the leadership of Duke Robert Guiscard (or the Cunning) they defeated the Byzantine army, commanded by the Emperor Alexius Comnenus in person. But before they could consolidate their triumph, Robert had died of typhoid at Phiscardo, the harbour in Cephalonia which bears his name today.

During the next century the Normans attacked the islands several times, while Byzantium's weakness necessitated the alliance with Venice, which gained its first footholds in the area. So when the Fourth Crusade captured Constantinople and dismembered the Eastern Empire in 1204, the Venetians added the Ionian Islands to their share of the booty. Although the Doge described himself as 'ruler of one quarter and a half quarter of the whole Empire of Romania', he and his colleagues realized that the Lion of St Mark had seized more than could be immediately digested. Therefore in July 1207, Corfu, Paxos, and the adjacent islands were transferred to ten Venetian nobles, on condition that the defences were maintained and an annual tribute of 500 gold pieces was paid. An especially privileged trading status was reserved for the Republic's subjects, although the Greeks too were protected, once they had sworn an oath of fealty, and the rights of the Orthodox church were respected.

In theory Venice had also gained Cephalonia, Ithaca and Zante by the treaty of partition. In fact these remained in the hands of the Orsini family, an Apulian cadet branch of the great Roman house. For the next 130 years or so they controlled their islands and expanded their power on the mainland through a series of ruthless and able successors to Count Matteo Orsini. Indeed, if Count John had not died in 1318, he would have been the most powerful as well as the most hated man in Frankish Greece.

Levkas was the only one of the Ionian Islands to remain in Greek control. Michael Angelus, a cousin of the deposed Byzantine Emperor, established his court at Arta, which formed a rallying point for the Greeks, submerged by the Latin conquests. The Despot of Epirus, as he styled himself, was careful to maintain a garrison on Levkas, to which, along with most of the rest of his dominions, Venice had laid claim. He soon expanded his power, capturing Corfu, where his rule acquired a solid foundation of popular support by wooing the Orthodox church and exempting the people from many taxes. The Angeli retained Corfu for some forty years, and Levkas for much longer, no mean achievement when almost all Greece was in Frankish hands.

Kythera's fate was somewhat different. In the partition it had been assigned to the Veniero family, on the grounds that the supposed birthplace of Venus should belong to the self-styled descendants of the goddess of love. Apart from a brief reoccupation by the Byzantine fleet, the island was to remain in the family's possession for centuries, while the neighbouring island of Antikythera similarly belonged to the Viari. However, the Republic in the mid-fourteenth century punished the Venieri for participating in the Cretan revolt, and thereafter Venice wielded the effective power.

Feudalism only came slowly to the islands. Corfu was not properly divided into fiefs until it was added to the dominions of Charles of Anjou, King of Naples, in 1267. Thereafter the island was divided into four bailiwicks and twenty-four fiefs. The land was either royal demense or held by the barons directly of the Crown. Already the elements of local institutions were apparent; a Council, originally composed of the Latin barons, but rapidly expanding to include many citizens and foreigners, a hierarchy of officials elected by the Council, and a High Court of Justice or *Curia Regis*. The Angevin regime was religiously intolerant but favoured Corfu as a strategic base and a lucrative asset. In the other islands the feudal system was neither so widespread nor so effective.

In the tortuous labyrinth of mediaeval Greece, many actors flit across the Ionian stage: Angevin, Aragonese, Venetian, Genoese, and Byzantine. Suffice it to say that the Eastern Empire was recaptured from the Latins, but under the auspices of the Palaeologi, not the Angeli; that the Despotate of Epirus, which had passed to the Orsini, was extinguished along with its rulers; and that a new dynasty, the Tocchi, had gained control of Cephalonia, Zante, Ithaca, and Levkas by the 1360s. Veteran Neapolitan courtiers, they were to remain distinctively Italian and Catholic, and were indeed destined to be the last Latin dynasty in the Levant.

For by 1400 all the petty rivalries of Greek and Frank were overshadowed by the gigantic looming threat of the Ottoman Turks. Their advance had been meteoric; the Byzantine Empire had sunk to the status of a tributary state, while the Balkan powers, Bulgar or Serb, had been crushed. If Sultan Bajazet 'The Thunderbolt' had not been defeated by Timurlane's Mongol hordes, Constantinople would certainly have fallen fifty years earlier. As it was, rulers like the Tocchi continually sent emissaries to Adrianople to assure the Sultan of their goodwill, and readily abandoned their allies in the face of a Turkish advance through the Isthmus of Corinth.

It was the Corfiotes' good fortune that their sovereign was no longer the decrepit Kingdom of Naples, but Venice, one of the few maritime powers able and willing to resist Ottoman aggression. After some years of anarchy, the barons had been unable to agree whom to acknowledge as their overlord. Those who advocated loyalty to the Angevin monarch, Ladislaus, were overruled by a faction, who offered their island to Francesco Carrara, Lord of Padua. He promptly sent troops to occupy the fortress. At this stage the Venetians intervened. The prevailing instability was bad for trade; while Carrara was their deadly enemy and the ally of Genoa. Thanks to the persuasive eloquence of Giovanni Miani, the Captain of the Gulf, the islanders hoisted the Banner of St. Mark again after 170 years, and the opposition groups soon came to terms.

By the negotiations concluded in 1387, the Doge guaranteed the observation of all the Corfiotes' traditional privileges, confirmed all fiefs and titles of nobility, and merely stipulated that justice should be governed by Greek and Venetian laws, while no native could be tried outside the island, except on appeal to him. In return, the community surrendered its time-honoured exemption from taxes and tolls, provided the walls were repaired. The Republic's promise never to dispose of Corfu, and to undertake its defence, was enshrined in the Golden Bull, thenceforth referred to as the charter of the island's liberties. The recently appointed bailie, Marino Malipiero, restored order and obtained the restitution of much municipal property illegally seized. Venice's rights of suzerainty were formalized in 1402, when Corfu and its dependencies were bought from the Angevins for 30,000 gold ducats.

During the fifteenth century the islands prospered. Levkas, or Santa Maura as it was called by the Latins, became the capital of the Tocco principality, and housed an elegant and erudite court inside a formidable castle. Cephalonia is recorded as having two large harbours; Same on the east and Argostoli on the west coast, over 6,000 houses, and a population of 40,000; while Zante held over 25,000 inhabitants. The Tocchi's revenues amounted to over 12,000 ducats per annum, almost enough to qualify the duchy for a kingdom. It was a pity that religious affairs were not handled with the same dexterity as were commercial affairs; only in 1452, fearing that their Greek subjects 'might prefer the mufti's turban to the Cardinal's hat', did the Tocchi revive the Orthodox bishopric of Cephalonia, with jurisdiction over their other islands.

It was, alas, too late. The next year Constantinople fell to the Turks, and within a few years the Ottoman armies had occupied Greece. Some 30,000 refugees, many of them of distinguished origins, poured into the islands.

Virtually unaided the Republic was forced to fight the strongest military power since Imperial Rome. The Tocchi quickly lost their dominions, and when they expelled the weak Turkish garrisons from Zante and Cephalonia in 1481, the irritated Venetians expelled them in their turn. By the treaty of 1485 the Republic ceded Cephalonia and Ithaca to the Sultan, keeping Zante on payment of a 500 ducat annual tribute. When war resumed in 1499, the recapture of Cephalonia and Levkas were among the few Venetian triumphs, nor would the Sultan make peace until he had had the latter restored to him. Six of the Ionian islands were indeed lucky to escape the cultural void and dulling oppression of Ottoman rule, which was to endure in Greece until Morosini's transient reconquest at the end of the seventeenth century.

Chapter II

A. THE CROSS AND THE CRESCENT

For the first thirty years of the sixteenth century a precarious peace prevailed throughout Greece. The cautious Venetians maintained a strict neutrality in the war then raging between the Ottoman and Habsburg Empires. Sultan Suleiman the Magnificent coveted the Ionian Islands, realizing they controlled Venice's trade routes to the Levant, and in 1537 found an excuse to attack them. The Turks were ferrying men and munitions across the Straits of Otranto from their base at Valona. An incident occurred in which one of their merchantmen, which failed to lower its ensign, was sunk by Venetian galleys. Suleiman sent a dragoman with two ships to Corfu to obtain an explanation. Unfortunately these too failed to make the proper signals, were fired on, and driven onto the Albanian coast. The Republic hastily apologized to the Porte, and brought the officers responsible home in chains.

However, the Sultan refused to be appeased. He moved his camp to Butrinto, which surrendered immediately, while his troops occupied Paxos. In late August an army 25,000 strong under Khaireddin Barbarossa with formidable artillery landed at Gouvia and invested the town of Corfu. Soon only the Old Fortress, and Angelokastro, the impregnable castle on the west coast built by the Angeli in the thirteenth century, which sheltered 3,000 refugees, were the only strongholds on the island left in Christian hands. This was the first serious invasion the Corfiotes had undergone for centuries; for the Genoese landings in 1403 and 1432 had been easily repulsed. Luckily the fortress was well defended by a garrison of 4,000 men, half Italian and half Greek, under Jacopo di Novello. They endured heavy bombardment, for Barbarossa had placed guns on both sides of the peninsula and on the isle of Vido, (then a nobleman's pleasure ground called Malipiero), but with 700 guns they replied briskly themselves.

The state of provisions within the citadel was much less fortunate. Within a week the position was critical. The old men, women, and children were driven out of the gates to beg bread in the Turkish lines. When this was refused, the wretches wandered helplessly in no-man's land, many dying in the ditch beneath the ramparts. But after another thirteen days the Ottoman forces were also close to starvation, and pestilence raged in their ranks. In several assaults they had failed to storm the walls, and on 11 September they reluctantly re-embarked.

In a siege lasting barely three weeks they had wreaked havoc. Throughout Corfu fields, farms and vineyards lay in ruins. Over 20,000 captives had been carried off, including Kale Kartanou, the girl who was to become the mother of Sultan Murad III. For the next four decades the island's population was only 17,500, just a sixth of the figure in classical times. Efforts to attract settlers from other Venetian colonies or even from Albania proved unsuccessful. En route to Constantinople, Barbarossa meted out a similar fate to defenceless Kythera. He sacked the town of Palaeokhora, taking away all its 7,000 inhabitants into slavery, a calamity so terrible that folk songs still tell of it, while the superstitious ascribed it to the judgement of God upon the prosperous but dissolute little community that had once existed there.

For the rest of the war the Venetian and Imperial fleets co-operated badly, mainly thanks to the malice of the Genoese admiral, Andrea Doria. In 1538 he missed his chance to bring Barbarossa to battle off Preveza, despite superior numbers abandoning his position to the enemy. The Turks were however too preoccupied with fighting the Persians and the Portuguese in the Indian Ocean to press home their advantage. In 1540 the Republic abandoned its ally and made peace, albeit on bad terms. The last of its mainland possessions, Monemvasia and Navplion, were ceded to the Sultan, and the evicted *stradioti* (military settlers) received lands in the Ionian Islands and Crete.

The Adriatic enjoyed a truce, but not an enduring peace, for the next forty years. Every summer the Barbary pirates terrorized the islands and interrupted commercial traffic, although they did no real harm. One enterprising corsair, Carazali, fixed his base for raiding the shipping lanes at Levkas. Venetian attempts to subdue him were unsuccessful throughout the 1550s, but Cristoforo da Canal, the *Provveditore dell'Armata,* captured many pirate ships, and died gloriously in battle after sinking four more of them. In 1560 there were complaints of raids under the very walls of the citadel, and the senate ordered the two Corfiote galleys to remain on constant alert. Meanwhile Venice stayed steadfastly neutral, even during the great siege of Malta in 1565, despite appeals from the Papacy and Philip of Spain. The election of a crusading Pope in Pius V, and the accession of an unwarlike Sultan in Selim II, failed to encourage a more belligerent stance.

Yet it was the Republic's fate to be attacked again. A power with such scattered possessions and an economy which depended on trade, while lacking the resources in manpower and material of the large nation states, did perhaps invite aggression. The Venetians had moreover ceased to take the Ottoman threat seriously enough, and had allowed their fortifications and armed services to decline. So when the Turks invaded Cyprus they soon conquered the whole island except for the fortress of Famagusta. Pius' exhortations to form a Holy League no longer fell on deaf ears, for the danger to the remaining Christian outposts, in particular the Ionian Islands, was all too obvious. As he wrote to King Philip: 'The Venetian fortresses are the antechamber of Christendom', and even that prudent monarch agreed. But so haphazard were the arrangements between the allies, that their joint relief expedition never reached Cyprus in 1570.

In May 1571 the Holy League was formally signed. Characteristically, Venice only acceded when her simultaneous negotiations with the Porte had proved fruitless. It was agreed that a combined force of 200 galleys, 100 roundships, 50,000 infantry and 4,500 cavalry should be despatched against the Turks or the Barbary pirates for the next three years, the costs to be borne two-fifths by the Republic and three-fifths by Spain, should the Papacy contribute nothing. So great was the allies' mutual mistrust, that their armada did not assemble at Messina until late August. Meanwhile an Ottoman squadron had raided Corfu, Cephalonia, and Kythera, undertaking no proper sieges but ravaging the countryside. They did not, however, escape unscathed, for the Corfiote galleys sank many of their ships at anchor, and an unsuccessful assault on Angelokastro plus five days' skirmishing cost the Turks over 1,000 men. Rumours that a large fleet was about to descend on the island were scotched by the news that the Holy League's armada was at last moving eastwards. The stage was set for the major confrontation of Cross and Crescent, and suitably enough the Ionian Islands provided the scenario.

> 'Don John pounding from the slaughter-painted poop
> Purpling all the ocean like a bloody pirate's sloop . . .
> Vivat Hispania! Domino Gloria!
> Don John of Austria has set his people free!'

In such magnificent verse G. K. Chesterton has immortalized the Battle of Lepanto, in which the forces of the Holy League, commanded by Don John, Charles V's bastard son, barely twenty-five years old, gained a signal victory. Their armada had arrived at Corfu on 27 September 1571. The Turks had hastily retreated, but bad weather hampered communications and they raided Zante unmolested. A council of war approved Don John's decision to pursue and engage the foe, so the fleet weighed anchor, although the big slow galleons had not yet arrived.

On 4 October the armada reached Phiscardo, and sailed down the Ithaca channel. Three days later the wind dropped, and a flat calm ensued. Don John's audacity had paid dividends, for on the morning of 7 October the opposing fleets faced each other near the Echinades Islands, between Ithaca and the entrance to the Gulf of Lepanto. The Turks too had suffered from divided counsels. Ali Pasha, the Commander-in-Chief, had only been persuaded to fight by Ochiali, the brilliant seaman who led the Barbary ships, after a direct order from the Sultan. The Ottomans enjoyed a slight numerical majority, 271 vessels to 235, but Don John also had six galleasses full of artillery, and his men were better armed and led.

When the signal-gun fired, everyone prepared for action. The Christian fleet was divided into three squadrons, the Venetians' sixty-three galleys on the left wing, sixty-four under Gian Andrea Doria on the right, while Don John commanded a further sixty-three in the centre, leaving Santa Cruz with thirty-five more and the galleasses in reserve. Ottoman dispositions were similar: Ali Pasha led ninety-three ships in the centre, stationing fifty-six under Mohammed Sirocco Pasha on the right wing, and ninety-three more under Ochiali on the left. Many of these were small galleys, and there was no effective reserve. The line of battle, over 7,000 yards long, stretched from the Acarnanian to the Peloponnesian shore.

Fighting began at 10.30 a.m., and Don John's squadron opened such a destructive fire, that the Turkish right wing, then the centre, were overwhelmed. Many galleys struck their colours. Ali Pasha was taken and decapitated. But on the left Ochiali outmanoeuvred Doria, drawing him away from the main fleet, then shooting like a thunderbolt through the gap. The Venetians ascribed the Genoese admiral's mistake to cowardice and jealousy. Anyway the Turkish losses had been immense—113 galleys wrecked, 117 others captured, 30,000 men killed or drowned, and a further 8,000 prisoners, while 15,000 Christian slaves had been liberated. The League had lost 8,000 dead, 21,000 wounded, including Cervantes with a shattered left hand, and only ten galleys sunk. Enormous plunder fell to the victors, 150,000 sequins from the commander's flagship alone. Lepanto was indeed a body blow to Ottoman naval power, from which it never recovered.

After couriers had been despatched with the tidings, it was decided to capture Levkas. The fleet arrived there on 13 October, but the Turks at once opened the sluices, thus inundating the fields, and set fire to the suburbs. A Greek peasant reported the castle was well garrisoned and provisioned, so the expedition was regretfully abandoned. The Venetians returned to Corfu, the Spaniards to Messina, and the Holy League steadily disintegrated. The following July its armada sailed from Corfu, minus Don John and the Spanish contingent, and on 7 and 10 August fought two engagements with the Turkish fleet off Kythera. But Ochiali, who had been re-equipped with 150 new galleys, again slipped away, and the campaign was inconclusive. In March 1573 Venice made its separate peace with the Porte, surrendering all her gains and prisoners, accepting the loss of Cyprus and limiting her fleet to sixty galleys. A war indemnity of 300,000 sequins was paid, and the annual tribute for Zante increased to 2,500 ducats. The Holy League was dead, and Don John's brief moment of glory gone forever.

The Ionian seamen had fought well in the campaign. All the major islands had provided galleys; Corfu had sent four and 1,500 sailors. One captain was captured and flayed alive, but another, Cristofalo Kondokali, took the Ottoman flagship, which was exhibited in the Arsenal. He received the title of *Cavaliere* and a grant of land near Butrinto. More important, Venice had belatedly extended the fortifications, mainly after the 1537 siege. In 1553 a bailie wrote home that further expenditure was useless, unless the defences were adapted to modern warfare. 200,000 ducats had already been spent, but an enemy could plant guns under the counterscarp. Supervised by Sammichali and then Vitelli, a specialist workforce laboured for years, intermittently as the money kept running out. The ruins of Palaeopolis were pillaged, many houses in the suburbs demolished, and by 1588 the New Fortress was completed, to protect Corfu on the landward side. Wells had been dug, a wall to the water cisterns built, and far more shelter for the population organized against another full-scale invasion. Yet the town was still not entirely walled, nor had earthworks on Mounts Abraham and San Salvator, which dominated it, been constructed.

The Castle of St George on Cephalonia, the Venetian headquarters, was strengthened, and on the west coast the peninsula of Assos, an extremely strong position, was fortified, the circumference of its curtain wall extending for over three miles. In Zante the castle overlooking the harbour was only rebuilt in the seventeenth century, and as half of it reputedly subsided in an earthquake in 1514, the island must have been virtually defenceless. Kythera was better protected, for the Venetians had strengthened and enlarged the fourtheenth-century fortress on its superb site above Kapsali Bay.

The incessant warfare in the sixteenth century created many problems for the islands. By the 1580s all were in deficit, with heavy expenditure on fortifications; Corfu's alone had cost over 1,800,000 ducats. Peculation by underpaid officials worsened the crisis. By mid-century Canal was demanding that an overseer be sent from Venice, as the provisioning of his galleys was wholly dishonest and unreliable. Bribery and maladministration of justice became a commonplace. One bailie accompanied the annual judges on circuit, illegally taxing every peasant five ducats, thereby forcing many to sell their animals. This was doubly disastrous as it was essential to revive agriculture. Bailie Francesco Morosini reckoned that Corfu could be as fertile as Lombardy, if the farmers were encouraged to cultivate more land, and the poor were subsidized to buy beasts of burden. He introduced millet with startling results, boosted the wine and olive oil harvests, and production from the saltpans. But he failed to make Corfu self-sufficient in food, while the prevalence of usury ensured the unalleviated poverty of the peasantry. Unless the situation improved, the Senate could neither offer sufficient subsidies, nor lighten the heavy burden of taxation.

Admittedly the Habsburg and Ottoman Empires had made peace in 1581. Spain's concerns thereafter were more with the New World and the Dutch revolt, the Sultan's with a Persian war. Thus by the 1590s the focus of world politics had shifted from the Mediterranean. By now however newcomers, the English and the Dutch, who grew adept at combining trade and piracy, had appeared in the area. Until Lepanto, the underlying fact of life had been Christian-Moslem enmity; so when the fresh ingredient of Catholic-Protestant rivalry was added, the balance of power shifted once more.

Trying merely to protect its trade routes and maintain neutrality whenever possible, the Republic was again the natural victim of aggression. A series of patrolling squadrons had already been organized, and the Provveditore dell'Armata, based on Corfu, had the thankless task of defending the Ionian Sea, while the southern sea lanes were guarded by the Cretan squadron of four ships, reinforced by another four in the summer. This naval armament sounds impressive, but in practice barely half the fleet was at sea at any given time, especially during the winter. The system of provisioning was woefully deficient, while as money only came from the capital, pay was usually months in arrears. It was anyway so inadequate that the free oarsmen, heavily in debt to their officers, were often worse off than the convicts who were being sent to the galleys at the rate of 500 men a year by 1604. The *sopracomiti* were disobedient and dilatory, causing endless delays, while they spent on shore the money sent to pay and provender their crews, or returned endlessly to the Arsenal for unnecessary repairs to get more leave. In fact the native-born commanders from the islands behaved more honourably than their Venetian counterparts.

Frequently the Ionian Islands were used as the battleground. In October 1584, Gabriele Emo, commander of the convict galleys attacked a twenty-six-bench Turkish ship of Cephalonia, and captured it after a six-hour engagement, slaughtering the crew of 300 and freeing 200 Christian slaves. In 1593 another Barbary corsair was easily taken, for 'the wretches had lost their compass and sailed for a good part of the night, keeping the lantern of our vessel always in sight, thinking it was the North Star. Only at daybreak, when in firing range, did they realize their mistake'. Other engagements were less successful. In June 1610 four Barbary galleys safely reached Levkas with their booty, although they should have been overhauled before Paxos if one Venetian captain had not delayed his embarkation for several hours.

There were many non-Moslem predators in Ionian waters. An edict of 1583 ordered all armed western vessels in Venetian ports to surrender their guns. That February a Maltese galley was surprised in Avlemona harbour and surrendered without bloodshed. Again, in July the Cretan squadron confronted four ships of the Knights of St John off Antikythera; the Grand Master's galley fled by changing tack, the rest were taken. Theoretically solely concerned with fighting the infidel, 'these pirates parading crosses', as the Senate described them in a complaint to the Pope, 'showed a curious inability to distinguish between friendly and hostile shipping, plundering several rich merchantmen off Cephalonia on the pretext they were bound for Constantinople'. The Spanish viceroys of Naples and Sicily, who secretly fitted out privateers, were no better. One vessel raided the Lazaretto at Corfu in 1596, abducting two merchants in quarantine there, a Jew and a Turk, plus all their goods. So when the Venetians captured a Sicilian galley, as they did off Zante in 1588, they hanged the whole crew including a cousin of the Viceroy's butler. Such enterprises continued, although when King Philip categorically forbade them, they ceased to enjoy official backing.

It was however, the northerners who inflicted irreparable damage to the Republic's commerce. Protestant seamen saw the Mediterranean as a new theatre of war, in which the struggle against Spain could be combined with some lucrative business. With a vested interest in the status quo, the Venetians were hardly likely to welcome them; anyway, the intruders treated all Latins and Catholics as equally hostile. By 1600 piracy had become overt, as this testimony by a sailor shows: 'About twenty miles of Kythera, we fell in with an English ship. They ran alongside, claimed to be friends, and told the master to come aboard. Then they fired off a round of musketry, and our captain in a panic with all the crew and four soldiers escaped in the dark. Ten of the English came aboard and slept on our vessel. Next morning they plundered it, taking everything, even the sailors' clothes, although they left my belongings, when I requested it.' The saddest and most typical point to emerge is that the master, with a bigger ship and crew, refused to fight, saying the cargo was fully insured anyway.

Maffio Michiel, the energetic provveditore in Zante, sent a stream of complaints to the Senate from 1603, writing: 'The English are becoming absolute masters of these waters; for apart from rapine and robbery perpetrated daily on every sort of vessel, especially on those of Your Serenity's subjects, they are utterly supplanting them in the carrying trade of the Levant, weakening the customs and ruining the merchant marine, as Your Excellencies must know.' The pirates in their *bertoni* or roundships, could continue their operations all year, unlike the galleys, and they grew ever bolder. One notorious buccaneer, John Ward, brought four ships within range of the Zante shore batteries in 1607, when pursuing the Syria and Egypt convoys, but was driven off. Endless protests to the British government did little good, while the Turks afforded sanctuary and encouragement to the corsairs. Michiel adopted counter-measures accordingly. Foreign captains were made to deposit a surety, amounting sometimes to 10,000 ducats before leaving port against any subsequent acts of piracy. When he captured privateers, he promptly executed them despite the protests. Doubtless he viewed the pirates' reprisals, when they burned a ship containing all his personal property, even strangling his wife's doves, with wry humour.

Piracy did certainly play a major part in the decline of Venice. But it did no such damage to the Ionian Islands, which benefited from increased naval expenditure, with more timber and provisions needed, more crews to spend money in port, and vastly expanded dry dock and caulking facilities at Corfu. Of course, the lack of security on the seas cannot have stimulated inter-island communications or trade, and occasionally the corsairs pillaged the countryside. Yet, compared to Barbarossa, the seventeenth-century Barbary raiders were gadflies, while the northerners were too commercially minded to see any point in destroying the islanders' prosperity.

Most Ionians were in fact only too happy to deal directly with the newcomers, unanimously loathing the Republic's protectionist policy, which by the ordinance of 1602 required them to send all their exports through Venice. Michiel shrewdly noted: 'All these disorders might easily be removed if the Senate would return to the original conditions, allowing free export to the west from these islands, subject to the new duty on currants. At present Your Serenity will lose the 36–40,000 ducats per annum, which it should bring in from Zante and Cephalonia.' Admittedly piracy had now turned into systematic plundering, transcending religious barriers, but a more intelligent approach by Venice would have turned the new conditions of trade to best advantage.

It was not apparent in the early seventeenth century that the balance of power had changed irreversibly, and that Venice had ceased to be a vital factor in European affairs. The Republic maintained its armed neutrality, carefully watching the Spaniards and their allies, lest they provoked a war with the Turks. After 1611 Christian fleets in Ionian waters endeavoured to foment a revolt on the mainland. Inevitably the Habsburgs cast covetous eyes on the islands as strategic and commercial bases. Spanish spies abounded, and in 1623 the Senate learned of a plot to seize Corfu. Venetian officials continually emphasized that the garrisons were inadequate, the guns obsolete, and the fortresses in a state of disrepair. Some works were undertaken and local levies raised, but it was fortunate that the islands were not involved in the crisis engendered by the Thirty Years' War. Further schemes by the Spanish Consul, Lipraroli, were thwarted; his son and successor died aged twenty-three, probably from poisoning.

Peace with Turkey did not last. By 1645 vast preparations were under way at Constantinople, and it soon became clear that the Ottoman objective was Crete. Despite endless rebellions, 'The Great Island' had been the jewel of Venice's Empire in the Levant since 1212. Now the Turkish army quickly conquered most of it, and settled down to the siege of Candia, the capital, which was to last for over twenty years. The cost to the Republic was enormous: 30,000 men killed at a price of four and a half million ducats. But neither side was strong enough to gain a decisive advantage. At last, in September 1669, the garrison with its commander, Francesco Morosini marched out with the honours of war, and all Crete, except three small fortresses, passed under Ottoman control.

The Ionian Islands had been the principal staging posts for troops and supplies. All had sent volunteers to Crete. The Corfiote and Zantiote military had gone there en masse, but the fearful losses suffered by the latter, (only eighty out of 800 returned), discouraged further recruiting. Many had fought heroically. The Aninos brothers, with their Cephalonian contingent, had been the last soldiers to get into Candia, while Angelo Delladecima commanded the Tower of St Andrew 'with faith and endurance', so the Doge's commendation ran. Their compatriot, George Charvouris, succeeded in holding the vital outer bastion, where he sustained two mortal wounds. Others behaved less admirably. The rich could purchase exemption from military service for 500 ducats, so the burden often fell on the peasantry. Another means of evasion was to enter Holy Orders; in 1666, 288 people did so in Corfu alone, and a special examination was set to halt this abuse. The mainland enclaves of Butrinto and Parga were attacked in the 1650s, but their defenders beat off the Turks, although a counter-attack on Levkas in 1658 was ineffective. Otherwise, none of the islands, including Kythera, were directly threatened.

Now, apart from Tenos, they were Venice's sole overseas possessions, in which a flood of emigrants from Crete settled. They were, furthermore, the springboard for any attempt to recover the lost territories. Corfu was the vital stronghold, and the engineer, Filippo Verneda made numerous recommendations, such as rebuilding the castle at Kassiopi to protect the northern channel, and levelling Mounts Abraham and San Salvator. Sadly, little was done, but after the repulse of the Turks from the walls of Vienna in 1683, the Venetian opportunity for revenge had come. Morosini was reinstated as Captain-General and in 1684 sailed for Corfu, where he made his winter quarters.

That autumn he launched an attack on Levkas. Its castle, a notorious nest of pirates, was reputed to be almost impregnable. All the main islands sent galleys to join the expedition, and among the 2,000 Ionian auxiliaries the Ithacans are particularly mentioned with the 150 monks and priests brought by the warlike Bishop of Cephalonia. After a sixteen-day siege Levkas fell, to be followed by the neighbouring islands Meganisi, Kalamos, and Kastos. The two latter were granted to a Cephalonian officer, Colonel Floriano, who took the title of Count Delladecima, as he received the tithe normally paid to the Republic. The capture of Preveza restored another valuable base, and command of the Amvrakian Gulf.

In 1685 Morosini took the field with a polyglot army 9,500 strong. Within three years he had conquered the entire Peloponnese except for Monemvasia, and had taken Athens, careless bombardment of which destroyed much of the Parthenon before its garrison surrendered. The last phase of the war saw Venice consolidating her gains. By the Treaty of Carlowitz in 1699 the Republic retained the Peloponnese, (or Morea as it was known), Aegina, and Levkas, while ceasing to pay tribute for Zante. The Sultan merely regained his territories north of the Isthmus of Corinth and bided his time for revenge.

The Morea's administration was modelled on that of the Ionian Islands, and trade flourished, at least sufficiently to pay the expenses of government including Kythera's and Aegina's. Yet the mutual antipathy between the Moreotes and Venetians grew during this fifteen-year occupation, until many Greeks secretly hoped for a return to Turkish rule. It was obvious to everyone that the Republic could no longer afford the necessary army and modern fortifications, and that its aggressively Catholic attitude was bound to facilitate a reconquest. By 1714 the Porte, having defeated Russia, was eager to begin such a campaign. The next year saw a string of Ottoman successes, after which the whole Morea and the last footholds on Tenos and Crete had been lost. Kythera and Antikythera capitulated, when the garrison readily handed over the castle, leaving such of the population as could to flee to their boats. In 1716 Levkas was abandoned, and that summer a Turkish army of 65,000 under Kara Mustapha Pasha marched across Epirus. Their objective was Corfu.

Advance warning of an impending attack had not been lacking. The Senate, alarmed by the collapse of their power on the mainland in 101 days, appealed for help to France and Spain, and recruited troops abroad. They also appointed a new Captain-General, Count Johann Matthias von der Schulenburg, a Saxon soldier of fortune, whose sister was George I's mistress. He had served with distinction under Charles XII of Sweden and Marlborough, and straightway embarked for Corfu. He repaired the fortifications as far as time permitted, and made a flying visit to Zante. All the citizens, even the Jews, were armed, and the town well stocked with provisions and munitions. But preparations were not completed when the Turkish fleet was sighted on 5 July.

Butrinto fell, and, as in 1537, the Ottoman army, 30,000 foot and 3,000 cavalry, landed at Gouvia. Meanwhile a Venetian relief squadron under Andrea Pisani burst through the enemy's blockade and arrived safely in harbour with the loss of one ship. The seaward defences of the town were formidable, but on the landward side, despite an array of new bastions, outworks and glacis which stretched from Garitsa Bay round to Mandouki, the commanding eminences of Mounts Abraham and San Salvator had still not been properly fortified. Against these the full fury of the Turkish attack was concentrated. After a second assault the troops posted on Mount Abraham were overwhelmed, those on San Salvator fled. Schulenburg was summoned to surrender—a summons contemptuously refused. Yet he could write 'I am in want of everything', and his motley garrisons of Greeks and Slavs, Italians and Germans, barely amounted to 8,000. Kara Mustapha Pasha next turned his attention to the New Fortress. Day after day his troops attacked. They were as regularly repulsed. The garrison even made a dawn sortie, although unfortunately the Slavs were attacked in error by the Germans, and some 200 were slain.

On the night of 17 August the Ottoman general led his whole force into battle. Everywhere outnumbered, the garrison fell back, and some of the enemy fought their way into the New Fortress. The record says that Mouktar, the grandfather of Ali Pasha, hung up his sword on the gate. After this fierce struggle had lasted six hours, Schulenburg with 800 men debouched from the Porta Raimonda, and at the critical moment took the Turks in flank. He drove them back to their lines, leaving 2,000 dead and twenty standards behind. By his reckless bravery he had saved Corfu. Nevertheless another assault was expected, and it seemed doubtful that the fortifications would hold. When the fateful morning broke there was no sign of the Turks. Closer inspection revealed a deserted camp and the army re-embarking. For the night before a terrible storm had washed their baggage into the sea. The Corfiotes believed that a procession of acolytes led by an aged bishop had been seen in the sky, and the politic Venetians fostered this belief in divine intervention. Actually the murmurs of the unpaid Janissaries, news of a major Turkish defeat on the Danube, and the approach of a Spanish fleet had been the determining factors. The Turkish losses after the forty-eight-day siege were heavy; 15,000 killed by sword and plague, and a further 900 drowned in the hurried embarkation.

Schulenburg was suitably honoured by a grateful Republic (his statue still stands on the *Spianada*). He recaptured Butrinto and Levkas, then the war dragged on uneventfully until the Peace of Passarowitz was signed in 1718. By it Venice gained Levkas, Kythera, and the mainland dependencies in perpetuity, while renouncing all other claims in Greece. Corfu was further fortified after the powder magazine in the citadel blew up, killing Pisani and 1,500 men. But with Kythera as her easternmost possession, and a declining Levant trade, Venice's Empire had become more of a liability than an asset.

B. VENETIAN FINANCE AND ADMINISTRATION

In the sixteenth and seventeenth centuries Venetian rule in the Ionian Islands assumed its final form, which it was to retain until the French annexation. While affording a real security and prosperity, at least until c. 1700, and guaranteeing their privileges, the Republic imposed a strict obedience on its subjects. Few changes had been introduced in Corfu after 1386, except for the decision to send two councillors from Venice to assist the bailie. The councillors appointed on a biennial basis, were meant to receive an annual salary of 300 ducats each and to live in the castle. They mostly presided over the Court, which sat five days a week and had three annual judges, (two Greek, one Latin) to act as its assessors. In 1423 however, their posts were abolished, and the new office of provveditore was created. He too was to reside in the fortress, to be in overall command of the garrisons and to judge in their disputes with the citizenry, although initially his authority was limited.

Paxos, having been the property successively of the Sant'Ippolito and Altavilla families, passed directly to Venice, but the expense of defending it so far exceeded the revenue it yielded that in 1513 the island was again sold to another noble house, the Avrames. Their rule must have been spectacularly bad, for most of the population fled to the mainland, and Paxos was re-annexed by the Republic and made an administrative part of Corfu. 'The Captain of Paxos', usually native born, was answerable to the provveditore, while an assembly of village elders, (there were no large landowners) met sporadically and represented the islanders' grievances to the authorities.

When Cephalonia reverted to Venetian control in 1503, the first priority was to repair the damage done by the Turks. As on Zante, a military colony of stradioti was planted, and more soon emigrated from the mainland. One provveditore, aided by two councillors, was considered sufficient to govern the island from the Castle of St George. But after the fortress of Assos was completed in 1596, a second provveditore whose functions were purely military, was appointed to command there. For so relatively large an area the administrative establishment seems none too big, although the Republic realized that in such rugged and mountainous terrain, with a fiercely independent population, its writ would only ever run to a limited extent in the interior.

Anxious to repopulate Ithaca, the Venetians offered new settlers land free of all taxes for five years, then at the rates current in Cephalonia. In 1548 the retiring provveditore there could write of 'my other island—Thiaki, very barren and steep with various harbours, especially one called Vathy'. He proceeded to enumerate sixty families, living much in fear of pirates, three hamlets, but no fort. He also mentioned one family, the Galates, who held the only feudal barony under the Venetians, originally bestowed on them by Leonardo Tocco. In 1536 a Captain Pugliese was appointed governor for life, and after his death, his successors were sent from Cephalonia, although twice they had to be removed for malversation and interfering in local affairs. The governorship was abolished in 1697, and two elders or *demogerontes*, held sole sway, while the principal men of the island met once a year to elect their officials. By 1750 the population of Ithaca had risen to 7,000, and considering all the difficulties, agriculture flourished amazingly well.

Zante also took several decades to recover from the Ottoman devastation. A swelling tide of immigrants from the mainland joined the stradioti already there, on the promise that they should be relieved of all tithes and feudal services for four years. By 1528, despite several plagues and earthquakes, the population had risen to over 27,000 and Zante had become the main port of call en route to Crete and the east. Eventually its administration was assimilated to that of Corfu, consisting by 1545 of one provveditore, two councillors, and a secretary, all Venetian noblemen.

The Republic had kept a *Provveditore e Castellano* at Kythera continuously since 1363, who exercised judicial, military, and executive powers from the great castle above Kapsali Bay. Until Candia fell to the Turks, Kythera was 'the eye of Crete', a coastguard was continuously on duty from March to October, and beacon fires were lit at night to appraise the authorities of the approach of a hostile fleet. Yet the protection provided by the three fortresses garrisoned by the Venetians was inadequate, Barbarossa's terrible raid proved that, and by 1545 the population had dwindled to 1,850, while the harvest was only a quarter of that yielded before the war. The provveditore reported that his annual income of 500 ducats was entirely consumed by the courier service to Crete and by official salaries. But the islanders complained that he bought up at a low price the corn and wine produced on the Republic's land and sold annually at auction, resold it to them by blackmail, and so mismanaged the foodstocks. Moreover, the Venieri let out their estates, now known as the *Commessaria*, to local usurers, who farmed the taxes and oppressed the peasantry. The Senate belatedly took remedial action, increased the subsidy, and instructed the provveditore to soothe agrarian grievances.

Such were the original Venetian arrangements for governing the islands. From the later sixteenth century, however, all the officials were overshadowed by a new supremo, known as the *Provveditore Generale del Levante,* whose responsibilities extended over all the Republic's Ionian territories except Kythera, (there too after 1718), and who also commanded the fleet, although he seldom took part in its campaigns. A great noble, appointed directly by the Grand Council in Venice for a three-year term, his arrival and investiture were scenes of solemn ceremony, regulated by exact etiquette. Dignitaries from every walk of life greeted him as he landed. The Jews provided carpets for the streets, the Catholic and Orthodox clergy both held splendid services, and the procession wound its way round the town until it reached the Church of St Spyridon, where the Provveditore Generale knelt before the relics of the saint, and vowed to respect the customs of the people he had come to rule.

By 1700 his staff had grown to include a secretary, an interpreter for Oriental languages, and a treasurer who collected all taxes and duties and controlled the military stores. These three were appointed from Venice, but the Provveditore Generale could choose his own Chancellor for legal matters, a Colonel-Inspector for the garrisons and four aides-de-camp. He was expected to keep considerable state in his palace within the Old Fortress, to employ four liveried servants, two messengers, and three musicians, who played the horn and trumpet alternately during meals. Receptions and banquets had to be given for all sections of the community, who was asked to what being of course strictly prescribed. He paid an annual state visit to the other islands, normally at the same season and in the same order. His arrival was marked by a public holiday, a joint service of both churches, and a banquet for the nobility and magistrates. Once again rigid protocol prevailed; he must first kiss the cross presented by the senior Catholic cleric present, then the gospels proffered by the spiritual head of the Orthodox Community. At the end of his term of office, the Provveditore Generale had to return straight to Venice, and give the Senate a detailed account of his stewardship.

Theoretically this sytem should have ensured the highest possible standards in public service. But as the expenses of a Provveditore Generale invariably exceeded his salary, so the temptation to corruption always existed, although, until the last decadent years, the incumbent was usually an aristocrat rich and high-minded enough to resist them. Even so, most hired their plate, furniture, and liveries from the Jews, debts which, in return for services rendered, they occasionally forgot to repay. How much stronger was the temptation for the lesser officials, normally men of modest means, who were appointed for two years by the state at a tiny salary, and who had to return home at their own expense afterwards. Rousseau mentions in his *Contrat Social 'le multitude des pauvres barnabottes qui n'approche jamais d'aucune magistrature et n'a de sa noblesse que le vain titre d'excellence et le droit d'assister au grand conseil'.* It was from the *barnabotti*, this depressed noble class, that colonial functionaries were appointed, exclusively so by the eighteenth century, when their behaviour became scandalous. By then it was notoriously common knowledge that a noble only went to the islands to make his fortune, although he should balance exploitation with dignity, decency with cupidity, and indeed with celerity, for there was no time to waste. It was reckoned that the provveditore at Zante made 20,000 ducats a year; the Doge only received 12,000. Doubtlessly the system benefited the Republic's finances, but it ended by destroying the probity of government.

In Corfu the provveditore, in command of the Old Fortress, the troops, and the night police, was deputy head of the administration. The bailie remained the chief judge, in charge of the day police with the two councillors (posts reinstated in the sixteenth century). Fourth in the hierarchy came the

Capitano Grande, the Commandant of the New Fortress. All these were Venetian nobles appointed by the Senate. Indeed, since annexation the Republic had kept all the posts under its own control, even those of dragoman, constable, and salt commissioner, but the fiction of local participation in government was assiduously maintained.

In 1386 a council of notables, eighty to 100 strong, had been formed to represent the interests of the Corfiotes. It was composed entirely of nobles, who alone could hold public office, bear arms, gain exemption from the corvée, and receive honours and emoluments. As more outsiders joined it, in 1443 the bailie was ordered to choose seventy prominent persons as a council. By 1490 the figure had risen to 150, which remained constant until the late eighteenth century. To qualify for membership, nobles had to be exclusively Greek or Italian, to have lived on the island for ten years or to be married to a native.

The council elected the three annual judges, the four *sindaci*, also the clerk of the court, two assessors of legal costs, the *giustizieri* (weights and measures inspectors), and a census officer. Also the post of castellan in such fortresses as Angelokastro, Butrinto, and Parga was in their gift. Butrinto, with its famous fisheries, yielded over 1300 ducats a year, but Parga was scarcely profitable. The inhabitants, although fiercely loyal to the Republic, sold the weapons sent for their defence to the neighbouring Turks. The luckless governor had to provide each family with five measures of salt a year, and a ceremonial dinner for the priests and landowners at Christmas and Epiphany, while a local council of thirty-two really ran the town.

As time passed more jobs were added to the list. Three administrators of the *Monte di Pieta* (the poor relief fund), three magistrates for the countryside, and three intendants of health. The prestige attaching to the Trierarch, or commander of the war galleys, whom the Corfiotes were allowed to choose, was enormous. In fact there was unfailingly fierce competition for election to all the offices, however honorary and unprofitable, and council meetings became the scene of elaborate political intrigue. Every post was held only for a year, to permit the maximum number of people to enjoy office. Sensibly enough the Venetians also awarded the rank of captain in the navy to a Corfiote after one campaign. The connection with the army was less direct, for the garrison always consisted of Slav and Italian regiments, but the nobles commanded the town militia of 500 artisans or *scolari,* who were granted exemption from taxation provided they drilled on Sundays, and the rural police for which each village furnished a small contingent.

After the 1537 siege, the residence qualification for membership of the council was reduced to five years, and with the drastic decline in population enough bourgeois families were admitted to make up the numbers. They had to submit an explanation of their claims to elevation and pay an unspecified sum to the public works. The Assembly continued to meet every October, but its functions were purely nominal, while the council began to show a preference for cabinet management. From 1627 it elected a *Consultà del Conclave* of the three judges, the four sindaci and five others, who held their sessions behind closed doors.

Later the nobles' names were inscribed in the *Livra d'Oro* as a permanent record (when Andrea della Marmora wrote his history in 1672, 112 families were listed). Since nobles were forbidden to engage in trade, lawyers proliferated, and the premium set on place-hunting grew. Yet the law of 1647 sounded the death knell for the old aristocratic oligarchy, as the Republic, which had retained the sole right to ennoble, in its desperate financial straits offered a patent of nobility to any rich citizen in the islands who would pay 500 ducats, or possessed a property worth 4,000. Of course this tax on vanity was extremely profitable, and the council reluctantly acquiesced, 'to help Venice, which has need of the money for the necessities of war'. A commission of the sindaci and annual judges was set up in 1691 to scrutinize and report on all applications. Yet this could not disguise the fact that the system had degenerated into farce. The professions of jeweller and chemist, but 'no other menial occupations', were now considered to befit a noble's dignity. Moreover the decree that only those nobles with an urban residence were entitled to vote in the council fatally divorced many landed proprietors from their estates, and hastened the decline of agriculture. The glamour nevertheless persisted until the end; a new noble was ceremoniously introduced and took the oath of loyalty, while a herald sounded the trumpet to proclaim his election. Then he was carried home in triumph by four ushers from the council, escorted by the Provveditore Generale's aide-de-camp, while the acclamations of the crowd outside his house sometimes lasted several hours.

The other islands had councils too. That on Cephalonia, formed in 1505, met in the Castle of St George, and elected three sindaci, four health commissioners, two censors, two advocates, three judges of first instance, six magistrates for the countryside, and a city chancellor. As the population expanded, to over 15,000 by 1548, so did the council. By 1593 it had 434 members, and the Senate decided to limit it to a constant figure of 150. This had already been done in Zante, where the community was divided into three classes, nobles, citizens and populace. It was stipulated that only lawyers, priests, notaries, teachers, artists, and jewellers were eligible for the first category. In Easter week the General Assembly met to propose candidates for the council, but its proceedings had become chaotic, and the council disposed of the usual offices, being now allowed, like the Cephalonians, to appoint the captains of their own war galleys. The nobles in Zante and Corfu enjoyed reciprocal rights to attend each others' council meetings, but both denied this privilege to the Cephalonians, whose sessions were increasingly unruly. An observer could write: 'There is neither means nor place of meeting', and a qualification of a mile's residence from the capital was introduced. Crowds of peasants gathered in the streets and greeted the election of the council's officials with applause or violent disapprobation.

At the inhabitants' petition, a council of thirty with a property qualification was founded in Kythera in 1573. Gradually this turned into a closed oligarchy, appointing two councillors who acted as assessors, three annual judges, and sindaci to represent the grievances of the people. The former proprietors played an ever smaller part; the Venieri died out by 1700, although collateral branches of the family maintained the connection, and Nicolo Veniero served as the island's provveditore thirty years later. By then the Viari too were extinct, although their descendants remained co-lords of Antikythera until 1797.

Interestingly Levkas' constitution, after its recapture by Morosini, was notably more democratic. Its first governor, the Count Delladecima from Cephalonia who had fought so gallantly, invited the islanders to submit their own draft to the Senate. Sixteen *capitoli* were sent in and approved as the privileges of the community. There were two provveditori: one ordinary, appointed for two years, who ran judicial affairs with a sindaco to assist him, and one extraordinary, sent out triennially, who controlled the civil, military, and fiscal establishments, and supervised Vonitza and Preveza under the Provveditore Generale's aegis. Under his presidency, a Civil Council of seventy townspeople was chosen, and in 1760 the election of countryfolk was permitted as well. The community's poverty was such that the usual local offices appointed by the council went openly to the highest bidder. By 1768 the abuses had become so flagrant that the Senate annulled this privilege, leaving all patronage in the hands of the provveditore extraordinary, whose choice was limited to council members paying a fixed sum to the public treasury.

The greatest triumph of Venice's colonial rule was that, although it seldom governed by popular consent, it brilliantly maintained the illusion of doing so. In his annual tour of inspection the Provveditore Generale was always available to hear grievances, and in fairness often redressed them. The Senate sent out 'Inquisitors into the affairs of the Levant' periodically, to see if the islands' administrators were abusing their powers. And all Ionians retained the right, (of which they regularly availed themselves), to send deputations to Venice to plead their case. For example, in the early seventeenth century when the Corfiotes complained about bad behaviour ashore by members of the fleet shore leave was temporarily suspended. Such sensitivity to public opinion is a remarkable tribute to any colonial power. Unfortunately the Venetians did not show an equal concern for the economic wellbeing of their dependencies.

The Republic's fixed policy was to have a managed economy in production and commerce, at all times and in all circumstances. Eventually the islands were divided into five fiscal chambers: Corfu with Paxos, Levkas, Cephalonia with Ithaca, Zante and Kythera. Each had its own system of taxation, and in each the number of duties was very large. The Venetians' respect for tradition made them keep taxes imposed by previous regimes, whether logical or not. In Levkas, for instance, there were customs dues of nine per cent. Although known to be too high, they were maintained while the government was happy with the six per cent it actually received. By the eighteenth century there were ninety-two different impositions: twenty-seven at Corfu, twenty-nine at Levkas, eighteen at Cephalonia, twelve at Zante, and six at Kythera; a large enough total, although dwarfed by the 217 taxes the Republic levied in its Italian possessions. In Corfu wine was taxed four times—on production, on sale, on import, and on export. The host of petty restrictions finally enraged everyone without yielding a decent revenue, while the spirit of blind conservatism prevented their repeal. Even the Senate's reform of all fiscal legislation in 1767 aimed at clarification rather than uniformity.

By far the biggest proportion of the revenue came from import and export duties. This is well demonstrated by the extract from the island's accounts, which the provveditore of Cephalonia sent to the Senate in 1622. On the credit side is 240,000 ducats accruing from export duties on currants, and 7,500 from wine, cotton, and sewing flax. The debit side is, however, formidable.

80,000 ducats paid for western cloth
2,500 for imported wines
4,500 for olive oil from the other islands
2,000 for earthenware pots and other utensils
40,000 for grain purchased from the mainland
5,000 for meat
1,000 for cheese
3,000 for salt fish
3,000 for furs and skins,

amounting to 141,000 ducats in toto. On top of these a further 45,000 went to the fiscal chambers of Corfu and Crete, and 30,000 more to pay for iron, wood, silk, and wool imported from Venice. Net revenue therefore amounted to little more than 30,000 ducats.

To many critics such a heavy reliance on indirect taxation seemed unjust and injurious to trade. But the Venetians understood better than earlier rulers that the Ionians, like all Greeks, loathed direct taxation, a lesson the British learned in their turn. Indeed, not until 1917 did the Athens government levy direct taxation on the islanders' incomes. For all its shortcomings, the old system could have worked, and the budget balanced principally on the basis of customs receipts. The trouble was that the islands, perennially short of grain, imported most of what they consumed, and exported more and more of their agricultural produce.

In Corfu trade had flourished initially under Venetian rule. As the ideal half-way house between the Lagoon and Crete, its harbour was never empty. The oil trade was fostered for the government gave twelve gold pieces for every hundred trees planted, so that they slowly spread throughout the island, and della Marmora could write of a now bare islet, Vido, that 'it resembles a forest swimming on the waves'. Export duties were fixed at fifteen per cent on oil, nine per cent on salt, and four per cent on everything else. Import tariffs were set at eight per cent on all foreign, and at six per cent on Venetian goods.

But by the sixteenth century Venice was applying the policy of '*La Dominante*' to her territories, whereby all commerce had to pass through the Lagoon, and thus a further set of import and export duties was imposed on the Ionians and everyone trading with them. As has been seen with the currant trade, local initiative combined with the traders' freebooting attitudes slowly eroded the effectiveness of this policy. Yet it did lasting damage to the islands' economies. Transit commerce dwindled away, and in the mid-eighteenth century, N. H. Grimani, the Provveditore Generale, could write that Corfu, although ideally placed between Italy and the Ottoman dominions, was being used less and less as a port of call. Similarly the prices of local products had to be reduced to keep them competitive, while foreign goods became progressively more expensive. Anyway Venice stifled the development of any local industry which might compete with her own, for instance forbidding the manufacture of soap on Zante.

The 1756 budget has been preserved intact, and well illustrates the Republic's financial administration. Overleaf is set out the income and local expenditure in sequins of the five fiscal chambers.

		Income	Expenditure
Chamber of	Corfu	20,422	4,424
	Cephalonia	19,269	2,350
	Levkas	6,649	2,298
	Zante	38,662	3,400
	Kythera	436	900

Apparently in impoverished Kythera alone does expenditure outstrip revenue; elsewhere it is a small proportion. Alas, this magnificent feat of economic management is illusory. In the general figures the total income for all seven islands and their dependencies is 318,229 ducats, while total expenditure is no less than 421,542, leaving a deficit of over 100,000 ducats (a sequin was then worth 2.74 silver ducats). The discrepancy is easily explained. Only the general budget includes provision for the military and naval costs, which the Republic continued to make the islands pay. Although it also includes Ionian revenue which Venice received direct, this does not begin to compensate for the outgoings. Indeed, of the modest sum of 13,000 odd sequins allowed for local expenditure, most was allocated to the salaries of Venetian officials and the Catholic clergy. Genuinely local items, such as the building of *lazarettos,* hospitals, or orphanages, plus public festivals and prizes for prolific farmers, amount to a mere 300 sequins. Is it surprising that travellers' accounts mention the lack of roads in the countryside, of water or sanitation in the towns, or of any provision for education whatever?

Grimani compared the figures for revenue differently, yet they show how much more money—twice as much in fact—the Republic derived from its policy of 'La Dominante', than from taxes received directly from the islands. He calculated that during his three year term of office the fiscal chambers had raised 247,000 ducats, the oil duties 338,000, those on salt 48,000, the currant duties 56,000. Venice had gained another 53,000 from freighting all this produce in her own ships, while charging the Ionians a further 50,000 for her senior representatives' salaries. These amounted in total to nearly 800,000 ducats, no small sum, when so little was spent for the benefit of the native populations, and from areas whose economies had been declining since the seventeenth century. Grimani, moreover, forgot the peculation of many of his own officials, and the extortion of the tax farmers.

Taxes were being farmed out on Cephalonia and Zante in the sixteenth century; later the idea spread to Corfu, and by the eighteenth century the French monarchy's system of *fermiers généraux* was adopted. The greed of the farmers, all nobles, was so appalling that in 1767 the Senate decreed from three to five years, depending on the circumstances, should be the duration of their contract, although their powers were in no sense restrained. The Republic always drove a hard bargain. For instance, the Corfu saltpans were farmed out to Count Sordinas in the 1760s. He had to furnish 4,000 measures per annum to the state, pay 903 sequins to the treasury, and could then, after all other charges, sell the remainder at a profit. Most contemporaries felt he had bought a bad deal. By then every tax was farmed; payment was made in cash only on arbitrary assessments with resort to coercion if needed.

However, the final decades, when Venetian rule had reached the stage of irrevocable decay, are not a good yardstick for the Republic's financial policies, which, when viewed in entirety, are by no means so bad. The fiscal burdens borne by the Ionians were undeniably heavy, yet were not unsuited to the character of the people and the complicated forms of property ownership prevailing there. The costs of protection were immense, and they saved the islands from a yoke infinitely more oppressive, barbarous, and predatory. In a mercantilist age it was unthinkable for any imperial power not to attempt to profit from its empire, and when the Republic's interests coincided with those of its subjects, the latter were encouraged: witness the growth in olive and currant production. The nineteenth century would, however, bring a new awareness of political economy, and point to a more civilized solution.

C. KING CURRANT

In his *Rare Adventures and Painefull Peregrinations* William Lithgo wrote about Zante in 1609: 'I was credibly informed here by the better sort that this little isle maketh only of currants, 160,000 sequins, paying yearly over and above this for customs 22,000 piastres [a sequin then equalled nine English shillings, a piastre six]. A sum of money which these silly islanders could never afford (they being not above sixty years ago a base, beggarly people from an obscure place) were it not for some liquorish lips in England of late, who, forsooth, can hardly digest bread, pastries, and—*verbi gratia*—bag-pudding without these currants.' The Greeks could never quite comprehend the English craze for currants. In Lithgo's words: 'I have heard them often demand in a filty derision, what they did with such liquorish stuff, and if it were carried home to be fed to the swine.' Sceptical of the currant's charms the Greeks may have been, but they soon realized its commercial importance.

About 1500, when the Republic controlled six of the Ionian Islands, it was one of the five great powers of Renaissance Italy and a major trading nation.

Despite all the territories lost to the Turks, Venice still dominated the commerce of the Levant. Their strategic merits apart, the islands were invaluable as staging posts along the trade routes. For shipping was only really active along the coast, much of it was local anyway, and for the rest the weather and the fear of piracy made the high seas undesirable, except for a direct crossing by the shortest route. Corfu, under the lee of the mountainous east coast was the obvious key to the position, where the Adriatic broadens out into the Ionian Sea through a channel only forty-five miles wide, from Cape Linguetta in Albania to Cape Otranto in Apulia. From classical times to the Steam Age, ships regularly made this crossing in a single day. But the islands were almost as well placed along the shipping lanes, which explains their invasion by foreign crops, whose justification lay in their importance in foreign markets and whose over-cultivation regularly threatened the equilibrium of the local economies.

Venice had enjoyed a near monopoly of the Levant trade with northern Europe for almost a century. Her merchants in England formed a colony sufficiently numerous to warrant their own consul. They received their wares from the 'Flanders Galleys', which carried goods from the metropolis at fixed seasons, usually after the *Galere de Mercato,* mostly from Beirut and Alexandria, had unloaded their cargoes. The Tudors, anxious to gain a share in this profitable business, began to raise tariffs, and successive wars so crippled the Venetians that no fleet of theirs visited England from 1509 to 1518; then trade declined steadily until about 1532, particularly after the discovery of the Cape route had led to the dislocation of the spice traffic. But from this date until about 1590 commerce flourished in the Republic, whose Ionian subjects benefited accordingly.

A rigidly protectionist policy had been followed consistently since the Senate Decree of 1458 that Venetian subjects might only carry English or French cloths via the Lagoon, whence they must be exported in conformity with other customs regulations. 'Divers tall ships' were reported early in the sixteenth century to be trading in Ionian waters in clear defiance of this edict, and of a subsequent one in 1518. But the Republic reasserted control, as the currant trade grew apace. During three decades in mid-century, it was reckoned that the revenue in Zante had increased fortyfold, and the island's council petitioned the Senate for leave to uproot the vines and restore some of the vanished cornfields. Instead a tax on currants was levied, the proceeds of which went to buy bread for storage. By comparison with their mainland counterparts, Ionian growers were heavily taxed. Yet the trade continued to expand, and by the 1580s Venice, exhausted by the Turkish war and the great plague of 1575–8, which killed over a quarter of the metropolis' population, was no longer able to monopolize it.

Queen Elizabeth issued letters patent to two English merchants to trade in Ottoman territory in September 1581, after their envoy, William Harborne, had overcome French and Venetian opposition, and signed a commercial treaty with the Porte. The Turkey Company's charter was limited to seven years and it expanded quickly. Meanwhile another group was granted the sole right to import olive oil, sweet wines, and currants from the Venetian dominions for six years from 1583, and was empowered to levy a tax of 5s 6d per hundredweight of currants imported by an outsider.

When both companies' charters expired, it was agreed there were many advantages in combining their operations. In January 1592 the Privy Council granted an enlarged charter for a twelve year period to fifty-three named members, with options for another twenty. The Company prospered; by 1600 it had twenty vessels freighted in addition to those it owned, and eighty-seven freemen. The import of currants or 'trash berries' from Zante and Cephalonia was the most lucrative, yielding annually a profit of £11,500 on 2,300 tons. After much negotiation with the government, a new charter was granted in perpetuity to 119 men in 1605, allowing anyone else aged over twenty-six to join on paying a designated sum. Under the charter giving a monopoly of trade in Turkish or Venetian ports, the Levant Company operated for the rest of its existence.

By now everyone recognized that currants were the staple of the Levant trade. Goods were being exported and imported into England to the value of at least £250,000 a year. The principal export was English cloth, with tin, lead, furs, spices and other East Indian goods, which were cheaper if trans-shipped. But at Zante, where two-thirds of the currant crop was purchased annually at a cost of £50,000, almost all payments had to be made in cash. At least ten ships called there and at Cephalonia every season to lade currants, as well as wax, honey, oil, and wine, and on straight barter this entailed importing far more than the islands could digest. Therefore cargoes were sold for cash in such ports as Lisbon, Cadiz and Constantinople, where sales always exceeded purchases.

The Venetians, however, still hampered the development of trade. Convinced that the popularity of currants was unfailing and knowing that only Patras with inferior Moreote produce lay outside their control, they continued 'their intolerable restrictions'. With the growth of the currant trade, most vessels called directly at the Ionian Islands, so in 1602 the Senate passed a law requiring all currants to be shipped to Venice, the staple for every shipment abroad. Inevitably a huge contraband trade developed, many businesses transferred to Patras, advanced money to the growers to encourage better cultivation and preparation techniques, and brought over skilled dressers from the islands. Moreover many currants were smuggled across to the mainland by night with the connivance of the Turkish authorities. Soon so few English ships visited Venice that the Company closed its consulate there, and in 1609 the Senate reluctantly repealed its prohibition on direct exports from Zante and Cephalonia.

By 1622 the provveditore was complaining that two English houses on Zante, and three or four on Cephalonia monopolized the business, forcing growers to sell at low prices. He suggested forbidding foreigners to buy currants beforehand, so that a fair price could be negotiated when the ships arrived, and restricting the harvest, which had grown from between four and five to between eight and nine million *staliri* in both islands. The Senate was repeatedly warned by its officials that payment for English cloth drained the economy and that too many currant vines were being planted. In 1624 the provveditore on Cephalonia was instructed to permit new planting only if a petition had been presented to the Doge and carried by a four-fifths majority in the Senate. Otherwise the vines would be uprooted, the land confiscated and sold to the highest bidder. To discourage smuggling no grower might have his house near the shore. 'We also desire your opinion whether cloth from our ports can replace this western produce, for some is sold at a low price, and may even be of of better quality', while to counterbalance the English monopoly extra duties on cloth, tin, and lead would be imposed. Nothing happened of course; the proposals were not enacted nor were exports curbed.

After a fresh quarrel in 1625, when some Venetian merchants who had chartered an English vessel were forced to pay consulage charges, the Senate forbade any vessel to lade a return cargo of currants in the Ionian Islands, unless it could be proved that at least two-thirds of the outward freight had been unloaded at Venice. Otherwise, an extra duty of five ducats per mille weight was payable by the purchaser. The indignant Company estimated this would cost 50,000 ducats a year more, and some merchants advocated abandoning the trade altogether.

Agreement was eventually reached. From 1 December 1628 prices were fixed to vary from sixteen to twenty ducats per mille weight, which represented a dramatic decline from prices a decade earlier. This seemed satisfactory, for many feared that in a free market the price might rise as high as forty ducats; certainly twenty-five was realistic with small quantity and high quality. Interestingly, Cephalonian currants always fetched two ducats less than those grown on Zante. Furthermore, no English ships should lade old currants after 1 July, or new currants until 15 December. John Cowley was appointed as the Company's 'public minister in the islands'. Yet the problem remained unsolved, for the quantity of currants imported was so large that there was little profit margin left on the prices. Proposals to buy a fixed quantity per annum, namely 2,200 tons, and to allot each member of the Company a fixed quota, proved impractical. Cowley reported that factors were dealing on their own account and for ships' Masters.

A special committee was appointed, which recommended the issue of an order forbidding the lading of currants until Christmas 1637, after which twenty-four or twenty-five mille weight at most would be bought at twenty-two ducats from August until Christmas, and twenty ducats for the rest of the year. A storehouse was to be built on Cephalonia to preserve the crop awaiting shipment. If cargoes were more than ten per cent shortweighted, the factors' commission would be deducted accordingly. A consul whose commission would be three-quarters of a ducat for every ton of currants bought, was to be made sole buyer in both islands. As Cowley had retired, and his successor had been summoned to Venice and detained there on various futile pretexts, an agent without the offending title of consul was appointed in each island. Matters seemed at least to have been resolved satisfactorily, if hardly amicably.

In 1641 the Senate wrote to its envoy in London: 'If you think it advisable, you will divulge that it is the Republic's intention that English merchants shall be well treated in this city, in Zante, Cephalonia, and all our dominions.' So undoubtedly it was the local officials who were to blame for continuing to raise tariffs and compelling merchants to buy spoiled fruit at high prices. It was reckoned that taxes paid to Venice now exceeded the cost of the currants. The Company petitioned Parliament to forbid the import of all currants until duties were reduced, and a bill to this effect was duly passed. The Venetians responded by excluding all English cloth from their territories until the embargo was lifted, and the Company recalled its agents. Much distress ensued in the islands, so the Senate lowered the duties in 1643. But the volume of the currant trade with a country riven by civil war greatly diminished, and did not revive until after the Restoration.

After 1660 the Levant trade revived rapidly, and the Company initially benefited from the lack of any serious competitors. The importance of the business it brought is shown in a despatch from the provveditore in Zante in 1665: 'I experience great difficulty in finding money to supply the wants of the troops with the restricted resources I have found here due to the prolonged absence of the English ships, upon whose appearance depends the value of the public capital and the general relief of this island.' Yet changes had taken place. The consul at Zante was henceforth appointed by the Crown on the Company's recommendation, not by the Court of Assistants, and was referred to as 'His Majesty's Consul'. Gradually the Company lost control of the currant trade. From 1669 to 1673 sixty-two ships from the islands are entered in the records, but by 1697 no currant imports are listed for 'Turkey and the Levant'. The reduced entries come under the heading of 'Venice', as they continue to do throughout the eighteenth century. The outbreak of war in the Mediterranean jeopardized the security of commerce, while the French, negligible competitors hitherto, gained paramount influence at Constantinople.

The currant trade declined only very slowly, although worried Ionian growers were soon proposing to charter ships and export their own crop. In 1675 Wheler found a consul and six merchants living on Zante and handling a considerable volume of business. But much of it was done with English traders in Italy, thus undermining the Company's monopoly. Currants constituted £51,000 of the £53,000 worth of British imports from Venice in 1697. In 1730 these figures had sunk to £44,000 and £49,000 respectively; by 1750 they were down to £27,000 and £31,000. Meanwhile the French had undercut their rivals and dominated the carrying trade of the Levant. As they had not acquired a similar fondness for currants, they largely excluded the Ionian Islands from their calculations. Moreover, having never had a network of local agents and suppliers there, they found it both easier and cheaper to lade currants in the Morea, where the Turks, after the reconquest of 1715, were most anxious to foster business and liked the specially designed lightweight French cloths.

The Venetians' folly exacerbated the situation. They still believed that the owner and carrier of goods should be the same, that foreigners should be denied freedom of contract, and that all the produce of their territory should pass through the Lagoon and bear double taxation on imports and exports. They ignored the fact that the world's changing trade routes no longer made Venice the natural emporium she had been in the Middle Ages. In 1662 the Senate repealed the import duty, but not the export duty, and after twenty years readopted it, arguing that the scheme had not attracted back the lost trade. They resolutely refused to consider the free transit of goods demanded by the English and Dutch. The last attempts at compromise broke down in 1733. Long before this the merchants had secured the right to lade where they wished in Venetian territory simply by taking it, while the Republic's blind conservatism had doomed the currant trade, and with it the islands' prosperity.

D. THE SERENISSIMA IN DECLINE

Many Ionians welcomed the Peace of Passarowitz. If the glory had departed, so too had the problems. The Habsburg alliance had been proclaimed eternal, so the only Christian power likely to covet Venice's territories in Greece was friendly. Ottoman Turkey no longer wished to expand. What it now valued was the status quo. As Constantinople's grip on the distant provinces weakened, semi-independent chieftains arose in Albania and Epirus, with whom the Republic maintained reasonable relations. The Barbary pirates were bought off by bribing the Bey of Tunis and other North African rulers; by mid-century the threat had virtually disappeared. The traders from northern Europe were now respectable merchants, not privateers, even if they did not always observe every detail of Venetian commercial policy.

Within the islands, however, lawlessness was increasing. The seventeenth century had been an age of almost continual crisis, and the people had grown steadily more disorderly. Back in 1616 the bailie was deploring the large number of crimes committed in Corfu, and the failure of the authorities to take the necessary measures. In 1628 riots occurred in Zante, when many citizens refused to accept the decrees of the provveditore or the island's council. Order was eventually restored, but the nascent opposition to aristocratic privilege was unmistakable. Simultaneously, social conflict was developing between the townspeople and peasants. The latter's lot, whether they tilled demesne land or private estates, had scarcely improved since the Middle Ages. Many were irretrievably in debt to speculators who had lent against the harvests, and with the misery engendered by the Cretan war, civil strife nearly erupted in Corfu in 1652. A gradual debasement of the currency and several outbreaks of plague further undermined morale.

Therefore the eighteenth century saw a deepening abyss separating the classes. The peasantry loathed those whom they regarded as their oppressors; the bourgeoisie, growing in wealth and self-confidence, resented the nobility's monopoly of public office and personal prestige. Lawlessness became endemic. In 1724 the Provveditore Generale reported that there were over 3,000 bandits in the islands, most in areas inaccessible to the police. He appealed to them to surrender and expiate their crimes in the Republic's galleys; regrettably few obeyed the call. With arms so readily available, most nobles kept a band of hired *bravi*. Brawls and vendettas became habitual; and soon one provveditore was not only accepting the realities of the situation, but profiting from it by charging a graduated tariff for wearing weapons.

By 1790 one traveller, Captain Sutherland, could thus describe the prevailing anarchy on Zante: 'By what I learned, the police are really shocking. The Governors are generally needy men, but by accepting fines as remission for murder they are soon enriched, perhaps by the ruin of the widow and orphans. Is your husband assassinated? Dry up your tears—your Governor is three guineas richer. Do you remonstrate? For three guineas you may let loose all the demons of revenge. So one murder produces another; whole families are involved in destruction, or else live in perpetual alarms. Justice never interferes, and society is of course destroyed.'

In addition, long-distance trade did not revive. High-cost shipping, low-quality crews, and discriminatory tariffs had debased Venice's commercial status so that now it was merely the hub of inter-regional exchange for the Adriatic and the Veneto. The Ionians might still find a market for their oil or currants, but they were tied to a stagnant economy. They were likewise part of a political system that had ossified. A few oligarchic families held power in the metropolis, and mollified malcontents by handing out a few crumbs of office. So the regime remained stable, while it was served by an efficient and fundamentally lenient bureaucracy which rendered it tolerable to the world. The economy had changed from a commercial-manufacturing to a rentier basis, yet the external fabric of Venice was preserved. What had been lost was that free-ranging Renaissance spirit, springing from new ventures. The Republic's outlook had contracted with its status, a trend exemplified by the attitudes of many officials in the islands.

One conscientious administrator descried impending ruin. In November 1760 the Provveditore Generale, N. H. Grimani, addressed a lengthy memorandum to the Senate. He listed the islands and their problems individually. Over half the oil produced in Corfu and Paxos was being exported illegally, for the customs receipts had dwindled and only a seventh part was consumed locally. He asked for two more vessels, equipped at public expense, to patrol the seas. He condemns the prevalence of usury, steeply rising prices, and 'the attitudes of Your Excellencies, which do not seem to encourage industry'. For example, all raw materials and consumer goods had to be imported. Yet enterprises like the two new silk factories at Zante which made excellent fabrics, were discouraged. Commercial laws must be relative, not absolute. If Corfu became a free port, it could again be an entrepôt of east-west trade and communications. Grimani concluded with the hope that his despatch had exposed the misery of his charges—*'quel degrado abbia patito l'affluenza de' colli sudditi.'*

Nothing was done, of course, and the administration slid further towards impotence and corruption. During the Russo-Turkish War, from 1768 to 1774, many Ionians volunteered to fight. When Russia deserted the Greek cause, refugees flocked to the islands. Venice, which had maintained strict neutrality, wished to hand them back to the Turks, and was only prevented by vigorous protests from Catherine the Great. Russian consuls were appointed in the three main islands, many Cephalonians emigrated to the Crimea while their merchantmen flew the Russian flag. When the war was resumed from 1787 to 1792 some islanders became corsairs and a general was sent from St Petersburg to Ithaca to direct their operations. Two of them, Lambros Katsones and Androutsos, (father of the redoubtable *Klepht,* Odysseus) became famous, although they seemed to find it difficult in their plundering to distinguish between Christian and Turk.

Belatedly, Venice sent its admiral, Angelo Emo, to Corfu as 'Captain Extraordinary of the Galleys'. He restored order and overhauled the naval establishment. The grateful Corfiotes presented him with a fine mural, the Zantiotes with a golden sword. He had shown what determination and integrity could still achieve. Alas, Emo's dedication was the exception, not the rule. In 1773 the Provveditore Generale, Pietro Querini, was caught selling military supplies to the Russians. With eight accomplices he was brought back to the metropolis for trial, but while his secretary was hanged, he was only imprisoned for three years in a darkened cell. Nor was his conduct unique.

André Grasset de Saint Sauveur, French consul in the islands from 1782, was an acute and informed observer. His writings contain an account of the grim situation then current. In Corfu the Provveditore General lived in grand state. When he went out he was escorted by two couriers and four liveried footmen. Five times a year he gave formal banquets—for the clergy, Venetian residents, the officers, local nobility, and principal citizens. An excellent meal was provided, which was a source of gain, not expense; indeed his surest source of income. For each guest on departure slipped under his plate a promissory note for so many measures of oil, payable in cash or kind after the first harvest. An aide-de-camp collected the slips and showed them to his chief, who modulated the warmth of his farewells accordingly. There was also the *Mancia,* a custom brought from Italy. Every New Year each noble or citizen had to throw a coin into the boxes by the gates, and along the palace corridors small tables were placed at which sat officials requesting gifts. The next day each regiment sent round a drummer and two soldiers to remind the richer inhabitants that their security and generosity were indivisible.

The Provveditore Generale might force his subordinates to lend him large sums at low rates, but his Chancellor was worse. Holes in the shape of lions' mouths were cut in the palace walls, in which, as at Venice, anonymous denunciations could be placed. Those denounced were brought before the Chancellor and told to deposit a caution, which they never dared reclaim. If the supply dried up, denunciations were 'arranged', while the halbardiers who fetched the victim were ordered to bring back some article from his house as 'evidence'. Every summer the Chancellor made the annual tour round the islands as his superior seldom bothered to do so. Once intended to correct abuses, it had become a way of sharing in the local officials' abuses, or improving on them. In Zante one infamous provveditore lent out the revenue to the peasants at usurious rates, while his wife shouted 'Oil, oil!' whenever she heard a shot fired, knowing he would receive oil warrants for acquitting the murderer. Justice was a farce, available to the highest bidder. During the last decade only three or four convictions are recorded from the scores of murders committed. One man who had killed ten others received a ten year sentence; another got twenty years for making disparaging remarks about the Provveditore Generale.

By the 1790s there was a meagre garrison in Corfu and virtually none in the other islands. It consisted of one regiment of artillerymen, 450 strong, and nine more of infantry. There were also two Slav regiments, probably the best troops, but altogether there were barely 5,000 men, whose pay was so far in arrears that they often had to find employment from private citizens to buy provisions. While the twelve engineers in charge of Ionian fortifications lived in the town, the cannons' mouths were clogged with earth and the ditches with crumbling masonry. The officers lined their pockets by carrying dead or disbanded men on their lists; but if soldiers were genuinely ill, they were put into hospital where they received no pay or food, and subsisted on public charity to survive.

It was the same story with the fleet. After the fall of Candia, Corfu had become Venice's naval headquarters for the Levant. The Republic maintained two squadrons there: one of twenty-five galleys, the other of twelve heavy sailing ships, mounting sixty-four to seventy-four guns. Each had a Vice-Admiral in command under the Provveditore Generale, and Ionian nobles were encouraged to make a career in the fleet. The squadrons were supposed to undertake one campaign a year in peacetime, and were repaired in winter in the Arsenal at Gouvia, constructed after the 1716 siege. The site was ideally placed, with forests on the mainland affording excellent timber for shipbuilding, but the Senate, anxious about its own Arsenal, confined activity at Gouvia to careening and basic maintenance. During the eighteenth century the number of ships diminished, and many captains disappeared for a year at a time on commercial rather than military cruises. No captain ever admitted his vessel was unseaworthy, lest he lose his subsidy, and when it could no longer float he scuttled it without informing the authorities.

The aristocracy still monopolized the municipal administration. The four sindaci paraded round the town in long black robes and huge wigs, surrounded by crowds of suppliants, although their functions were increasingly futile. The health inspectors continued to enforce the quarantine regulations, by which an entirely healthy crew could be left to die on the small hot islet, on which stood the lazaretto. Yet their vigilance was so suspect that Corfiote quarantine was disregarded in Italian ports. Although most of the council's posts were unpaid, they were deemed so lucrative by needy noblemen that they were put up for auction.

Affairs were no better in the other islands. Agriculture had stagnated. The biennial olive harvest averaged 200,000 barrels of oil, but sales were so slow that the presses remained full for the ensuing eighteen months. The wine no longer enjoyed the reputation it had had in classical times; thick and sweet, it did not keep, and more was imported from Dalmatia. Almost all the wheat was imported too; there was even insufficient maize, the peasantry's staple diet. Fruit and vegetables grew in abundance, but were usually ruined by swarms of insects. Livestock rearing had never properly developed, while all timber, for fuel or shipbuilding, was brought across from Epirus. Foreigners now operated the fisheries, usually Italians, 'who made the Corfiote pay for his laziness'. If trade flourished in the port, it was in goods of alien origin: rice, sugar, smoked and salted fish, woollen or silk fabrics with caviar, coffee, and spices from the orient. The currant trade had declined so much that the consul's was the only English merchant's house left on Zante. Overburdened by duties, the buyers had gone to the Morea, where the growers might easily have sold out and been paid for their next crop, while Ionian stocks were still intact. Saint Sauveur saw much of the harvest thrown away or given to the pigs.

Efforts at reform were invariably disjointed and sporadic. Since the 1720s the inadequacies of hospital facilities for the garrison, with a staff of two surgeons and two barbers, had been deplored, and the sick entrusted to the care of priests. Suddenly in the 1790s a plan was made to build a huge military hospital. Needless to say it never came to fruition. Grimani had tried to revive the *Monte di Pieta.* For a few years it provided much needed poor relief; then it collapsed again. To improve finances the government had levied a tithe on the clergy's considerable property, but did not repeat it. To combat usury a state pawnshop to lend money at a moderate six per cent was established, but never given sufficient funds. As the countryside in Corfu had relapsed into poverty, the proprietors lacking the capital and the peasantry the energy to make improvements, an attempt was made to improve the roads and ease the transportation of farm produce. In 1794 five roads radiating from the town were begun by voluntary subscription, but were never finished, like the modernized water supply, until the British Protectorate. The project to naturalize coffee, sugar, and indigo on the slopes of Mount Aenos on Cephalonia was a dismal failure.

Political changes were equally abortive. In 1786 Nicolo Erizzo was appointed Provveditore Generale, with special powers to reform the islands' constitutions. He reduced the Grand Council from 150 to sixty, to be chosen by lot from among the nobility, not freely elected by the General Assembly, as hitherto. The Assembly would still hold its annual session, but was to be composed solely of the local authorities, office holders and nobles aged over forty. The bourgeoisie, seeing themselves deprived of all political rights, petitioned the Senate for permission to form a separate body, with their names inscribed in a special book. The nobility opposed this attempt to differentiate them from the humbler classes, and the request was refused. Erizzo's nerve failed, and he introduced reforms in only one other island, Levkas, where the council was reduced by an equivalent amount.

At first the impact of the French Revolution on the Ionian Islands was limited. The Corfiote citizens renewed their petition to Venice against the nobility's privileges; in Zante some riots occurred. However when war between Britain and France broke out in 1793, it ensured the final ruin of the islands' trade. Venice was now quite unable to patrol the seas. The 1791 budget merely provided for six galleys, three ships of the line, and three frigates as the entire Levant fleet. Pirates from Albanian harbours, emboldened by the total lack of naval activity, began to raid coastal shipping. When the Provveditore Generale retired, the garrison mutinied for lack of pay and had to be mollified by a levy on the richer townspeople. He left a message of welcome for his successor, Carlo Aurelio Widmann. A message of condolence would have been more appropriate.

The Widmanns were a new Venetian family, descended from a German porter at the Fondaco dei Tedeschi, who had made a fortune and bought his way into the *Livra d'Oro.* One of four brothers, Carlo Aurelio Widmann, born in 1750, had had a brilliant career in the navy and gained respect by his patriotism and honesty. He arrived in July 1794 with the best of intentions and the worst of illusions. His sole escort was one frigate, not the customary fleet. Dressed in the traditional garb—a long red satin robe, a gold cloak, an immense Louis XIV wig, and red shoes—he landed to a tumultuous reception. A triumphal arch had been erected on the Spianada (the Esplanade in front of the Old Fortress); all the main streets were covered with multi-coloured carpets and decorations. The festivities, complete with fireworks and a musical tableau, lasted three days, until Widmann had to disperse the crowds, who were starting to insult the memory of his rapacious predecessor.

Soon the Provveditore Generale realized how desperate his position was. The oil harvest was already mortgaged, the currant crop had been disastrous. At most the islands contained enough food for another four months, after which more would have to be imported from the mainland. In Corfu a quarter of the land belonged to those who had abandoned it, over half the rest to townspeople who never visited it. The visible deficit of imports over exports was around 100,000 ducats, and would have been worse but for the many sailors on voyages, and the labourers who worked on the mainland. The treasury was quite empty: the tax farmers and moneylenders would advance no more. Once again the garrison's pay was months in arrears. Well might Widmann write to the Senate, defining his position as '*Lo Squalore*'!

In a crisis of such magnitude, he boldly appealed to public generosity. Disaffection might be general, but he reasoned many people would feel that if the present régime was bad, any likely replacement would probably be worse. Using threats, pleas, or subtle logic he won his point. The Jews advanced 2,000 ducats and armed some soldiers at their own expense. The Zantiote landlords raised 30,000 on an extraordinary levy. The Cephalonians offered 20,000 and the magistrates waived their emoluments for two years. Levkas, which was not rich, promised 6,000 ducats, while the four towns of Butrinto, Parga, Preveza, and Vonitza, having no funds, offered men, which offer had to be rejected, as there were no uniforms for them. The Provveditore Generale himself went far beyond the call of duty, giving lenders his own signature, presenting 8,000 ducats to the Treasury and advancing a further 30,000. Indeed, he ended by pawning his own silver.

He begged the Senate to send more funds, but that worthy body knew little about money. In 1796, when contemplating war with France, they decided to defend five fortresses, of which Corfu was one, blandly ignoring the Republic's insolvency and the ruinous state of Ionian fortifications. That summer they summoned the commander of the Levant fleet with his four serviceable ships to defend the Lagoon, leaving the islands completely unprotected. In November poor Widmann wrote that with all available credit and his personal resources exhausted, he was forced to seize the little money in the Monti di Pieta and the savings and bank deposits, in the public service. He dared not disband his troops or dismantle his frigates, otherwise chaos would certainly ensue. Besides, he had heard of the approach of French and Russian vessels, whose motives he justifiably doubted. The Senate replied commending his zeal for his country's welfare, and yet again failing to enclose any money.

'I am on the brink of a catastrophe', wrote Widmann as 1797 dawned. He had reached the end of his tether, quarrelling violently with Saint Sauveur over granting asylum to two emigrés. Amazingly, all the islands remained calm. If French propaganda was reaching the peasants, which he doubted, it was having remarkably little effect. He heard that the Republic had declared war on France, after which the couriers had stopped. He did not know that on 30 April, the Senate had resolved to send him 30,000 sequins to pay the soldiers' and officials' salaries. When Widmann walked in solemn procession, the populace pelted him with flowers—a fitting tribute. He believed now that he could only pray for divine intervention, but it was to be Napoleon, not God, who intervened.

1 *Above*—The villa on Madouri islet off Levkas belonging to the Valaoritis family. Built during the nineteenth century in the Venetian style by the poet, Aristotelis Valaoritis, it reflects the Italianate tastes of the Ionian aristocracy, as do most of the country houses, portrayed in the following pages. The Church architecture however is much more a blend of Eastern and Western styles.

2 *Opposite, top*—General view of the façade at Sarakina, formerly the Lunzis family's mansion on Zante, now an empty shell gutted by fire.

3 *Opposite, bottom*—Colonnade under terrace at Sarakina.

4 *Above*—Steps to the garden entrance at Sarakina.

5 *Opposite, top*—Interior of the Zoïs family house at Varres, Zante. On the wall is a portrait of Dionysios Solomos.

6 *Opposite, bottom*—Interior—The drawing room at Akrotiri, the Chronopoulos family's house on Zante, built for Sir Frederick Adam.

7 *Above*—Interior at Akrotiri. On the table lies a crusader sword, and above it a copy of the Treaty of Union between the Ionian Islands and Greece.

8 *Opposite, top*—Afra, Corfu—home of the Kourkoumelis family. View of the main façade.

9 *Opposite, bottom*—Façade and garden wall of the Giallinas family's country home at Kavalouri, Corfu.

10 *Above*—Steps at Afra.

11 *Above*—The grand staircase at the Achilleion, Corfu. Today a casino, it was built for Empress Elizabeth of Austria, 1887-1892. The neo-Pompeian decor, if totally out of keeping with the Corfiote countryside, manages to evoke the atmosphere of the period.

12 *Opposite*—The Kaiser's desk at the Achilleion, with its saddle-shaped seat designed to overcome the handicap of his withered arm. Above it hangs a photograph of him in yachting clothes.

13 *Opposite, top*—View from the Manessis family house at Ayios Stephanos, Corfu, looking out to sea over the tower of Benitses Church.

14 *Opposite, bottom*—The arcades at Kombitsi, Corfu, formerly a Carmelite Monastery founded in 1742 and recently converted into a private house by the late Spyros Harokopos.

15 *Above*—The Dracoulis family house at Vathy, Ithaca.

16 *Above*—Gate and campanile of Anafonitria Monastery, Zante.

17 *Opposite, top*—The Monastery of Mirtidia, Kythera.

18 *Opposite, bottom*—Church of Ayios Nikolaos-sto-Molo, Zante, with a Stele commemorating the Battle of Lepanto, 1571.

Η
ΖΑΚΥΝΘΟΣ
ΤΗΝ ΣΤΗΛΗΝ ΤΑΥΤΗΝ
ΤΗΣ ΝΑΥΠΑΚΤΟΥ

19 *Opposite, top* — The Church of Ayios Yeorgios-tou-Latinou, Zante.

20 *Opposite, bottom* — Icon in this Church, on which members of the Philike Etairia are meant to have taken their oath to liberate Greece in 1819.

21 *Above* — Campanile of the Church of Ayia Maura at Makheradon, Zante.

22 *Above*—The Campanile of the village church of Ayios Nikolaos, Zante.

23 *Opposite, top*—The rebuilt 19th century church at Ayios Nikolaos.

24 *Opposite, bottom*—The 13th century Byzantine church of S.S. Jason and Sosipater, Corfu.

25 *Above*—Ayia Ekaterini, Zante. The Church is a dependency of the Monastery of Saint Katherine in Sinai. Outside is the plaque to Damian Zagorisky, the Russian vice-consul in 1803 who is buried here.

26 *Opposite, top*—The early 19th century church of Isodia tis Theotokou, Levkas.

27 *Opposite, bottom*—The Metropolitan church at Ipapandi, Paxos.

28 *Above* — View of Campanile of the Church of St. Spyridon, Corfu. Twice the miraculous light which has shone from the top of it has saved the islanders from the plague and from the Turks.

Chapter III

THE CULTURAL SYNTHESIS

'The whole fabric of modern Corfiote society, the conditions of land tenure and the habits of the people are still largely based on the Venetian polity' wrote a noted authority on Greece, William Miller, some fifty years ago. Today this is less true of Corfu, while the other islands were never as Italianate. But the fact remains that the Ionians have a cultural legacy from Venice unique in Greece, both for its long duration and the deep roots it struck. Placed as the islands were on the edge of two worlds, they transmitted eastern values to the west and vice versa. Not that this always endeared them to their rulers. In 1615 in his celebrated tract *As to how the Republic should govern itself at home and abroad,* Padre Paolo expressed it thus: 'For your Greek subjects greater watchfulness must be exercised, because the Orthodox faith is never to be trusted. Perhaps they would not much stick at submitting to the Turk, having the example of the rest of the nation before their eyes. Therefore they should be observed attentively lest, like wild beasts as they are, they find an occasion to use their teeth and claws . . . wine and bastinadoes should be their share and keep good nature for another occasion.'

Luckily Venetian policy was usually more trusting and enlightened. At the time when six of the seven islands had come under her sway, Venice was at her cultural apogee, one of the chief centres of learning in Renaissance Europe. The theological faculty at Padua University, under the Republic's control since 1405, advanced many ideas attractive to the body of Orthodox churchmen, sympathetic to Latinizing and humanist trends, who desired some rapprochement with the West. After the Fall of Constantinople the prospect of a reunion of the churches faded over the horizon, and with the deaths of pro-Catholic Greek prelates like Cardinal Bessarion, such contacts as still existed were maintained through Venice and her territories.

By about 1500 Aldus Manutius with a group of Greek scholars was producing editions of the chief classical authors, while other presses were printing many texts, pagan and Christian, to be shipped from the Lagoon to eastern Europe. Most of these Greeks were Cretans, although some came from the mainland, Corfu, or Zante. For instance the Callergis Press, entirely devoted to publications in Greek, employed as one of its correctors George Moschos, who had previously taught rhetoric and medicine at Corfu. His learned brother Demetrius also taught there before moving to Italy. Later in the sixteenth century another distinguished copyist was the Corfiote Antonios Eparchos, poet, soldier, and ardent Hellenist. For many years he directed the Institute in Milan founded by the Pope, and modelled on the Greek college in Rome. Other scholars were less oecumenical. Pachomius Rhusanus from Zante, a good theologian and grammarian, also studied at Padua and wrote many anti-Catholic tracts.

The linchpin of this cultural interchange was Padua University. A Chair in Greek was endowed in 1463, and an Aristotelian school of philosophy emerged. Two professors were regularly appointed in most subjects, and were indeed expected to lecture simultaneously. Ecclesiastical interference was kept to a minimum. The Jesuits were admitted to Venetian territory, but were forbidden to undertake higher education. Similarly the Inquisition was permitted to function, although lay magistrates continued to participate in their trials. For Venice was a secular-minded society, where the world's first commercial theatre was established in 1565, and the traditions of the *Commedia dell'Arte* soon spread throughout her dominions. At Padua scientific and medical discoveries were still made, for the professors declined to view knowledge as a closed system, discoverable from an authoritative text, and maintained as an act of faith. The Venetians came to identify these open-minded ideals with local patriotism, by comparison with the obscurantist theory of papal supremacy. The sensuality prominent among the richer classes stood in stark contrast to the puritanical ethos of the Counter-Reformation.

Common targets of militant Catholicism, Venice and the Orthodox church drew closer together from about 1570–1630. Some sixty Greek graduates a year were now obtaining degrees at Padua, and returning to the Levant. Almost all the privileged Ionian youth attended the university, whence they often graduated without sitting an examination. They left imbued with such Aristotelian ideas as the mortality of the soul and the immortality of the material world, which were clearly heretical. In 1577, in an attempt to recover lost ground, the Pope founded the College of St Athanasius at Rome, but it gained few converts. Most Greeks and certainly most Ionians remained firmly wedded to Venice. A Corfiote like Iakovos Trivolis naturally went there to publish his *History of the King of Scotland and the Queen of England* (a verse imitation of the novels of Boccaccio). In 1626 Flangines, another Corfiote, founded the famous school named after him there.

The tragedy was that the Republic remained adamantly opposed to improving educational standards on the spot. A few Greek and Latin teachers were paid in Corfu; only one in each of the other islands. It was not surprising that those who could afford to do so sent their sons to be educated in Italy. By the seventeenth century talented Ionians found few cultural stimuli at home. Gone were the days when visitors like Cyriacus of Ancona found it easy to buy good Greek manuscripts in mid-fifteenth century Corfu, because it contained so many cultured citizens, or when monks in Cephalonia were copying the works of Origen and Chrysostom, and paraphrasing Homer in octosyllabic verse under the patronage of the Tocchi.

Venetian ecclesiastical policy was less bigoted than that of most Catholic powers. In accordance with its ideals, the Republic preserved a balance between Pope and Patriarch, although the essentials of the earlier system were retained. In Corfu the chief Orthodox priest was still the *Megas Protopapas,* while the Archbishop was a Catholic and an Italian. The chief priest was elected as before, by thirty chosen members of the Assembly and the 'Sacred Band' of thirty-two town priests, usually for a five year term, although he could be re-elected subsequently. Influence and simony played a greater part in his appointment than sanctity, and on gaining office he was encouraged to recoup his expenses. In each of Corfu's four bailiwicks and in Paxos there was a *protopapas* under him, who controlled the local clergy. Suspicious as ever of outside interference, the Venetians only allowed him to correspond with the Patriarch through their bailie at Constantinople, thus severely restricting his initiative. On the other hand the Senate upheld the privileges of the Sacred Band and the thirty-three rural priests, while thwarting any attempts from Rome to tamper with Orthodox services.

Local relations between the Churches remained fairly good, for the Orthodox Creed had always permitted mixed marriages, although the children were often gained as converts. The Catholics joined in the great processions; the Orthodox prayed for Pope and Archbishop at annual banquets in the latter's palace, and both held communal services in St Arsenius' Cathedral. The rural clergy were also prepared to excommunicate refractory villagers at the government's request, a practice that survived in parts of Greece until this century. In all its 400 years of rule in Corfu, the Republic only once curtailed the freedom of its Orthodox subjects, when to prevent an influx of refugee clergy after the Fall of Constantinople, the Sacred Band was forbidden to hold its normal meetings, and priests who had been resident for less than ten years were forced to leave.

In structure the churches changed little from the Middle Ages. Cephalonia was elevated into an archiepiscopal see with jurisdiction over Ithaca and Zante (where a Catholic bishop also resided). The Zantiotes repeatedly protested against this arrangement, which was settled by a senatorial decree that the Cephalonian clergy should retain the right to elect their own prelate, provided they chose someone from the other island every third time. In Kythera the Orthodox bishopric, dating from the thirteenth century, survived. One incumbent in the 1590s, Maximus Margunius, tried hard to reconcile the doctrinal differences between the two churches, but was accused of being a Papal agent and then prosecuted by the Inquisition for writing anti-Jesuit tracts. Everywhere nepotism and corruption flourished, with the nobles interfering in clerical elections; yet everywhere there was a basic toleration of the rival creed. Indeed such wise Popes as Leo X and Paul III expressly forbade meddling with Orthodox services, and allowed the islanders to retain the old-style calendar when the Gregorian version was introduced. Mixed marriages persisted to the advantage of the Greeks, so that by 1775 there were only two noble families left on Corfu who were still Catholic, while in Cephalonia it was solely the garrison. The superficial Romanization of the Orthodox church was belied by the steady gain of converts from the Roman faith.

Various Ionians were also involved in an interesting dialogue between the Orthodox and Protestant faiths. Several of Luther's disciples were deeply interested in Hellenism, particularly Philip Melancthon, who approached Eparchos with a proposal that both sides should hold talks. However Eparchos rebuffed him, denouncing the Reformation's divisive influence. Subsequent approaches to the Patriarch proved equally abortive. But in the early seventeenth century a remarkable cleric, Cyril Lucaris, ascended the Patriarchal throne. Holding much sympathy for Calvinist views, he determined to reform education and send Greek children to Protestant countries. He persuaded a Cephalonian, Nicodemus Metaxas, who had set up a printing press in London in 1625, to move it to Constantinople, although the Jesuits persuaded the Grand Vizier to order the destruction of such an unpleasant piece of wizardry. For ten years the quarrels raged, and the Jesuits were expelled from the Ottoman dominions, until Lucaris published his *Confession of Faith,* which shocked most Orthodox believers by its overt Calvinism. The Sultan, bored by the squabbles, had him deposed and strangled.

Yet the Calvinist faction remained strong. Another Cephalonian, Hierotheus, the Abbot of Sision Monastery, travelled to Leyden where he translated Protestant tracts into Greek. Contacts with the Anglicans lasted longest, for both churches had hierarchies with an Apostolic succession and subscribed to the charismatic quality of bishops. A Greek colony grew up in London with its own church and college, while students went to Oxford and Cambridge. The Levant Company fostered this development; as late as 1701 Ionian and other Greek prelates visited England, although the doctrinal differences, especially the belief in Transubstantiation, proved irreconcilable.

Long before this, Venice, economically and politically enfeebled, had ceased to oppose the Counter-Reformation. The terrible plague of 1630–1, which killed a third of the population, must have seemed like a judgement from heaven on the tolerant, pluralist society which lived by the humanist ideals of the Renaissance. The new mood of baroque piety, invaluable in reviving flagging enthusiasm for war against the Turk, was ill-suited to compromise, and the intellectual petrifaction which ensued scarcely appealed to most Greeks. By 1700 the Ionians, with the rest of the Orthodox world, had started to look to the rising power of Russia as the prop of Hellenic aspirations and cultural traditions. Padua ceased to be a centre of intellectual innovation, although its standards remained high, and a stream of students, mainly medical, still came from the East. Indeed the Collegio Cotunios was founded for them there in 1653. But teaching stayed on the Aristotelian scientific-philosophical pattern, while advances elsewhere sprang from a mathematical-mechanical mentality. During the eighteenth century the fossilized system either ignored or suppressed the ideas of the rationalist Enlightenment.

To be fair, the Republic had not deprived its Ionian subjects of all cultural stimuli. An Academy of Thirty, the '*Assicurati*', was founded in Corfu in 1656, to promote intellectual development, only to be abandoned after the Turkish siege of 1716. About then too a literary society was formed, and a second one in 1732. The Catholic Archbishop Querini wrote a lengthy treatise entitled *The Antiquities of Corfu*. Meanwhile the Jesuits with their officious management of propaganda had partially succeeded in diverting local culture in the main islands from strict Byzantine traditions towards the Baroque. The protopapas invoked the Pope's name at the end of the service, and petitions from Zante asked permission for the Greek clergy to officiate in Catholic churches. Many Orthodox worshippers, attracted by the pomp and ritual, attended mass. Two distinguished artist priests in Zante, Nicholas Koutouzis and Nicholas Kandounis, introduced the Roman liturgy and ornaments, shaved their beards, smothered the buildings in flowers and hangings, and chanted in Western fashion. Koutouzis was finally defrocked in 1810 for writing bitter, satirical verse at the expense of the local worthies.

Some of their compatriots were less easily led astray. In Cephalonia one priest, Elias Meniates, refuted Catholic doctrine with the eloquence of a

Bossuet. Two more, the Likhoudes brothers, journeyed to Moscow at the Patriarch's suggestion, prevented the imposition of a Latinized Eucharist on the Russian church and acquired much influence over the Tsar. When in 1763 the Patriarch reacted to complaints that many of his clergy were illiterate by founding an academy for monks on Mount Athos, the centre of Orthodox learning, the first professor he appointed was a Corfiote, Eugenius Voulgaris. The latter however proved so modernistic in his views that he was rapidly dismissed. With his friend Nicephorus Theotokis, Voulgaris became the great pioneer of the revival of demotic, or popular Greek, which flourished in the next century. Yet how could any genuine intellectual regeneration, from a Catholic, Orthodox or secular viewpoint, be practicable in a society deprived of a printing press or any facilities for higher education? In the 1790s, so Mario Pieri claimed, a grammar and a Latin dictionary were the only books readily on sale in Corfu, and these had to be bought from a chemist's shop.

Venetian rule was the great age of the Patron Saints, who still play an important part in the life of the islands. St Spyridon, born and bred a shepherd in Cyprus, rose to be Bishop of Trymithion in the fourth century, and attended the Council of Nicaea, where he supported the disputed doctrine of the Trinity by casting on the ground a brick he was holding from which fire and water gushed at once. Famed for his piety and charity, he died aged over ninety, with many miracles attested. Soon exhalations of sweetness and a spray of red roses sprang from his coffin; suitable steps towards beatification. Moved to Constantinople to escape the Saracens, his remains were kept there until they were smuggled out after the Turkish conquest. Their owner, a rich priest called Kalochairetes, also possessed the embalmed body of another Saint, Theodora. He slung both over a mule, so the legend goes, which carried them to Epirus and thence to Corfu, where they were laid to rest in the chapel of St Michael the Archangel in 1456. The casket containing Theodora's relics was soon presented to the community, but Spyridon remained, a figure of awe to the faithful and of profit to his owners, although it took the entreaties of the entire island in 1489 to prevent his being removed to Venice.

By 1500 his relics had passed to Kalochairetes' granddaughter, who married into the Voulgaris family, in whose possession they stayed until 1925. Spyridon was reputedly never invoked in vain by invalid or traveller. Even Greeks from the Morea and the Aegean islands readily offered part of the profits from their voyages in return for his protection. The church especially built for him was begun in 1589; it was the richest on Corfu and its campanile the highest in the town. Four great processions were held every year in his honour: on Palm

Sunday, Easter Saturday, 11 August, and the first Sunday in November. They were the island's most splendid festivals, in which the whole community participated.

The Palm Sunday procession dates from the seventeenth century. According to della Marmora, Corfu was struck by a deadly plague on Christmas Eve 1629. The source of the epidemic was traced to a servant of the Public Health Commissioner, who had bought ten woollen kerchiefs from a Turkish ship in port. The poor man was held responsible, interned and shot on the Lazaretto islet, but the plague spread throughout the island. Crowds gathered to pray to St Spyridon, a light like a small lamp appeared at the top of the campanile each night and thenceforth the number of deaths slowly diminished. The epidemic stopped on Palm Sunday. The Easter Saturday procession commemorates the relief of Corfu from famine in the mid-sixteenth century. The legend goes that no grain ships could reach the harbour because of contrary winds. On Easter Eve vessels laden with flour sailed into port, for the Saint had spoken to their captains in a dream and induced them to change course for Corfu, to sell their cargoes to the starving citizens. The August procession refers to the 1716 siege, when Spyridon is meant to have frightened away the Turks; while that in November recalls another of his miraculous interventions to quell the plague in 1673, when for three nights the townspeople saw a bright light in the campanile and a vision in the sky holding a crucifix. Indeed his most recent miracle dates from the Second World War, where he caused a bomb to explode in mid-air, which would otherwise have landed on his church, killing hundreds of people sheltering there.

Both order and dress were strictly prescribed in the four processions. The colours were magnificent: the provveditori in red, the bailiff and councillors in black, the soldiers in uniforms varying between the yellow tunic and breeches with grey surcoat of the artillery, the white with blue fringes of the Italian infantry, and the red ruched jackets with long blue trousers of the Slav regiments. The nobility wore Venetian, the populace national dress. This consisted of a red woolly bonnet, a short jacket with silver buttons, and baggy black trousers with a silk belt, through which a dagger was stuck, 'not purely for ornamental purposes'. The women wore a trimmed blouse with a skirt in a contrasting colour, an apron with embroidered flowers, and high-heeled shoes. The most beautiful costumes came from the villages, passed down through generations, and like the hairstyles all differed slightly. The belt might be fastened with two golden clasps, the skirt edged with gold or silver motifs, or the blouse trimmed in violet or purple velvet.

For the preceding eight days the doors, windows, and belfry of the church were decorated with branches of laurel and myrtle. At the belfry's four corners stood four trophies, one each for Venice, Russia, and England, while the fourth might be Danish, Swedish or Dutch but never French or Turkish. The bells rang incessantly, and on the eve of the procession the casket of ebony with gilded drapes worked with precious stones was exposed to the veneration of the people. Sixty soldiers barely sufficed to control the crowd, who thronged to implore the Saint's protection. The next morning six priests carried the casket under a canopy borne by all the high officials, including the Provveditore Generale. From every side the batteries fired off a twenty-one-gun salute, as did the galleys, whch left their moorings beneath the Old Fortress to follow the procession as it wound its way along the ramparts.

Other major celebrations took place on the eve of Good Friday, when each church had its own procession, and the women who usually appeared in the *janizzeo*, a kind of stand with a grille, moved freely around in the nave. In early April there was a feast for the Resurrection of Lazarus. A figure paraded through the streets waving a multi-coloured banner, dancing and reciting a popular poem on the subject in Greek. On 19 January, the festival of St Arsenius, the clergy of both denominations officiated in the Latin Cathedral, until it was destroyed in the huge explosion of 1718. Lastly the investiture of the Megas Protopapas was a very grand occasion. The new incumbent, dressed in scarlet, holding his ivory pastoral staff was carried into the Orthodox Cathedral by six bearers to the firing of salvoes and the pealing of bells. No wonder visitors remarked that Corfu seemed perpetually en fete.

Gerasimos Notaras was born of a good family at Trikala in the Morea in 1509. He took his vows on Mount Athos, travelled throughout the Levant, lived in Jerusalem, and eventually came to Cephalonia in search of a more ascetic life. He rebuilt a ruined church in the Omala Valley, and was persuaded by the villagers to found a convent there for their unmarried daughters in 1554. Famed for his saintliness and healing powers, Gerasimos is said to have had magical gifts of making crops grow and divining water, once finding a well in the middle of the dusty avenue leading to his convent. His death on 16 August 1579, and his beatification two years later were celebrated with services and processions. But as patron saint of Cephalonia his record of intervention on behalf of the islanders is less spectacular.

During the sixteenth century Zante too acquired its patron saint. Dionysios Sigouros was born there of aristocratic parents in 1547. Archbishop of Aegina, then of Cephalonia and Zante, he retired to spend his last years as the Abbot of Anafonitria Monastery, founded by the Tocchi, where his reputation for sanctity was much enhanced by sheltering his brother's murderer. He died in 1622, and was beatified in 1703. Originally his remains were buried on the Strophades, but when a Turkish fleet sacked the islets in 1717, two monks escaped with them to Zante. The relics were reinterred in a church specially built to house them in the town. The splendid rococo coffer with the silver casing by George Baffas still exists, although the Church is the third on the site. On 24 August and 17 December solemn processions were held in his honour, although St Dionysios' subsequent exploits are not recorded.

In remote Kythera the Mirtidia Monastery was built on the spot where a shepherd boy found a miraculous icon in the fourteenth century. Every year on 7 October the islanders celebrated the festival of their patron saint, Panayia Myrtiotissa, Our Lady of the Myrtle Bough, whose image, carried on the waves and found hanging in this tree, represents the Christian version of Aphrodite arising from the sea. An equally charming story concerns little Ithaca, known since mediaeval times as Val di Compare, supposedly because a sea captain, who had anchored near shore one stormy night, saw a light shining through the darkness and found it came from a hut containing a newly-born child, to which he stood godfather (*koumbaros*), and so named the island.

The society of the Ionian Islands, like their religious life, reflected a blend of east and west. To judge by their origins, the nobility were certainly a heterogeneous collection of families. In Corfu the Marmoras, Theotokis, and Prosalendis were of Byzantine extraction, the Capodistrias and Giallinas from Dalmatia, the Voulgaris from Epirus, the Sordinas from the Veneto while the Pieri were French. Since Angevin days there had been a divison between Greek and Latin nobles, which had nothing to do with their professed creed, but defined the former as Byzantine, Cretan or mainland Greek families, the latter as of French or Italian stock. The increasingly artificial distinction was not abolished until 1691, although the other islands never copied it.

In Cephalonia the Aninos, Carantinos, Foca-Cosmetatos and Metaxas families had come from Byzantium, the Corafas were Neapolitan, the Delladecimas from Crete and the Typaldos Roman. Zante was even more cosmopolitan. Of its noble families the Sigouros and Rossis descended from Norman invaders, the Mercatis were from Tuscany, the Carrers from Cyprus, the Lunzis and Comutos from the Morea, while the Messalas and Romas claimed direct descent from Imperial Rome. To add to the confusion many aristocratic houses had cadet branches, which settled in the other islands; sometimes the whole clan moved, as did the Kourkoumelis and the Flamburiaris from Cephalonia to Corfu. By about 1600 a *Livra d'Oro* was in being in each of the three main islands. However so many lines died out that, with the high incidence of bastardy and the frequent ennoblement of bourgeois families by the Republic in later years, the *Livra d'Oro* two centuries later bore faint resemblance to the originals. In the small islands, Kythera, Ithaca or Levkas a *Livra d'Oro* was never formally established, while the origin of distinguished names like Petrisopoulos and Valaoritis remains obscure.

There was however one constant thread running through Ionian social history. The Venetians who came out to administer the islands intermarried with their charges extremely seldom. As the number of Catholics dwindled steadily, religion was the ostensible dividing line, yet in reality 'the humblest Barnabotte would have blushed to marry the daughter of the grandest local noble'. Whatever their origins, all were regarded by the Venetians as Greeks and thus an inferior race. Instances like the Countess Theotokis who married an Albrizzi and had a celebrated salon in mid-eighteenth century Venice are very rare. Generally the Ionian nobility married less and less outside its own ranks, although there were exceptions. In the 1760s the Lunzi brothers, Counts Francisco and Athanasius, were so close that when one travelled or fell ill, the other knew immediately. Francisco met a Danish lady, Countess Martens, at Venice, proposed to her, then sickened and summoned his brother to take his place. In accordance with his dying wish, Count Athanasius married her, but she could never bring herself to love her husband, forever regretting his more handsome brother. Although she lived on Zante for years and bore him many children, the ghost of her dead fiancé was always before her, or so she used to tell her friends.

By the eighteenth century the richer Ionians were becoming increasingly Italianate. From 1693 Corfu had its own theatre in the merchants' loggia. Three tiers of boxes, shut with jalousies, surrounded the stalls. They were taken for the season, extending from early autumn until Lent; each was decorated individually and crammed to capacity. One of the naval commanders, entitled *Preside del Teatro,* was responsible for engaging the troupe of Italian actors, who played the Commedia dell'Arte. By tradition Harlequin was always a Bergamasco and Pantaloon a Venetian. Initially women were not allowed in the theatre, then they frequented the boxes, later the stalls if masked, and soon all restrictions had lapsed.

The carnival took place every year from 18 January to Ash Wednesday. Among the festivities was a *chiastra*, a sort of tournament, fought in the streets opening out onto the Spianada, where stands and lists were erected. A ball was also organized by each of the four *casini*—of Venetian and Corfiote nobles, and of naval and army officers. Each offered the facilities of a club – gaming, a special smoking room, newspapers from the metropolis, and a café on the ground floor, whose tenant worked as hall porter. When a famous actress attended at one of these social functions, it turned into a *cavalchina* or masked ball, during which she stood at the entrance with a silver bowl receiving the guests' donations. By the late eighteenth century opera houses existed on Corfu, Cephalonia, and Zante, where the behaviour was no better and the musical standards no worse than in many cities in Western Europe.

To a point the middle classes participated. But, bitterly resentful as they mostly were of the nobility's monopoly of privilege and office, they tended to hold themselves aloof. On Zante especially they formed trading guilds, which with rising prosperity formed a rival force in the community. With strict laws of apprenticeship and a carefully graduated hierarchy, these tended to become closed corporations. Already in 1628 the guilds had challenged aristocratic ascendancy in several bloody riots, but the Republic successfully mollified many citizens by permitting them to buy patents of nobility. As every guild supported a church, which it tried to make the finest in the island, they became important patrons of the arts. By 1811 the number of churches on Zante had proliferated to 1410, half of them private chapels. St Nicholas was the Church of the Guilds of Corn Merchants and Seafarers, the Bricklayers worshipped at St Basil's, the Merchant Tailors at St Athanasius' and so on. Midway between the westernized habits of the nobles and the oriental primitiveness of the peasantry, the guilds made an invaluable contribution in fostering a sense of civic pride.

Under the Republic's sway the Jews occupied an anomalous position. They had been tolerated by the Angevins, and a ghetto with a rabbi was well enough established to be mentioned by 1365. The Greeks however hated the Jews although ironically the earliest known Greek vulgar prose is a translation of the Book of Jonah for the Corfu synagogue. Government officials were constantly reminded to treat them justly. During the fifteenth century the ghetto expanded; there was a fresh influx from Spain and Portugal in 1492, followed by one from Italy. The townsfolk would not allow them to take part in public processions or hold any office, despite the precedent of David Somos, one of the island's five ambassadors sent to treat with the Doge in 1386. Absurd tales abounded that Judas Iscariot had come to Corfu; his castle near Butrinto was pointed out, and a lineal descent even devised, ignoring the Gospels' clear assertion that the traitor had hanged himself. Perhaps there was some genuine confusion with the ancient name of Scheria.

Suspicion gradually replaced the open-minded tolerance with which the

Venetians had once viewed the Jews. Yet only in the Ionian Islands were they exempted from the taxes levied on their compatriots in the metropolis, and they alone were spared in the general decree of banishment for their race enacted in 1572. Theoretically they had to live within the ghetto at Corfu, but when it was razed in 1524 to make way for new fortifications, many families moved out into the town or the citadel. In the mid-seventeenth century the Jews had 500 houses in the reconstructed ghetto, their own council and officials, and controlled most of the business of the port.

Soon they spread to the southern islands, although no other community approached that of Corfu in size. Greek hostility did not abate. 'As a substitute for the custom of stoning, which does so much damage to the houses', in the words of the 1532 ordinance, the Jews had to wear a yellow badge or hat. But they evaded the prohibition on their owning or leasing any property except their own homes, by a system of mortgages. Their indispensability to a succession of Venetian officials ensured this was never challenged. Allowed to practise as advocates, they frequently defended Christians as well as their fellow countrymen. Only at Easter were they in real peril, when the mob might have attempted a massacre, if the ghettos had not been closely guarded. An eighth of the town of Corfu's population was Jewish by 1797, split into two groups, each with its own synagogue and traditions. The quarter is known as the Hebraika to this day.

Of all the classes, the material and intellectual condition of the peasantry changed the least. The Republic had retained the fief system in Corfu, and later in the other islands, even after the majority of the original families holding baronies were extinct. Serfs fell into three categories: those belonging to the barons, the Catholic Church, and the state. Sometimes they could buy their freedom; yet they enjoyed less rights than under Turkish rule. They lacked any political status, belonging absolutely to their lord with his other property, moveable and immoveable, so that their sole escape from a harsh master was to run away. Serfs on the demesne lands, which the Republic normally let to the highest bidder on a twenty-nine-year lease, were slightly better placed. All except the priests were theoretically liable to forced labour, but in practice they could gain exemption for a small sum. Certainly there were grumbles about working on government projects during the grape or corn harvests, and about having to pay taxes on oil in years when the olives did not bear. But della Marmora's assertion that the peasants rose against their lords at the slightest provocation is quite inaccurate; Venice never had a serious jacquerie, nor was there evident discontent with the regime until the seventeenth century.

By then agriculture had decayed, thanks to the Republic's deliberate policy of monoculture—of the olive in Corfu and Paxos (there were over two million trees on the former in 1797), of the currant in Cephalonia and Zante. Only in barren Ithaca, in Kythera, and to some extent in Levkas, did a mixed agronomy survive. Since property, like power, was in the hands of the few mainly absentee landlords, any incentive to better the lot of the rural poor was lacking. In years of food shortages, they were naturally the first to suffer. It is therefore the more remarkable that they retained the essence of village life and customs, whose hold on superstitious minds was as strong in 1797 as three centuries before.

Unlike many townspeople, the countryfolk had kept to their traditional oriental costumes. Both sexes wore earrings and their hair long, which the men hid under a red bonnet, while sporting enormous moustaches. The women only appeared in public masked, and if a stranger called, forthwith retired. If only relations were present they came down to meals, but did not sit and join in, staying huddled in a corner of the room gathering up the scraps left by their husbands, which they shared with the children. Their most noteworthy feature was their extreme pallor, not their beauty. The men were regarded as agile and supple with savage tempers, and in this era the vendetta became established in the islands. Passed down from father to son, it often involved entire villages and endless bloodshed. By the eighteenth century it was aptly said of the Ionians: 'the fig seller and the butcher boy are equally armed'.

Wedding customs were long established. After the marriage service, the entire congregation followed the bride to the nuptial house to the sound of clarinet and tambourine, and examined her bed, on which were placed the two candles topped with crowns, used in the ceremony. A few minutes after everyone had retired, the husband usually appeared and signified his satisfaction by firing a pistol. Music started, and the villagers danced round the happy couple's home all night. The next morning a table covered with drinks and sweetmeats was put in the hall, and a reception held. One superstition ran that if a guest tied three knots in his scarf at the moment the groom said 'I will', the luckless man would be deprived of the joys of married life. To rid himself of such ill fortune he had to hide under his pillow a pistol used in several murders. If his family felt he was showing insufficient zeal, they threw a black cock, a lock of his hair, and one of his treasured possessions into the fire. This always did the trick. The Cephalonians never married in May, following the old adage that only donkeys should procreate during that month, so solely an evil woman would wish to do so: '*Malae nubent Maia*'.

Funerals were governed by rules no whit less strict. Directly a dying man had expired, and sometimes before, he was wrapped in a robe leaving room only for his hands and head, laid on a dais covered with a red cloth, his face turned to the east and a candle at his head and feet. Immediately keening women surrounded the corpse, beating their breasts and rending their clothes. The priest rapidly recited the prescribed prayers, leaving the relatives to recount the deceased's virtues, to explain why he had departed the world, and to close with funny stories.

When the cortege left the house, the vase used for washing the dead was smashed on the threshold, to show it would never be used again. Water was poured in the coffin's wake to give nourishment to the deceased, and after the funeral service the corpse was embraced on its nose, mouth and eyes, with whispered messages for those already dead, and was left in a cellar. Every three months it was brought grain, bread, wine, and oil, while it was considered in poor taste to change its shroud before a year had elapsed. The wreaths, used by the ancient Greeks to adorn the dead, were only placed on the brows of virgin ladies as proof of an uncontaminated life. If a husband predeceased his wife, their wedding wreaths were buried with him; if he was a priest, his sacredotal oil lamp was interred too.

The country priests, as indigent and ignorant as their congregations, were ill-fitted to enlighten them. Usually married, their only home was the chapel, where their bed faced the altar. After conducting their first mass, their assembled patrons placed offerings on a salver, but occasionally the new priest, unsure of the takings, sold his collection to a broker beforehand. One way of supplementing the meagre income from christenings, marriages, and funerals, was to paint the patron saint in an identical style and colour on a gilt background. Every house in the islands contained at least one icon. However their main livelihood was in excommunication. An Ionian, wishing to avenge himself on a co-religionist, appealed to the priest, who stood before the designated house in mourning garb, carving a black candle and accompanied by his church personnel. After suitable prayers he launched a terrifying curse, gesticulating at the victim, who was thenceforth excluded from all dealings with his fellow men; ostracized, abused or exploited by those unable to refuse him their services. In his turn he could purchase the excommunication of his accuser; thereby both anathemas were annulled, and only the clergy, muttering '*Miserere Domine*', actually profited.

Much Ionian folklore was undeniably bizarre. All girls called Mary were meant to meet in uneven numbers from Tuesday to Friday in Easter week, and begin making a man's shirt as midnight struck. If it were sewn, washed and pressed before dawn, it assured the immortality of him who received it. A fertility rite took place on all the islands on 1 May, when parties went into the countryside to pick flowers and blades of corn, which they twined into chains or plaits, and hung from doors and windows. On the eve of 24 June, the birthday of John the Baptist, bonfires were lighted, the young men danced in the streets while the unmarried girls told each other's wedding prospects. On 29 August, in memory of his martyrdom, people drank the juice of black grapes, because of its resemblance to human blood. Pagan beliefs lingered on in remoter districts, the hoot of the owl and the howl of the dog being considered bad omens. Nymphs could be seen in a dust cloud raised by a gust of wind, or by anyone who slept in the shadow of a tree and then fell ill. Vampires possessed the spirits of those who had led dissolute lives. This welter of superstitions was handed down virtually intact into the nineteenth century, a proof of the immutability of peasant life in the islands.

From the era of Venetian rule much information about the Ionians and the lives they led can be gained from travellers' accounts. In the late fifteenth century B. de Breydenbach published the first sketch showing the citadel of Corfu in his *Opusculum Peregrinationum ad Sepulcrum Christi,* (published 1486). A Florentine, Nöe Bianco, copied it thirty years later in his *Viaggia al Sacro Sepulcro,* and soon sketches also showing the town were published. The large perspective plan included in G. Braun's *Beschreibung der Vornehmster Stadt der Welt* (Vienna, 1574), indicates no walls, but many houses visible among the trees. Pietro della Valle, who visited Corfu in 1614, described it as: 'on the points of a triangular elevation, washed on two sides by the sea; on the third, thanks to the Venetian engineers, it is separated from the rest of the island by a double ditch, walls, and bastions'. He found that 'the town is small and disagreeable, although the landscape is beautiful'.

At this time the Spianada is first mentioned. Its origins were undoubtedly military, to allow a free field of fire for the garrison of the Old Fortress. But it was now used for a parade ground, as a favourite promenade for the citizens, and for the civil and religious festivals so dear to their hearts. On 1 May all the fief holders paraded there, with a good horse and a fixed number of retainers, until the custom lapsed. Among them were the gypsies, who had been in Corfu since about 1400, and who, although only 100 strong, formed a separate fief under the exclusive jurisdiction of their lord, who could inflict any punishment short of death on them. The government had no power to make them perform any feudal obligation or serve in the galleys. The Hugot family held this fief, which was later given to Eparchos, for his bravery in the siege of 1537. The Spianada was the ideal setting for such ceremonies; it remained the centre of the town's life even when the assortment of barracks, arsenals, and casemates bordering it was built during the seventeenth century.

The other islands were less frequently mentioned. In his *Travels* (London, 1673), G. Sandys admired Sappho's Leap on Levkas, and scathingly dismissed Ithaca and Cephalonia. He was however fascinated by Zante. 'It is impossible that so little a portion of earth so employed should be more beneficiall: the mountainous part being barren and the rest comprised within two or three not very ample valleys, but those all over husbanded like an entire garden.' He observed many roads on the island, but only one harbour, and liked the motto above the castle gate:

> *'Hic locus odit, amat, punit, conservat, honorat,*
> *Nequitia pacem, crimina, iura, probos.'*
> (This place hates, loves, punishes, keeps, honours,
> vice, peace, crime, law, justice.)

Sandys disliked the people. 'In habits they imitate the Italians, but transcend them in their revenges, and are infinitely less civill. They will threaten to kill a merchant that will not buy their commodities; and make more conscience to breake a fast than to commit a murther.' He sailed on past the Strophades to Kythera, where he noticed: 'In the towne, rising two furlongs up from the haven, stands the celebrated Temple of Venus, (the most ancient that the Grecians had of that goddesse), and therein her statue in compleate armour. Here it is said Paris made a rape of Helena.' All traces of the temple have, alas, completely disappeared today.

In 1678 Dr Spon of Lyons and Sir George Wheler brought out *A Journey Through Italy, Dalmatia, Greece and the Levant,* which contains much about the islands. They described the Virgin's shrine at Kassiopi and its supposedly miraculous powers: 'Strangers that have a mind to know whether their friends are alive or dead, go to the Picture, and clasp a piece of money on it, thinking of some friend. If the person they think of be alive, the piece will stick fast; but if dead, it will drop into a sack placed underneath, so that dead or alive, the priest is sure of the money . . . The Picture is painted upon the walls, very smooth and shining, so that I attributed the sticking to some clamminess in the varnish, which they make sure is never wanting.' They also mentioned the ruined castle, actually destroyed by the Venetians, although, according to the legend, its inhabitants had been poisoned by a dragon's fiery breath. The travellers collected some rare plants on Corfu, were kindly received by della Marmora, the local historian, and sailed on south.

The description of Levkas, then under Turkish rule, is particularly interesting. 'Their houses are very low and built of wood. But to make amends, they themselves go very well cloathed, and are great pirates in those seas. The Pasha of the Morea came thither this year on purpose to burn their Gallies; whereof Durag Bey, a famous pirate of Lepanto, had formerly seven or eight under his command . . . There are about five or six thousand inhabitants in the Cittadel and suburbs. Without the fish we carried with us, we had very hard cheer there; for we found nothing but bad wine, bad bread, and worse cheese. There are about thirty villages in the Island, inhabited by poor Greeks that manure the land and catch fish; being under the jurisdiction of a Bishop whose revenues are but mean. The Isle is fruitful enough in corn, oranges, limons, almonds and pasture for their Cattel; being about thirty or forty miles in compass.'

In Zante they experienced one of the earthquakes so recurrent in the area. 'The town is well built of free Stone; but the buildings not very high, by reason of the frequent earthquakes; which in the spring occur some years, once or twice a week, and so shake all the houses that the walls of them are full of great cracks. One happened while I was there, at my return from Athens, during my quarantine in the pesthouse. That day the sun was of a yellowish colour, which was looked upon as ominous. I was sitting leaning upon a table; when on the sudden the Earth was so prodigiously shaken that I thought the place would have immediately fallen on my head. But the inhabitants are so used to it, that they make little or nothing of it.'

Such were the impressions of contemporary travellers. By this time the main islands, especially Corfu and Zante, contained sizeable foreign communities, whose contacts with the local inhabitants were more frequent, and usually more favourable. Wheler and Spon, writing of the merchants at Zante, said: 'They have left few marks of religion in their lives or at their deaths . . . They have neither church nor chapel nor pastor; they live without salvation and die without hope.' In fact the community was both more pious and more reputable than they inferred. By 1700 several merchants had built large houses in or near the town; the present Romas residence was constructed by an English consul as a dowry for his daughter. A tradition of long-established family businesses which was to survive with the Sargints and Crowes until well into this century, had begun. The British cemetery at Zante, with its magnificent tombs, displays the wealth and standing of many of its occupants, even if it also attests to the fever-ridden climate, which left many with 'a languid air, yellow complexion, and dropsical bellies'. One of the best known English residents was Sir Clement Harby, a formidable diplomat and Consul during the 1670s, whose correspondence bespeaks a profound knowledge of and affection for the islands, notwithstanding intermittent quarrels with officialdom.

Despite the gradual paralysis of government, the visual splendours of Ionian civilization increased. The seventeenth century was the golden age of building on Zante, where the baroque *palazzini* of the nobility along the Platia Rouga provided an architectural spectacle unique in the Levant. Even a small church, like Kyria ton Angelon, built for the Hairdressers' Guild in 1687, is a gem, while the Faneromeni completed in 1659 was a magnificent and sophisticated construction, until its tragic destruction in the 1953 earthquake. Many country churches, such as Makherado, were breathtaking for their ornate and sumptuous decoration, while some aristocratic residences, like that of the Lunzis at Sarakina, were conceived on a scale as grand as their counterparts in Western Europe, albeit in a far more restricted setting. The Venetians can scarcely be blamed for singing of this idyllic isle—'Zante, Zante, fior di Levante'.

In Cephalonia too, although the available wealth was never comparable, houses sprang up on a scale undreamed of a century earlier; particularly in the expanding port of Argostoli which, after the earthquake of 1756 had forced the Provveditore and garrison to abandon the Castle of St George, became the capital. On the smaller islands, little building was done; virtually none on Ithaca and Paxos. Yet even in Kythera, after Barbarossa's raid had led to the abandonment of Palaeokhora with its seventy-two frescoed chapels, a Venetian settlement grew up at Kato Khora, complete with its own miniature fort and churches. After the recapture of Levkas, the town (then known as Amaxikhi probably from the number of carts, *amaxia,* which unloaded produce there) spread rapidly. Churches like Ayios Minas were erected, country cousins perhaps by comparison with Zante, but large and imposing nonetheless. And in the eighteenth century the Valaoritis family built what must surely be one of the most delightful of all Ionian houses, the elegant pink villa on the islet of Madouri.

Of course it is simplest to envisage Venetian Corfu, for so much of it is still standing. Yet even here the explosion of 1718 and another in 1789 destroyed much of the Old Fortress, while the British cleared away more to make room for uninspiring barracks. In the town, the Campiello quarter still has an atmosphere redolent of an earlier age, although the bombardments in the Second World War demolished many buildings. The Kokkini well-head, the Loggia on the Town Hall with its defaced plaque to Morosini, the Vlakherna and Platytera convents, and a few arcaded houses all date from Venetian times. In the countryside, the architecture of the nobility's residences shows that distinctively Ionian blend of Greek and Italian styles. The Theotokis house at Karoussades, the Giallinas house at Kavalouri, the Kourkoumelis house at Afra all date from the sixteenth century, and the trend continues up to eighteenth century buildings, like the Manessis house at Ayios Stephanos.

In their art took the Ionians reflected their unique position between East and West. After the Fall of Constantinople, many painters emigrated to Crete, but some found their way to the islands. Two outstanding icon painters, Theodore Poulakis and Emmanuel Tzanes, lived for part of their lives and died in Corfu; others like Michael Damaskinos and Emmanuel Lombardos have left numerous examples of their work in the island churches and museums. The Cretan school was increasingly influenced by Western ideas of perspective, composition and colour by the mid-seventeenth century, yet, despite their new-found realism, they kept to the traditional themes of Byzantine iconography.

With the Turkish capture of Crete, the last bastion which preserved the aesthetic ideals of the Eastern Empire had fallen. More artists settled in the Ionian Islands, although many others swelled the colony in Venice centring round the Church of San Giorgio dei Greci. This was the age of sustained realism in art, apparent in the treatment of light and shade, of minutely detailed backgrounds and of carefully delineated human expressions and anatomical forms. The evangelist of the gospel of the Baroque to the Ionians was Panayiotis Doxaras. Born in the Morea, he settled in Zante in 1662, and studied under one of the Cretan emigrés, Leo Moschos. After further apprenticeship in Italy, he returned to introduce the virtues of Western painting, in particular of the Bolognese school, to his adopted homeland. As he taught his disciples 'The ideal is to work from nature; the task is to consider with a lucid eye whatever nature offers you at its grandest and most perfect', and in 1726 he published his guide to artistic technique. Doxaras' masterpiece was the seventeen paintings executed for the roof of St Spyridon's church, although unfortunately they were painted over in the nineteenth century.

Doxaras' efforts were to have far-reaching results. His was the first Ionian Academy of Arts, later to be revived under the French and then the British. His son Nicholas carried on these traditions, but tragically his finest work, the ceiling of the Faneromeni Church, was lost in the devastation of the 1953 earthquake. In turn his pupil was that Koutouzis already mentioned. Probably endowed with a more fertile imagination and a better sense of design than his master, he nevertheless lacked Doxaras' painstaking approach. Koutouzis' surviving works, and those of his associate Nicholas Kandounis, are extremely variable in quality and often too hastily painted to do justice to the artists' talents. By the time of the French Revolution, artistic standards had sunk to the level of their environment, of mere petty colonies, which reflected in a sybaritic society and a corrupt administration the decay of their metropolis.

Ionian culture, like so much else in the islands, was deceptive. Superficial westernization obscured the reality of the fundamental and immutable Greek character of the population. But the three, or in Corfu's case the four, centuries of Venetian domination had left a profound mark. In many ways the Ionians could pride themselves on their role as a bridge between East and West, for they had transmitted much of value in both directions. Without the subtle guiding hand of the Republic, for all its shortcomings, this could never have been achieved, nor would the unique blend of two contrasting civilizations have occurred. Well might Wordsworth lament, when he heard the sad news of Campo Formio:

> 'Once did She hold the gorgeous East in fee;
> And was the safeguard of the West: the worth
> Of Venice did not fall below her birth,
> Venice, the eldest Child of Liberty.'

29 *Above*—The Arsenal at Gouvia, Corfu, built by the Venetians after the siege of 1716. Today its three roofless naves belie its importance in providing for the proper maintenance of the Republic's galleys. Unfortunately it was built only when Venice was in irretrievable decline, but it remains as one of the many momentoes of her long rule over the Ionian Islands.

30 *Above*—Plaque to Francesco Morosini 'Il Peloponnesiaco' on the side wall of the Town Hall, Corfu.

31 *Opposite, top*—Facade of the Town Hall, Corfu, built as a loggia in 1693 and converted into a theatre in 1720.

32 *Opposite, bottom*—The Liston, Corfu, begun by the French in 1807 in imitation of the Rue de Rivoli.

33 *Opposite, top*—The Old Fortress, Corfu, as seen from the sea; from Byzantine times to the 19th century the strongest point on the island.

34 *Opposite, bottom*—View over Vido islet, Corfu, looking towards Mount Pantocrator.

35 *Above*—View over the village and castle of Assos. This promontory on the west coast of Cephalonia was fortified by the Venetians during the 16th and 17th centuries.

36 *Overleaf, top*—Ramparts and ruined chapel in the fortress of Santa Maura, Levkas.

37 *Overleaf, bottom*—Sea wall of the fortress.

38 *Above* — Turkish style house and the Cyclopean walls of ancient Levkas.

39 *Below* — The Main Street, Levkas.

40 *Above* — The 17th century Kokkini wellhead in the Campiello quarter, Corfu.

41 *Opposite, top* — Main Gate of the Castle on the hill behind the town, Zante.

42 *Opposite, bottom* — Detail from same, showing the Venetian lion.

T
F
P

43 *Opposite, top*—Gateway of the miniature fortress at Kato Khora, Kythera, with the Venetian lion, dated 1566.

44 *Opposite, bottom*—Ruined building in the fortress at Khora, Kythera, used as a gaol by the Venetians and the British.

45 *Above*—Ruined 18th century courtyard and fountain at Kombitsi, Corfu.

46 *Opposite, top* — The Venetian fortress at Khora, Kythera.

47 *Opposite, bottom* — View over Khora, Kythera, looking away from the castle.

48 *Above* — One of the old houses in Kato Khora, Kythera.

49 *Above* — The coat of arms with the double-headed eagle comes from the house of Yeorgios Petrochilos, Kythera.

Chapter IV
A Time of Transition

A. THE ADVENT OF REVOLUTION

'The islands of Corfu, Zante, and Cephalonia seem of more importance to us than all Italy. The Turkish Empire is decaying; the possession of the islands would enable us to support it if that were possible, or to take our share.' The despatches which Napoleon wrote to the Directory from Milan in the summer of 1797 show the importance he attached to a French annexation of the Ionian Islands. It was in France's interests to dominate the Mediterranean and Levant as much as it was in the interests of England, Austria, or Russia to prevent her. The idea had come to obsess Bonaparte. 'The time is not far off when we shall feel that to destroy England we must seize Egypt and the route to the East', he wrote, and to be master of the Adriatic was an essential prerequisite for him. The islands' strategic worth was greater than Malta's or Sicily's, and he realized that Russia with the advantages of a common Orthodox faith had long coveted them, that the English too wanted a base in the area, and that even the King of Naples was now pressing his claims on the grounds that they had belonged to his predecessors in the Middle Ages.

For the Republic of St Mark had ceased to exist, and the Ionian Islands no longer had a master. On 8 May the Venetian Senate had sent envoys to receive whatever terms Bonaparte cared to dictate. Widmann's brother sent him the terrible news by secret courier. Immediately the Provveditore Generale summoned the chief citizens, the Jewish leaders, the clergy, and the magistrates together, and read them the letter, which disproves subsequent accusations that he had kept the facts from the public. He had heard no news for six weeks although he had had some warning, for on Palm Sunday two French frigates had appeared off Corfu and asked for water. Uncertain what he should do, for France and Venice were then at war, Widmann had typically chosen to obey the laws of humanity and supply their needs. Some sailors had disembarked, and watching the St Spyridon procession, had passed irreverent remarks about 'the old fossil in its glass case'. A riot would have broken out, had the garrison not restored order. The French ships hastily weighed anchor leaving behind sour memories of the blaspheming Revolutionaries. In March too the Senate had informed Widmann that Italy was in turmoil, and bade him use the good offices of the clergy to retain his charges' loyalty. But otherwise he was in complete ignorance of the momentous events that had ended more than a thousand years of Venetian independence. A packet boat sent to Otranto soon returned with further news. Venice was in the throes of revolution, the aristocracy's hereditary privileges had been abolished, the Grand Council had renounced its sovereignty and declared for a government on the French model, while Bonaparte's troops had entered the Lagoon in a fleet provided by the city. On 1 June the new Provisional Municipality sent its Proclamation to Corfu, exhorting the nobles 'to make a glorious sacrifice of their titles' and the people 'to enjoy the benefits of democracy'. Widmann remained unconvinced that the Ionians wanted an overthrow of the status quo. The nobles did not of course respond to the appeal, nor did the people show any signs of wishing to profit by the rights which the mother country seemed determined to bestow upon them.

Napoleon was not, however, wasting time. In May he offered to lend the Municipality some troops to overcome the 'ill will' of the officials and nobles in the islands. After much pressure, the Venetians agreed to supply some ships, and four of their vessels, with eleven French ships, were assembled with an expeditionary force of 3,525 men. The command was given to the Corsican General Gentili, who had successfully fought the English in his native island, and whose origins were considered suitable to recommend him to Ionian affections, while he was told to evoke 'the memory of Greece, of Athens and Sparta' in support of his mission. With him went Arnault, a member of the Académie Française, who was deputed to make an exact report of the islands' artistic treasures, although he was to find nothing worthy of his notice apart from the statue of Schulenburg. After many delays the expedition set sail on 13 June but, as a total calm prevailed in the Adriatic, Corfu was only sighted on the 28th. Gentili had sent an officer ahead to prepare for the billeting of his men, and at first Widmann naturally failed to understand this was an 'allied' force. But what could he do? With no troops or fleet, and with enough powder in the magazine for one round from each gun, he could scarcely resist. Moreover, Gentili claimed to be coming as an ally to reinforce the garrison. Widmann was a loyal and conscientious administrator, he was not of the stuff from which heroes are made. He published an order that the newcomers should be received as friends.

'On the 10th Messidor, our troops landed and were welcomed by an immense crowd of people, who testified their joy by shouts of enthusiasm such as never fail to animate those who recover their liberty. At the head of the people was their Papa, well-informed and seemingly very old. He approached General Gentili and addressed him thus: "Frenchman, you will find in these island a people ignorant of those arts and sciences which distinguish other nations, but do not despise them on this account. What has been before can be again; learn to respect them by reading this book." The General opened the book with great curiosity and was not a little surprised to see that it was the *Odyssey*. The people of Zante, Cephalonia, and Levkas have expressed the same ardent desire for liberty, and hope under our protection to recover their arts, sciences, and long-lost commerce.' So ran Napoleon's despatch to Paris. And in the first few days the rejoicing was indeed universal. The people thought to see the deposition of the proud aristocracy, the nobles confident of their intellectual superiority and ill-informed as to the practice of democracy, believed they could control the new government as they had the old.

Gentili was careful to change nothing at once. Widmann and the magistrates remained in office. Yet his quarters were filled with those demanding aid or justice from the Republicans, and the General imagined that an annexation decree at that moment was possible. 'Say the word, and the islands are ours', he wrote to Bonaparte, but he understood neither the customs, character, nor political aspirations of the Ionians. Arnault advised him to create a provisional Council of Twenty-Four to reorganize the municipal administration, and ten of the chief citizens were called upon to produce a list of forty names each. From these the ones that occurred most frequently were chosen, and the Provveditore Generale, the Protopapas, the Head Rabbi and the Latin Archbishop were added to this body, as well as six farmers nominated from the chief villages of Corfu to represent the countryfolk. A sincere attempt had been made to balance the religions, for the Council had eighteen Orthodox, four Catholics, and two Jews. The first session opened under the presidency of Count Spyridon Theotokis, for Widmann had declined the honour. In a grandiloquent speech he enunciated the ideas imported a week before, he welcomed his fellow-citizens and urged them to show unity, tolerance and fraternity. Alas, this was asking too much. The next day one of the Greek priests resigned on the pretext that Holy Writ precluded his taking part in public affairs, while audibly telling his colleagues that the real reason was the shame of sitting down with the Jews. A tailor then followed this up by demanding the exclusion of the Rabbi and the Archbishop. His supporters noisily applauded and called for an immediate debate on the motion. When the President refused, uproar ensued and the Council was ejected by a mob. Thus emboldened, they pursued the wretched Jews, who barricaded themselves in their houses, and only when the troops were called out did the mob disperse. Few of them were impressed with Arnault's philosophic reflection that 'Jews were no more dogs to the Greeks, than Greeks were to the Latins.'

As the Council had dissolved, a Committee of Public Safety was formed, which promptly lived up to its name by proposing mass arrests and executions. Its members were soon unpopular enough to have to ask the General for a guard. One ardent patriot suggested proscriptions, and began by declaring his neighbour, then travelling in Albania, suspect, because he wanted his carriage. Fortunately, Gentili squashed this embryonic Terror. The Committee was given executive powers under his supreme authority, and seven other committees were set up—for commerce, education, the army, police, health, finance, and the arts. All could propose laws and appoint officials. The President of each changed every month, and the public were admitted, although only in such numbers that in case of a riot they did not outnumber the Councillors.

Small detachments were sent to the other islands. On Ithaca they were greeted with particular enthusiasm. On Zante, where the Provveditore was cordially hated, one party wanted the French, another the Russians. When Gentili's soldiers arrived, a tree of liberty was planted, and the *Livra d'Oro* ceremonially burned. The mob wished to burn the Provveditore's wig as well, and when he protested that it had cost thirty sequins, some rich patriot promised to reimburse him. A municipality similar to that established at Corfu was set up, the year was dated from One, and a vote passed to the French people 'thanks to whom we are free as at the time of Pericles, Aristides, and Solon.' Nevertheless, the Zantiotes raised the Russian flag three weeks later, and the small French garrison had to quell the demonstrations. In the other islands similar scenes prevailed, for the people were pleased to see the privileges of the hated nobles removed, while the Orthodox priests were delighted by the humiliation of their Catholic rivals.

On Corfu Gentili tried to effect reforms which were then to be introduced elsewhere. Justice, the prime scandal under the old regime, was overhauled, and nine justices of the peace appointed—three for the town, three for the suburbs, and three for the countryside, who were to give judgements on the spot. There was also a Court of First Instance with three judges, and an Appeal Court with ten magistrates, of whom nine were needed to form a quorum. Three criminal courts were to try crimes of violence, although a jury system could not be introduced so quickly. Everyone was amazed how rapidly and cheaply appeals were now heard. To celebrate the new order, open-air banquets were held, young men wrestled, and those representing the new ideals won of course, to return crowned with laurels, while the girls' elaborate costumes symbolized virtue reborn. Wine flowed in the fountains; the poor received alms. To demonstrate their rejection of the past, the Corfiotes threw down the Lion of St Mark and replaced it with the Gallic cock. On 16 July a Tree of Liberty was solemnly planted on the Spianada, but as 17 July dawned, it was found defaced. In vain did the Committee of Public Safety promise a large reward to those benefactors of their country who would denounce the guilty parties, in vain did the Protopapas pronounce his most terrible anathemas; they were never caught. Yet Gentili remained the idol of the mob for the moment, and Widmann's attempts to defend the Venetian record went unheeded.

The truth was, however, beginning to dawn: the French had come with many fine words and no money. On Napoleon's orders, Admiral Brueys' fleet arrived bringing further reinforcements and munitions, but no funds or provisions. All the previous regime's obligations were cancelled, and the former bailie was reduced to begging on his knees for help, or he would die of hunger. It was soon found necessary to levy a new export tax, to step up the old duties and to institute a 'hardship tax'. These measures principally alienated the higher classes, but the contempt shown by the French troops for popular superstitions was to make them universally hated. The devout Corfiotes saw them working on Sundays, refusing the last rites, and worst of all ridiculing their most sacred beliefs like 'the old carcass of St Spyridon'. For the great French miscalculation was to think their presence and example alone could detach a population from its age-old traditions. Originally the Protopapas had declared that the principles of the Revolution conformed perfectly with Our Lord's teaching. But when the Republicans suggested compelling priests to wear the tricouleur, expelling all those not native born from the island, and converting the Rosaria Church into a barracks, his attitude changed. Moreover other grievances such as billeting, an epidemic among the cows, even the maintenance of public order, excited popular resentment against the garrison.

These feelings were to crystallize through a club which the French had imprudently allowed to form. The islanders' ignorance, so sedulously fostered by Venice, had appalled the newcomers, and the foundation of a patriotic education society had seemed a good idea 'to be a light to inspire among the Greeks those heroic sentiments which had been the glory of the nation'. The society opened its doors to a wide public, meetings were crowded, debates stormy and more concerned with the propagation of revolutionary theory than with the development of Corfiote education. Gentili began by protesting his good intentions, when the clubists first criticized him. Then, seeing his moderation mistaken for feebleness, he proclaimed that anyone plotting against the government would be put in irons. Proprietors of cafés where the malcontents met were held responsible for their clients' behaviour. A huge petition was drawn up against the municipality in reply, indicting its duplicity and non-democratic basis. Arnault, while agreeing that purely liberal principles had been violated, argued that the people were inadequately prepared to exercise their rights and too disorderly to run their own affairs; he therefore refused to make concessions. Gentili declared that the municipality had been installed on the direct orders of Napoleon, and would not be changed until the island's fate had been decided. To all good patriots, the liberator had become the oppressor, and French difficulties were increased by a reduction in the garrison to 1,500 men for reasons of economy.

The malcontents posed the general an unanswerable question: if he had come as the Venetians' ally, why had he abolished their authority, if as the Corfiotes' liberator, why would he not let them enjoy their independence? Plots were hatched incessantly to massacre the garrison at a stroke, and if the Russians had not been so far away their aid would have been invoked, while in their absence the Austrians who had advanced in Dalmatia appeared as a potential ally. The conspirators reckoned that the best way of exciting the people's hatred against the French was to organize the intervention of St Spyridon. 'When the Saint leaves his coffin, then the island will dance', as the saying went. But to remove the relics exclusive access to them was necessary. The sanctuary had three keys: Papa Piero, head of the Voulgaris family owned one, the bailie had given him another before his departure, but the dutiful Widmann had delivered the third to Arnault. Papa Piero undertook to get it back. Every morning he went to discuss Homer with the Frenchman, but the latter, equally wily, would not be drawn into mentioning current events or handing over the key. So the priest devised a new plan. He requested a guard for the chapel in such troubled times. Gentili agreed and went to inspect it. A rumour was then started that the French wanted to despoil the rich sanctuary, and the general himself had gone to organize its sack. Arnault riposted in kind. Papa Piero was brought before him with two or three others who had complained of the profanation of the chapel. As they had claimed to witness the sacrilege at first hand, Arnault asked them why they had not resisted then, and warned them that their silence was bound to be viewed as compromising. Voulgaris had to sign a declaration attesting that the treasure was intact and under the vigilant guard of the French. This was fastened to the chapel door, and order was restored with the threat that if anyone so used St Spyridon again, he would be sent to join Our Lady of Loretto in the Directory's dungeons.

The Corfiotes' grievances found an echo in Venice, where the Municipality headed by Widmann's brother resented the military occupation, and complained to the French plenipotentiary that the expedition had been intended to protect the Ionians, not to annex them. In the other islands unrest was growing, so Gentili, although ailing, decided to visit them. He was warmly welcomed in Cephalonia, where he calmed the agitation provoked by the conflicting claims of Argostoli and Lixouri to be the capital. Thence he went to Zante, where the Russian flag had been raised eight days earlier. The peasants demanded some reduction in taxation, and remained unconvinced by Gentili's assurance that liberty could never be bought cheaply. In Levkas, where overt grumbles were less but fundamental hostility to the new ideas greater, the general was given a good reception by those who rejoiced at the overthrow of the nobility. Tranquillity had returned, at least superficially, and by September the municipality was declaiming on 'the honour for the isles of the Levant to form part of the Great Nation'. Suddenly annexation seemed a serious possibility.

During the preliminary negotiations to the Treaty of Campo Formio, Napoleon had strongly insisted that France must keep her important acquisitions in the Adriatic. 'The Court of Naples,' he wrote, 'has grand notions of annexing the Ionian Islands, and half the Papal States, especially Ancona. Their pretensions are too funny; I believe that in exchange she is willing to cede us Elba. The Republic's maxim must be never to abandon Corfu'. Nevertheless the Directors seemed inclined to accept this strange bargain, and Bonaparte had to emphasize the strategic value of the islands, which were, he assured Paris, perfectly provisioned and fortified. After averting a new threat to cede them to the Duke of Modena, he had his way. When the Treaty was signed in October, Article 5 contained an explicit recognition of the Republic's complete sovereignty over the seven islands and all the former Venetian enclaves on the mainland. Napoleon was as proud of this as of his greater triumphs in Italy. In a letter to Talleyrand, he stated: 'We are gaining the most precious part of the Venetian Republic for ourselves. When France has Mainz and the Rhine, and a well fortified stronghold in the Levant, what more can she want?'

His sixteen-year-old stepson, Eugene de Beauharnais, was sent to Corfu to announce the annexation. He landed on the last of St Spyridon's four feast days in the year, and the assembled crowds welcomed the news rapturously.

Beauharnais was offered a sword of honour, which he must have received with mixed feelings as he had just narrowly escaped an assassination attempt by three masked men. A pyramid was to be erected in the middle of the Spianada to commemorate the victories of the Army of Italy (it never was), and a deputation travelled to Milan, where they expressed the Ionians' gratitude to Bonaparte in such fulsome terms that they had to be reminded that the Directors were the supreme authority. The islands now treated as French territory were divided into three departments. Corcyra (i.e. Corfu, Paxos with the adjacent islets, Butrinto and Parga) had M. de Corbigny as its administrator; Ithaca (i.e. Ithaca, Levkas and its archipelago, Cephalonia and the dependencies of Preveza and Vonitza) was governed by M. Pocholle from its capital Argostoli; lastly the Department of the Aegean (based on Zante, with the Strophades, Kythera and Antikythera) had the writer M. Rulhière at its head. The designation was chosen deliberately, for although it did not comprise one Aegean island, Napoleon hoped to gain more territory from the Ottoman Empire.

From December 1798 each department also had the right to send an elected deputy to the central legislature in Paris. Despite the theoretical abolition of the aristocracy, the department of Corcyra elected Count Andreas Sordinas as its deputy by a large majority. Thirty places in a college in Paris were similarly reserved for talented Ionian youths, and though it was specifically stated that it was no advantage to be of noble birth, most of the applicants were well born.

A Directory of five members ran each department. The Commissioner General, who was the chief administrator, had overall powers, and he nominated the members of the municipalities, the judges, and most of the officials. Aided by a Secretary General, who had to be native born, and by three magistrates, he also ran the police and the finances. Each department was divided into cantons with a commission of seven in all those with under 10,000 inhabitants, and nine in the larger ones. In each canton a justice of the peace 'nominated by the most respectable heads of families would ensure the return of public morality'. It was all very neat on paper, and on 7 November Bonaparte himself published the charter, for which he was largely responsible. In Zante a public holiday was proclaimed, in Corfu solemn services held in both denominations. Moreover the Directory hastened to exploit the commercial possibilities of their new conquest, in the belief that Corfu could become the entropôt for all their Eastern and Adriatic trade. Passports were sent to the leading Greek merchants, the Ministry of the Interior published a detailed list of products from the Levant, and an

Inspector General of Trade arrived to make an assessment on the spot. Similarly the French strengthened their strategic position, forming the islands into one military unit under a general aided by a paymaster and directors of the engineers and artillery. As the general had discretionary powers of High Police, he exercised an unlimited authority in practice. To protect the islands against the Barbary pirates, a flotilla of two frigates, two cutters, and six barks was assigned to him, while a regular post service to Otranto ensured communications with France. These arrangements seemed guaranteed to ensure the success and permanence of the annexation, for which Napoleon had striven so hard. Unfortunately, one factor had been left out of his calculations.

Ali of Tebelen was a redoubtable figure. Pasha of Ioannina, which he had subdued after forging the firman which specifically excluded him from it, he now controlled a wide area in Epirus and Albania, and carried on an incessant campaign against the Suliotes. Reputedly the murderer of his brother, ruthless and ambitious, he dreamed of becoming an independent sovereign, and could only be a dangerous neighbour for the Ionian Islands. In 1793 Widmann's predecessor had described him thus: 'rich, powerful, devoured by the desire to rule, he knows how to estimate the exact resources and strength of his opponents.' Straight after Campo Formio he had written to Napoleon, expressing his esteem and offering his friendship. The Pasha affected great enthusiasm for the principles of the Revolution and the religion of the Supreme Being. Indeed he declared his willingness to be instructed in the Carmagnole, which he imagined to be a republican deity rather than a dance. He even wore the tricouleur in his turban.

Napoleon was completely deceived and imagined that their mutual interests would make Ali a reliable ally. So Gentili received orders to be friendly, and Adjutant-General Roze was sent to Ioannina to effect a reconciliation. Ali welcomed him lavishly, giving him Zoitza, a black-eyed seventeen-year-old beauty and probably his daughter, as a bride, and Roze returned with an ample dowry singing his father-in-law's praises. The latter meanwhile was secretly gathering a fleet and 5,000 men in the Gulf of Arta, which surprised the Suliote villagers from the sea and massacred 6,000 of them. Venice had always defended them; indeed the Treaty of Passarowitz prohibited Turkish vessels passing the Corfu Straits, and when Ali had tried this ploy before, the Venetians had armed and called his bluff. As the Suliotes were now supposedly under French protection, the challenge was clear enough. Unfortunately, since the French had already conceded the right of free navigation in the Adriatic, there was little to be done. And the islands did of course depend on a friendly neighbour on the mainland to supply their habitual wants—grain, meat and timber. The Pasha, quite unabashed, promptly demanded Butrinto as the price of his allegiance. When Gentili indignantly complained to Bonaparte of Ali's duplicity, he was assured that the latter's friendship was essential to French interests, except in the inconceivable event that he posed a threat to French territory. The bewildered Gentili asked for leave, but died en route home to his native Corsica.

On 20 December his successor General Chabot arrived in Corfu, while a Commissioner General for all the islands, Citoyen Bonhomme Comeyras was also appointed. A typically crafty and devious Jacobin official, he went no further than Ancona, where, after hearing of the emptiness of the treasury and the paralysis of the administration, he remained. The garrison had not been paid for four months, the sailors for even longer and all had to find work to earn their daily bread. The barracks were so dilapidated that in one, when the roof fell in, the troops had to be lodged in the cellars. The veterans were in a state of near mutiny, and Chabot had to levy another special tax on the chief citizens. Well might the discontented Corfiotes grumble that all their revenue went to the army. Yet a public address to the Directory was fruitless, as financial help was far less forthcoming than political reform. Comeyras was granted viceregal powers, and Zante and Corfu were divided into four quarters with the symbolic names of Liberty, Equality, Unity, and Fraternity. Each district in town or country now had its council, each canton its directory. Twelve miniature ministries were created, the courts again restructured, and the magistrates, all government nominees, were concentrated in the local capitals. It was but too obvious that the islanders' ancestral privileges were being gradually abolished.

When one of the three printing presses Gentili had ordered actually came, it began to produce grandiose declarations about the Ionians' future in the new Europe. But to be of any use, the population had to be literate. A primary school teaching reading, arithmetic, and French history and language to the children of all races had already been founded, and Chabot deputed an artillery officer to give lectures on the art of war. Otherwise public education languished, for the Patriotic Society after its unruly beginnings had achieved little. Nevertheless, it was felt to be a duty to impart the new doctrines of Theophilanthropy to the Corfiotes. Wanting no more innovations, they protested and recalled the promises not to meddle with their religion. The Latin clergy, whose churches had been looted by the French and whose Archbishop Fenzi had been evicted from his palace, fanned the flames, while the Protopapas supported them. The malcontents were encouraged by rumours of an impending evacuation, for Admiral Brueys' fleet had suddenly weighed anchor. Chabot acted swiftly; the Archbishop was deported, the Slav regiments disbanded, and several manifestos published proclaiming France's destiny in the East in such aggressive terms that the Porte complained. It was made a capital crime to have relations with the Russians, and ships trading with Russia were liable to confiscation.

The anniversary of the French arrival was celebrated with great pomp in June 1798. An altar of peace was erected on the Spianada, and that evening the town and forts were illuminated, and 'a concert of harmony' was given. Soon afterwards came the news of the capture of Alexandria, an auspicious opening to Napoleon's Egyptian campaign. Many who had scoffed at his achievements now began to wonder if he really might free their compatriots from the Turkish yoke. The prestige of France rose again, discontent temporarily abated, and some soldiers even married island girls. If this were not the Age of Gold originally promised, it was certainly better than the twilight of Venetian rule, as even those who loathed the Revolution were forced to admit.

In July Comeyras did finally appear with some funds, for he had extorted a forced loan from the city of Ragusa. His first act was a blunder, as he issued a proclamation that the Directory would reward public-spirited priests and severely punish those who abused their spiritual authority. He then abolished the old municipality and did not replace it, 'since my enquiries have not revealed a sufficient number of citizens whom I can deem worthy of fulfilling their municipal functions'. It was replaced by a commission. Comeyras set about adopting suitable French laws for the islands, and had started a systematic persecution of the nobility and clergy, when he went too far. He wrote to Paris demanding the recall of Chabot and Roze, and imputing the blackest crimes to them. In reply they alleged that he had been too dilatory in taking up his appointment and too zealous in filling it, and in fact it was Comeyras who was recalled, though he died of fever on reaching Ancona. Luckily his successor Dubois was to prove more enlightened and tolerant.

That autumn brought the news of Nelson's crushing victory at Aboukir Bay. Admiral Brueys did not follow his instructions to seek refuge in Corfu harbour, but Napoleon sent Chabot orders to send provisions to Egypt by organizing a dozen rich Ionian merchants to begin an exchange trade. The enemies of France revived. In August Sultan Selim had formed an alliance with Tsar Paul I. The next month they declared war and a united expeditionary force was assembled in the Bosphorus. Ali again saw his chance. He had recently had another visit from Roze, in which fresh assurances of eternal friendship were exchanged, although he had refused to revolt against the Sultan unless given 10,000 men and 100,000 sequins. Now he offered to reinforce the Corfu garrison with his own troops, if all the mainland enclaves and Levkas were ceded to him. Chabot disdained to answer; instead he set off to inspect the defences of the other islands. Proof that these precautions were well justified was afforded by an attempt by Ali's son, Mouktar, to capture Preveza by a ruse. When forestalled by the tiny French garrison, he blandly explained that his men were escorting a Prevezan warrior who had been maltreated by the Venetians and whom he wished to 'reintroduce' to his native town. The 'escort' were prudently refused entry. However the Pasha got his revenge elsewhere. Having invited General Roze to a meeting on the mainland, he threw him in irons and sent him to Constantinople, where the poor man died in prison.

The French position was perilous in the extreme. Their garrisons had never amounted to more than 4,300 men, plus 900 Italians from the Cisalpine Legion, and 2,000 or 3,000 Slav militia. With all the reductions they numbered little more than 3,000 in toto by October. Except for Corfu all the fortifications were in ruins, while the arsenals and magazines were almost empty, for Gentili had foolishly left them in the hands of their former custodians, who had sold most of the stores. Chabot was at Lixouri when he received official confirmation of the Russo-Turkish declaration of war, and a report that Ali, after concluding a truce with the Suliotes, had invested Butrinto. Taking 300 men to reinforce the garrison the general hurried there, but on attempting a sortie was left behind by his soldiers and almost captured. After several days of fierce fighting the town was abandoned to an overwhelmingly superior enemy, and a few days later the fort too was evacuated. Panic reigned on Corfu, where Dubois formed an extraordinary council of seven, all Frenchmen, to take over the entire administration in the emergency.

Forthwith Ali marched on Preveza, where thanks to clever agitation the projected defence works remained uncompleted. Reinforcements were rushed over from Levkas, but altogether there were only 700 French troops, sixty Suliote auxiliaries, and 200 unreliable Prevezan militia. The Pasha's men mounted a furious attack at dawn, and although the defenders performed prodigies of valour, the Suliotes in the middle of the line broke and fled. The Albanians surrounded their brave adversaries and massacred them amid the ruins of Nicopolis. The survivors retreated to find the militia had closed the two gates against them. These were forced, and a relieving squadron sighted on the horizon. But the treacherous boatman who promised to row out and tell of the garrison's peril, told them instead that the town had fallen, so the ships sailed away. Resistance soon ceased and the remaining Frenchmen were forced to help in the execution of many of the townsfolk. A pyramid of skulls, duly shaved and washed, was erected to be sent to the Sultan as evidence of this great victory. Then the prisoners were force-marched barefoot and waterless from Arta to Constantinople. 147 began the journey; virtually none completed it. Soon Ali was at the head of 15,000 men and controlled the whole seaboard except Parga. He had the effrontery to write again to Chabot proposing an alliance, and excusing his arrest of Roze on the grounds that he needed an interpreter. The general, who knew that he was simultaneously urging the Pargiotes to evict their garrison, did not bother to answer.

The Russo-Turkish fleet assembled at Hydra and rounded Cape Malea. On 5 October Captain Michel, commandant of the garrison on Kythera, was attending a ball when he was shown Admiral Ouchakov's proclamation to the islanders, urging them to sieze the French soldiers at a stroke. Michel gathered his men, fifty at the most, and shut himself up in the citadel at Khora, which was impregnable from the sea but vulnerable to attack from the landward side. Of the forty guns, few were in working order; there was a handful of bullets and one barrel of powder. The allies landed 2,500 men and Ouchakov threatened the garrison with annihilation if they remained obdurate. After two days' heavy bombardment, a deputation was sent to negotiate a surrender. Michel, however, demanded the honours of war for his troops, their repatriation and no punishment of any Francophile Kytherans. The talks were broken off, but when the allied officers stayed to dine at the castle, they were assured that he was ready to blow it up with everyone in it. Eventually a capitulation was signed on the gallant captain's terms.

A fortnight later the expedition appeared off Zante. Here everything was in chaos. Rulhière had gone to seek help from Paris, most of the municipality's members had fled to the interior and the pro-Russian forces waxed stronger daily. Ouchakov promised the islanders independence and a republic if they so desired, while the Patriarch's manifesto damned the French as atheists and blasphemers, and called on all good Orthodox believers to assist in their expulsion. The singularity of the Autocrat of all the Russias suggesting a republic, and the Patriarch recommending an alliance with the infidel Turk went unremarked, and these proclamations had great influence. Countervailing appeal to the Greeks' love of freedom and classical virtues went unheeded, and Colonel Vernier, who commanded the garrison, found treachery everywhere. The fishermen claimed they had not seen an enemy sail the day before the allied fleet arrived. When Ouchakov began a general bombardment, the French defence was paralysed by 8,000 peasants who swarmed into the town. The outlying batteries had to be abandoned and a retreat to the castle was ordered. Baulked of their prey, the peasants opened the prisons, pillaged the town hall and the archives, then looted all the houses in which the soldiers had been billeted. Finally they sacked and burned the Jewish ghetto, raping and killing its inmates. Meanwhile the nobles, who had incited them to fury, embarked and sought refuge with the Russian admiral. The next day a full-scale assault was launched on the castle, and Vernier, with only 400 men, offered to surrender. Less proud than Michel, he allowed his troops to be disarmed and made prisoner, only half of them being repatriated to France. No stipulations were made for his supporters among the Zantiotes, who, thoroughly alarmed, quitted the island en masse.

Cephalonia was the next target. Here too agitation had done its work and the garrison had had to commandeer provisions and sternly suppress discontent. Thus the peasants, the clergy, even the municipality members appointed by them, were all Francophobe. Colonel Roger had only 350 men, and any systematic defence of an island as mountainous and disjointed as Cephalonia was obviously out of the question. So the decision was made to concentrate at Assos, whither all the various detachments were summoned. Two hundred of the French were ambushed in a defile in the interior, where, with rocks crashing down on them and vastly out-numbered, they agreed to surrender. The mountain folk promptly broke their pledges and stole their money, belongings, and clothes as well. In terrible distress the survivors reached a village where they were even refused water until the priest intervened. When at last they reached Assos they found the steep path down to the isthmus blocked by an armed mob, and they were locked up in a chapel where they would assuredly have died had a Russian officer not arrived and conducted them back to Argostoli. Here they found their colleagues whose ship had been seized by the townsfolk at Lixouri before it could set sail. All the soldiers were sent as prisoners to Patras.

Next Ouchakov turned to Ithaca. But here the islanders' behaviour was very different. As the allied fleet approached, they offered to help Captain Millet and his twenty-five men escape. 'If we can lead you to safety and then fall into our enemy's clutches we will die if need be, but without regrets if we have saved your lives and freedom!' Before departing, everyone sat down to a communal feast, the ship that was to carry the French was garlanded with flowers and the Ithacans waved farewell so long as it remained in sight. On the second day at sea they met a Russian squadron, but by raising the Turkish flag they escaped unscathed, and Millet with his entire contingent landed safely on

Corfu. In Levkas too great alarm reigned that Ali would seize the island and treat it like Preveza. When the Pasha's decree urging the population to drive out the French was published, the municipality advised the garrison to retire. Then the tricouleur was thrown down and the Russian flag hoisted. Colonel Mialet's 300 men were an insufficient deterrent, yet before retreating to the fortress were restrained with difficulty from firing on the crowd. On 28 October some allied ships appeared and bombarded the walls, killing about fifty soldiers. Nevertheless Mialet, short of provisions and ammunition, held out for a fortnight. He only capitulated when granted the honours of war, and his officers were repatriated with him. Some of the French soldiers were driven overland to Constantinople, where they were brutally treated; the rest were taken to the Crimea and humanely imprisoned.

Many blamed Chabot for dividing his forces and sacrificing over 1,000 soldiers, who would have been invaluable for the defence of Corfu. Certainly Napoleon did not make a similar error in 1809, but with the attitudes prevailing in 1798 the general would have been accused of treason if he had ceded a yard of the Republic's territory without a fight. With the loss of the other islands, Corfu was now directly threatened. Dubois wrote: 'The place is in a wretched state of defence, and there are barely eight days' worth of provisions in the stores.' Of the 560 artillery pieces which Napoleon had proudly enumerated to the Directors, scarcely 150 were serviceable, and a further 300 were brought into use by the end of the siege only with great difficulty. The Old and New Fortresses were impregnable from the sea, but from the landward side the town was decidedly vulnerable. The three forts of San Salvator, San Rocco and Abraham connected by trenches and redoubts did strengthen the unbroken circuit of the walls, but they could be overlooked, particularly from Olivette Hill which rose above the suburb of Mandouki. In some sections, particularly around Fort San Salvator above Garitsa Bay, the houses abutted on to the ramparts, impairing the defence, while in others the ditches had silted up and the walls were in a ruinous condition.

The short respite they were granted by the enemy was used by the French to best advantage. The energy they showed amazed the Corfiotes, accustomed to the lethargic Venetians. Even general staff officers helped to dig ditches and raise ramparts. Every available gun was moved into position by 400 mules and the 200 artillery men. Chabot wrote to Paris that he needed 10,000 men to conduct a proper defence. As it was he had 1,800 and fifty Corfiote policemen. Despite Dubois' emotive appeal to the islanders, hardly any enrolled; there were just enough volunteers to form one company of gunners and one troop of cavalry, and most of these were Jews. Overestimating the population's hostility, the general took severe measures. All liberties were suspended, all local councils and courts dissolved. On 18 October Chabot announced a state of siege and delegated full powers to the all-French Committee of Public Safety. As the public treasury was empty, and there were barely 200,000 francs to supply the garrison's needs, thirty-two of the principal citizens were summoned and a large forced loan demanded of them. Naturally they protested strongly; the threat of being interned on board the frigate *Généreux* for the duration of hostilities made them agree. Only the young Capodistrias, who had been included not for his modest fortune but for his Françophobe sentiments, preferred to be interned.

Public discontent grew, and the clergy and nobility fanned the flames. Chabot decided to forestall them. On 22 October the Corfiotes awoke to find their streets patrolled and barricaded, most of the troops were drawn up on the Spianada in battle order, and the gates were barred. Officers went from house to house requesting that all arms should be handed over, and menacing any who lied with an immediate firing squad. In the town this step proved completely effective, but in Mandouki the villagers had the reputation of fighters. They had been enraged by the requisitioning of their boats for the evacuation of Butrinto, and were now determined to resist. That night the women, children, and old men were sent into the countryside, while the men mustered on the heights behind the town. When a French officer rode up to tell them to lay down their arms and disperse, their answer was the same as the Spartans' to Xerxes at Thermopylae: 'Come and get us!'

An hour later the frigates opened fire, reducing the village to rubble. The men, too proud to surrender and too frightened to advance, stood and watched the destruction of their homes. But when Chabot marched out of the town at the head of 800 men, they kept their positions along the heights. Only after an engagement lasting seven hours were they eventually dislodged. During the action the convent nearby caught fire, and some French soldiers slipped into the chapel and began removing the sacred vessels. They were stopped by Papa Piero, who deposited the treasures in the church of St Spyridon. The priests of course exploited this scandal and at their instigation the countryside rose in rebellion. Provisions only reached the town in a trickle, and the crisis was exacerbated by Ali's closing the whole mainland coast to French trade. Still the garrison had gained a breathing-space by their vigorous action, and the inhabitants of San Rocco and Garitsa hastened to bring in their arms.

The advance squadron of the Russo-Turkish expedition was sighted on 4 November, and anchored in mid-channel well out of gunshot. The next day a flotilla of boats mostly filled with nobles put out to join the restorers of their power. At the same time a deputation landed and offered Chabot favourable terms. If he surrendered, the garrison would be given the honours of war and transported to the port of their choice. However the general remained defiant: 'You will need 40,000 men to capture Corfu. Let us drink to each other's health. Tomorrow we can take each other's measure.' Then the envoys were conducted to the threatre, which was brilliantly illuminated, with the audience in full dress. The opera and ballet given was *The Entry of the French into Cairo*. Such was the heroic mood of the garrison, when Chabot announced to the Corfiotes: 'The Ottoman standard, symbol of a barbarous slavery, is unfurled before us. But before you fall under its yoke, you will see Frenchmen dying for you and with you!' Unfortunately the islanders, who had no objection to others dying for them, had no intention of dying themselves. Hearing that the fortifications were mined, and that before the town fell its defenders would lie buried in its ruins, many made a hasty exodus. The entire countryside was in Russian hands, so a blockade existed, and there were other perils, for bands of peasants styling themselves Jacobins roamed pillaging the houses of the rich and any unwary travellers. The Committee of Public Safety declared that the protection of the laws would no longer be accorded to anyone leaving the town without a pass. Arrests multiplied, and the death penalty was prescribed for anyone caught signalling to the enemy.

By 20 November Levkas had fallen and the whole allied fleet had gathered in the channel, consisting of seventeen rather elderly Russian ships and thirty Turkish vessels, new and well-built. Some Turkish troops were landed at Palaeopolis but most of the Russians remained on board. Operations proceeded slowly, and the garrison made a sortie to capture Mount Olivette, took seven Corfiote prisoners and promptly shot them. Meanwhile Capodistrias and his father-in-law had broken their parole and escaped; sentence of death was pronounced against them. Otherwise hatred of the French increased daily, especially after gun salutes for the St Spyridon procession were forbidden. The suburb of San Rocco was burned to prevent attacks from the shelter of its houses, while Garitsa, whose normally timid inhabitants were refusing to sell provisions, was systematically plundered. The wine was seized, the oil sold to the Jews by the public treasury, and the rest of the booty, even the church ornaments, shared out among the soldiers. Then the village was razed.

Ali Pasha, although neither of the allies had asked for it, continued to pour troops onto the island. Some 6,000 Albanians, all intrepid fighters, were set to harassing the garrison. One evening they captured Fort San Salvator, where they were only dislodged after an heroic assault by a grenadier battalion. They almost recaptured Mount Olivette too, for the Corfiote auxiliaries supposed to defend the batteries quickly fled. Some Russian infantry arrived, and a fierce battle developed. Although the French were at length forced to retreat they did so in good order. The *Généreux* also made a bold sortie causing havoc in the fleet, which now surrounded the town in a wide semi-circle, and even fired at the Russian flagship before retiring unscathed to port. Still awaiting his reinforcements from the Black Sea, Ouchakov had insufficient forces to order an all-out attack. Anyway, he had no wish to see the Turks alone benefit from the fall of Corfu. Thus he retained a defensive posture, and in early December violent storms imposed a halt to all operations. The French profited by it to repair the forts, erect a battery above the commercial harbour, and dig some trenches on Vido islet (or the Isle of Peace as they had renamed it). The allies completed a continuous line of entrenchments on the landward side, but their intermittent shelling did little damage. Biagio Colonna published his famous *Letters about Shells* in the press to warn people what to do when they saw one pass.

The assault was renewed on 14 December. A large corps of Turks and Albanians stormed Fort Abraham, whence they were only repulsed with difficulty. The garrison's problems were growing. A proclamation offering an amnesty to all Corfiotes who laid down their arms within a fortnight had, not surprisingly, been ignored. Famine now tightened its grip on the town; with no wheat, mouldy biscuit had to suffice for bread, all the dried vegetables and all horses and mules not vital to the artillery had long since been eaten, while the wounded were fed on broth made from the few fish that could be caught. A turkey was worth at least fifty francs, a chicken twenty, a pigeon twelve, a cat six and a mouse three. Deaths were numerous and the hospitals contained over 400 invalids. The population, suffering from equal privations, no longer bothered to conceal their loathing for the French. Every time a sortie was prepared, it was betrayed to the enemy. Then the Committee of Public Safety decided that all former nobles and Venetian officials were to be evicted from the town. Terror reigned and the prisons overflowed. The government officials no longer shrank from wholesale looting; every day a house was plundered on some pretext and its contents sold to the Jews. Hardship taxes redoubled: in October 400,000 livres had been demanded from the Corfiotes, in January a further 200,000, yet the Treasury only contained 120,000 francs. A curfew was enforced, the ringing of bells forbidden in case they were used to signal to the enemy, most of the shops were closed.

To counteract this general demoralization, Chabot made the Italian troupe of actors, who had been caught by the siege, give two free performances a week. The anniversary of Louis XVI's execution was solemnly celebrated with a parade on the Spianada and a torrent of grandiose orations. When the bombardment of Fort San Salvator began in earnest, the general led 600 men, almost his entire available strength, in a sortie, and after fierce fighting pushed back the Albanians, who were installing more guns on Mount Olivette. At last the promised reinforcements of 3,000 men, which the French had so eagerly awaited, did embark at Ancona in three frigates with a convoy of provision ships. The plan was for them to land on the west coast of Corfu and march towards the town, while the garrison by a concerted effort broke through the enemy lines. Unfortunately the officer sent to direct them had been captured by the peasants, so on disembarking they found no one, and their commander took fright. He imagined the whole allied fleet was approaching, and hastily set sail again for Italy having achieved nothing. Chabot in his desperation resolved to send the *Généreux* for help, and after a sharp engagement she broke through the blockade and gained the open sea.

The siege had now lasted more than three months. Yet no general attack had been ordered, and the fall of Corfu seemed far from imminent. In late February an English naval officer, Lord William Stuart, arrived to try and expedite matters, for Nelson was clamouring for some of Ouchakov's force to be released for operations in Italy or Egypt. Stuart's practiced eye soon discerned that Vido islet was the key to the position. Indeed, Admiral Brueys had declared it was worth ten warships, for it commanded the town, the Old and New Fortress, and both harbours simultaneously. The French engineers had already fortified it to the best of their ability, but the forty guns, mostly taken from old Venetian ships, had an inadequate trajectory.

For some days the winds remained unfavourable and the allies made their preparations. Then it changed, and twenty-eight vessels mounting 800 pieces of artillery approached Vido. The fire they opened was so intense that the very sun was obscured by the shells, and such olive trees as had not been felled, shivered into fragments. There was not a single shelter on the entire islet, and the French gunners found the wind blew the smoke from their guns back in their faces. The noise was appalling, the pall so heavy that it was impossible for the crowds gathered on the Spianada to glimpse what was happening. After superhuman endeavours, the 400 defenders retreated into the middle of the islet. Over 2,500 Turks and Albanians with 1,500 Russians were then ferried across to launch the assault. In vain did Chabot send reinforcements. After losing half their strength, the French surrendered. A massacre ensured; the Turks and Albanians gave no quarter even to the wounded, remembering that their officers had offered a reward for every head they brought back. The

Russians did try to protect them, and all the survivors who reached their ranks were saved. But as no measures had been taken to provide for a retreat, only fifty from the original complement of 700 effected their escape. The engagement had lasted three hours.

Meanwhile Ali's troops were assailing the town from the landward side, and again Fort San Salvator bore the brunt. Twice it was almost captured; bitter fighting raged all day and when dusk fell forty-five Frenchmen and 600 Albanians lay dead on its ramparts. That evening Chabot gave the order to evacuate it, after blowing up the redoubt and spiking the guns, for the garrison could no longer reinforce it. He knew the position was now hopeless and requested a twenty-four-hour truce from the allies. Before the defence council he maintained a belligerent attitude, demanding the abandonment of the town, which he proposed firing, and a retreat to the Old Fortress, which would be held to the end. But it was pointed out that this would only prolong resistance by forty-eight hours, as batteries from Vido must inevitably demolish the walls. So counsels of prudence prevailed, and Dubois was entrusted with the task of justifying the surrender to the Directory.

On 3 March, four French officers were sent out to Ouchakov's flagship to open negotiations; that evening they returned with a Russian delegation. Kadir Bey, the Turkish admiral, had raised objections. He was furious at being deprived of the chance of capturing a fortress deemed impregnable and after so much hardship he wished to give his troops the compensation of some plunder. Also he cavilled at the expense of transporting the French soldiers home. However when it was discovered that only 1,000 fit men remained on Corfu he relented. The terms of the capitulation accorded the garrison the honours of war, provided they undertook not to serve against Russia, Turkey or the coalesced powers for the next eighteen months. A complete amnesty wa offered to all those Corfiotes who had compromised themselves as Francophiles, or had held office under the occupation. For their part, the French undertook to leave the town and fortresses as they stood, with all the artillery, munitions and stores they contained.

Two days later the allied fleet took up its positions and the French ships were seized, with the Russians taking the lion's share. When their soldiers entered the town they were greeted with wild enthusiasm and the pealing of bells. Ouchakov landed to be received by the Protopapas, all his clergy, and a throng of nobles, and went straight to the church of St. Spyridon to render thanks. The garrison was disarmed and interned, but the officers were treated courteously. Kadir Bey and his staff called on Chabot; Ouchakov dined with him. These good relations lasted until the garrison was embarked, Russian soldiers even assisting at the burial of a French lieutenant. The convoy was escorted to Ancona, although a Barbary galley captured one of the transports en route, and Napoleon had to redeem his men from slavery in Algiers. The Turks were left in provisional control of Corfu and the other islands, although the Russians showed no signs of departing. Ali Pasha on the other hand withdrew his 12,000 Albanians across the straits, much discomfited. Even an hour's looting had been denied them; the Russians disputed his sovereignty over the coastal towns and compelled his retirement from Levkas. Thus after eight major battles and a protracted siege, the French gave up Corfu, where in a twenty-month stay they had initiated more changes, aroused deeper passions and greater expectations, than had the Venetians in four centuries. Nothing could ever be quite the same again.

B. THE SEPTINSULAR REPUBLIC

'The extraordinary and unnatural alliance between Russia and Turkey, when displayed in a joint intervention in the government of the Ionian Islands, could not but lead to misery and confusion', wrote Kirkwall over sixty years later. Without benefit of hindsight this was far from obvious in 1799 amidst the universal rejoicing after the eviction of the French.

The question now was what should be done with the islands, for their return to the defunct Venetian Republic was manifestly impossible. The Porte proposed three solutions: their cession to a second-class power (which was bound to be Naples), their creation into a republic, or into a principality under effective Ottoman sovereignty. The Sultan imagined that the Tsar's Orthodox and absolutist prejudices would rule out the first two solutions. However he received the reply that the Ionians, with the fortunate example of the Republic of Ragusa before them would do well to emulate it, and that any Turkish protectorate must be guaranteed by the other powers. The two governments' views remained diametrically opposed, with the Russians arguing that the arrangements made for the Danubian principalities were quite unsuitable for the islands. Paul was, in fact, as violently liberal abroad as he was despotic at home, and his obstinacy was eventually to triumph.

The Grand Councils were revived in all the islands, and they chose eighty-three delegates to a central body, called the Senate, which met at Corfu, with the ubiquitous Count Spyridon Theotokis as its president. Ouchakov promulgated a temporary constitution by which the Senate had to approve the local legislation and pass general laws binding on all the Grand Councils.

These were composed, as in Venetian times, entirely of the nobility, although the term 'noble' as defined in 1800 is of interest: 'to have been born of legitimate marriage, or legitimised of Christian parents, in one of the seven islands; to possess an annual revenue at Corfu of 1,800 Ducats, Cephalonia 675, Zante 1,350, Levkas 540, Kythera 255, Ithaca 315, Paxos 540; not to exercise any mechanical or other art; not to keep a shop; to have always led a decent life, and to be able to read and write in one of the languages used by Government; never to have been found guilty of infamous crimes or fraudulency.'

The Senate prepared a provisional constitution of its own, and chose twelve envoys to present it to the Powers. The work was hampered by the class and local rivalries which were disrupting all the islands. In Cephalonia Argostoli and Lixouri were virtually at war again, in Zante a deliberately misdirected vote of thanks to Nelson invited a British protectorate. The chief negotiators were to be the Zantiote Count Nicholas Sigouros, and Count Antonio Capodistrias. This Corfiote aristocrat had produced four sons of whom one, John, then twenty-three years old, had already distinguished himself. A medical graduate from Padua University, he had been one of the foremost opponents of the French occupation, and had seemed sufficiently formidable to be sent to gaol, from which, as mentioned above, he had soon escaped. For the present he was occupied with the post of chief physician at the military hospital, to which Kadir Bey had appointed him. His father and the other envoys set off for Constantinople and St Petersburg to win approval for their schemes.

Russia and Turkey concluded a convention on 21 March 1800, which created the Septinsular Republic, 'to be governed by its own notables' as a tributary vassal of the Porte. Every third year an embassy had to be appointed to take the tribute of 75,000 piastres. Both powers guaranteed the new state's territorial integrity, and undertook to send in troops only if needed for its defence. But the four mainland enclaves were to be ceded to the Sultan, although their privileges were respected. Meanwhile Ouchakov, who had proved himself a most sympathetic administrator, tried to keep order in the islands, and spared the towns from the pillage they would undoubtedly have suffered from the Turks. He had become alarmed by the impetuosity of the Senate, which had voted the restoration of the *Livra d'Oro* and all the traditions of the old regime, although they had substituted Greek for Italian in public acts, and had recognized that the ties with Venice had been severed for good. Therefore he published a decree reminding the Ionians that he was the arbiter of their independence. As Ouchakov considered the nobility selfish and far too ready to make a deal with the Turks if it suited them, his ideas for a constitution became increasingly liberal, and he proposed that all posts, including the Senate, should be open to the people. The nobles were horrified, so when forwarding his proposals to their envoys, they added their own secret instructions stressing the vital importance of preserving the principle of aristocratic rule. By skilful diplomacy both courts were persuaded to accept that this was the only feasible solution.

By the end of 1800, the constitution was promulgated and put into operation. It was essentially federal in concept, keeping a Grand Council in each island composed of all the nobles aged over twenty-five. The Senate sitting at Corfu presided over the federation. Its composition was determined by population ratios. Thus Corfu and Zante had three, Cephalonia and Levkas two members, Kythera one, while Paxos and Ithaca had one alternately. The Senate, whose President was to be styled *Archon,* would conduct foreign relations, choose ministers and consuls, command the armed forces, and ensure the smooth running of the federation. To finance communal expenditure, each island must donate three-quarters of its local revenues. The other central body, the Assembly, had by contrast no less than 240 members, elected on an annual basis from the islands, and was far too large and unwieldy to be effective. The defects of this constitution were obvious. A French observer remarked: 'In an aristocratic system which is a democracy in regard to the nobles and a despotism in regard to the people, each noble may become a tyrant, and the government, powerless to repress the nobles, can only oppress the people.' The small body of troops meant to maintain order had more officers than men; all were noble, and all were overpaid. Despite the pledges given, the Francophile party was persecuted, and many preferred exile to prison. The arrogance of the ruling class became intolerable; if the new government outraged its opponents by denying equality, it also encouraged particularism. Every island was encouraged to view its neighbours as competitors and rivals, and the inevitable result was conflict. In February 1801 the Union Jack was raised in Zante, and a spontaneous decision reached to request an English protectorate. Forresti, the British Consul, was ordered to express his disgust at 'this action by an anti-Turkish minority', and to disown Callender, an impostor who had encouraged the Zantiotes by claiming he was entrusted with a special mission from the Foreign Office.

The Senate decided that their envoys should tour the islands to explain the Constitution. As Count Capodistrias pleaded the infirmities of age, John was appointed in his stead, and from the first he was to dominate Sigouros, his older colleague, and show an impressive maturity of judgement and a capacity to act in a world of revolutionary change. He was to need it in his first port of call. In Cephalonia three struggles were taking place simultaneously: the democrats were demanding from the aristocrats the political rights they had enjoyed under the French; the townspeople of Lixouri were demanding their own lawcourts and harbour administration, with the eventual right to secede from the control of Argostoli and become an independent member of the federal republic; while the two great families of Metaxas and Aninos were fighting as usual. Eustathios Metaxas had been appointed Secretary of the Provisional Municipality after the Russians had recaptured the island, only to be dispossessed forcibly by the henchmen of Savvas Aninos. Such was the situation when the envoys arrived.

Capodistrias made an excellent speech, and Aninos organized an elaborate welcoming ceremony. That same evening Metaxas returned from Zante with money and reinforcements, and established his headquarters in Troionata. The only hope of avoiding bloodshed lay in a personal appeal to him. So Capodistrias set out after dark and on foot for the village to meet him. His appeal was successful, for Metaxas agreed to lay down his arms provided his rights were respected. Under the envoys' aegis an amnesty was granted to his followers on condition that he left the island. Two of his brothers remained at large however, and only after a Russian warship had come from Corfu and landed troops could order be restored. The Metaxas faction was crushed by force; a sharp engagement at Phokata in June dispersed their men, and the countryside remained quiet for some time thereafter, although most of the villagers had not handed in their arms.

An equal problem was posed by Lixouri. Here riots ensued after two of the townspeople had been condemned to death by a court at Argostoli. Capodistrias showed great firmness by having the two felons executed, then quieting the clamour from Lixouri by threatening to use force while guaranteeing the town's rights *vis à vis* Argostoli. When the envoys left Cephalonia in June it was at peace under a new government elected through the constitution. They next visited Ithaca, which proved equally difficult; after a week Capodistrias departed with the problems unsolved. Luckily he was spared a visit to Zante, where the pro-British protectorate movement had collapsed. If his first taste of public affairs had not been entirely pleasant, at least it had established his reputation for statescraft at an early age.

In March 1801 Tsar Paul was assassinated, and his successor Alexander reversed many of his policies. Anxious to maintain good relations with

Napoleon, he readily agreed to evacuate the islands, and forced the Sultan to follow suit. By August the last of the Russian and Turkish troops had been embarked, leaving the Septinsular Republic in chaos. Cephalonia and Ithaca declared themselves completely independent; the Zantiotes again raised the Union Jack. In Corfu the peasants in the countryside rose, estates were pillaged, and the town virtually besieged. It was indeed remarkable how a people who had calmly endured foreign rule for so long, could become quite unrulable when theoretically autonomous. The Ionian Senate, powerless to restore order, followed Theotokis' advice and resigned, after calling on the chiefs of the democratic party to assume control, and convoke the popular assembly they had been demanding.

Sixty-four delegates, chosen on the spot by the crowd, formed the new government at Corfu. The constitution of 1800, nicknamed 'the Byzantine', was abrogated, and another substituted, solely applicable to Corfu, leaving the other islands to choose their own. A unicameral assembly was to govern through a delegated executive, and all classes of society were represented, each class electing its own members on the principle of universal suffrage. By October the nobility's titles and privileges had been once more abolished. The *Onoranda*, as the popular assembly was called, behaved moderately at first while waiting to see if its measures won general acceptance. But the nobility, although they had submitted in terror to their own degradation, and had not been deprived of their estates, remained irreconcilable. They sent an appeal to the Turks, who, only too glad of another pretext for intervention, despatched a fleet. The Onoranda responded energetically. The town was put in a state of siege; large numbers of armed peasants manned the fortifications. When the Turkish ships appeared, their admiral was informed that if he landed more than a dozen men it would be treated as an act of war, and intimidated he retired. The Porte then sent an order to the President of the Onoranda to restore the Byzantine constitution. The President was none other than the indestructible Theotokis, who had probably requested this himself. As an English squadron was in the vicinity he asked for help in enforcing the order. 300 men were landed at night, and the democrats shut themselves into the Old Fortress and prepared for civil war. The subtle Theotokis again intervened, and arranged a compromise whereby the Onoranda was to continue to hold power while three of its members went to Constantinople, Paris, and St Petersburg to gain approval for a new constitution.

Scarcely had the envoys been sent off and the drawbridge lowered than English troops marched in, and the Onoranda was declared dissolved. An immediate revolt was only averted by their presence, but it was to be of short duration. Russia demanded their evacuation, and within a few weeks they were withdrawn. The peasants rose against the nobles, and anarchy resumed its sway. Ali Pasha realized his moment had come, for with outside help so desperately needed he could make his own terms. With the Porte's concurrence he began to mass his soldiers along the coast near Butrinto. Only a Russian ultimatum made him abandon the enterprise. The consuls of the three great powers now refused to intervene again in the islands' internal affairs, and only Romieu, the French representative, attempted to mediate. Anyway, he was the sole foreigner trusted by the people. But his freedom of action was restricted by the provisions of the Treaty of Amiens, by which France had recognized the Turkish protectorate. The envoys had gained approval of their proposals at Paris, but the other two powers continued to prevaricate. And in the meantime a civil war of proportions unmatched since the bloodbaths of the Peloponnesian Wars loomed closer daily. It was certainly fortunate that the Tsar, believing that he had established a stable peace with France and anxious to pose as the champion of Orthodox Christendom, executed yet another characteristic volte-face in policy. On 3 August 1802 five Russian ships with 1,600 men aboard sailed into the harbour at Corfu.

Relief was universal. The Russian plenipotentiary, Count George Mocenigo, was an experienced diplomat, and of Zantiote origins; both parties hoped he would settle their conflicts and restore tranquility and prosperity. A constitution, the third in two years, was rapidly published. In it Mocenigo espoused the liberal ideas propounded by Ouchakov, indeed he expanded on them, for power would not reside only with the nobles listed in the *Livra d'Oro* but also with all those whose abilities entitled them to be included. This 'constitutional nobility' would choose a college in each island of a varying number of Regents under a Président or *Prytanis*. The latter would manage local affairs, aided by the Regents whose functions were advisory but who could in certain circumstances exercise a veto on his decisions. The powers of these colleges were restricted, their sessions were only biennial, and any communication between them was forbidden as the federal principle was in disfavour. Their chief role was to nominate delegates to the legislative body. This would consist of a chamber of forty members to vote legislation, and a senate of seventeen to exercise executive powers. The Senate would really be a Directory, divided into three departments for finance, internal affairs, and foreign relations. Its chief was to bear the title of Prince. Three censors would supervise the workings of the law and maintain respect for the constitution. Orthodoxy was to be the state religion, but Catholics were accorded a special recognition and protection.

Alexander himself had drawn up these proposals, but Mocenigo had his doubts about the viability of the new constitution. It was immensely complex and detailed, containing 212 articles. All too soon it was obvious that amendments were necessary, and seven jurists were set the task of revising it. Meanwhile the Senate continued to try and govern. The young Capodistrias had been made Secretary of State with responsibility for foreign affairs, the merchant marine, commerce, and education. He appointed as his deputy his childhood friend, Mario Pieri, and together the budding diplomats undertook the formidable task of not giving offence to any of the great powers while satisfying the Tsar's plenipotentiary. Napoleon was still interested in the islands, and sent General Sebastiani on a tour of them. Slowly the situation began to improve, and the Senate drew up schemes to revive trade, reform the fiscal system, and create an embryonic army of 1,200 men. As Ephor or Inspector of education, Capodistrias took his duties very seriously. He had already formed the National Medical Association to promote improvements in medicine, and the Society of Friends, a group which met regularly for cultural and literary discussions. Now he enlisted the aid of a fiery nationalist, Khristophoros Perrhaivos, and of a good scholar, Andreas Idromenos, both priests from Parga, in founding more schools and improving the curriculum. Monastic funds were made available, new primary schools and a grammar school were opened in the catholic monastery of Tenedos in 1805, the catechism was revised and a public library founded, for which the monks' collection of 4,000 volumes formed a basis. There were even plans to found a university on Ithaca. A writer, Andreas Moustoxidis, was commissioned to produce a history of the islands.

During 1803 Capodistrias, with two colleagues, made another tour, and addressed large crowds in Cephalonia and Zante about the workings of the constitution. On the whole they were well received, but their trip was curtailed by the outbreak of a fresh European war. The Septinsular Republic followed Russia in declaring its neutrality, much to the irritation of Spyridon Forresti, who had been promoted to British Minister from his post as Consul in Zante. In October the Assembly met and heard a memorable speech by Capodistrias in which he admitted that the Republic was 'a mere name, the shadow of a state', although he attributed this to the Ionians' unfamiliarity with self-government after centuries of alien rule. He proceeded to list the benefits already gained, and forecast that a national army could be formed if it were strengthened by foreign, which of course meant Russian, cadres. The Assembly readily agreed to meet in private, to limit their debates to the matters before them, and to leave the legislative initiative with the Senate. Extremely restrictive as all this was, the constitution was at least functioning and every one of its 212 clauses was passed unanimously by the assembly in a single session. Perhaps the mixture of paternalism and aristocratic rule, based on wealth and education as well as birth, might work after all.

The Tsar however was dissatisfied. In bland contravention of the treaty of 1800, he wanted an explicit recognition of Russia's role as the protecting power. In practice this was the position anyway, but the Senate hesitated to acknowledge it publicly. Moreover, he wanted the democratic elements in the constitution reduced, for he now feared he had conceded too much. Mocenigo managed the next elections, and Capodistrias reluctantly acquiesced. With Russian troops as the mainstay of the regime he had little choice. And when Alexander signed a treaty with the Porte in September 1805, whereby the Sultan under British pressure permitted Russian warships to pass through the Dardanelles and recognized their Ionian garrisons, now in excess of 10,000 men, the independence of the Septinsular Republic was further circumscribed. It was obvious that the constitution would be modified in the same spirit.

That inveterate traveller Colonel W. H. Leake journeyed through the islands at this time and his report is of interest. In Levkas he observed a meeting of its College of Regents: 'The President opened the proceedings with a long speech in Greek pointing out the importance of the business on which they were met, and supporting his arguments by examples from ancient history. In fact not one of those present was ignorant that the meeting was entirely a farce, and that they had all been nominated a fortnight before by the emissary of the Russian plenipotentiary.' Elsewhere he found much the same state of affairs. In Ithaca the garrison had attempted to disarm the natives even of the small knives they wore in their girdles; in Kythera two Russian officers with one company of troops and a few Albanian Suliotes exercised an iron control.

The new Assembly finally met in November 1806, and a revised constitution of ninety-eight articles was presented to them, although Capodistrias explained that a fresh draft would be needed to secure the Tsar's approval. A legislative body was to be created, divided into upper and lower chambers and with its membership drawn from 'the constitutional nobility'. Elections were to be held every four years. Executive power would be transferred from the Senate to a Regency of five members, whose appointments, like those of the members of the legislature, had to be submitted to the Tsar, or rather his representative. Capodistrias had tried to secure permanent sessions for the legislature, not just for four months in the year, but he had been overruled. He had also urged that each island should have a chance of participating in the executive by limiting to two the members eligible from one island at any particular time. Again no concessions had been made. The five Regents elected for a five-year period were to be known as *Capi della Repubblica,* and were particularly enjoined to keep law and order, to command the armed forces and 'to act in the name of the nation'. They could choose ministers and coadjutors to help them, and together with them would form a general council to discuss important issues. But the Russian minister resident had the right to name all the officials of the executive and the judiciary; only for the first time, admittedly, and from lists of eligible candidates which the islanders would provide. Capodistrias had few illusions: the 1806 constitution would effectively cede Ionian independence entirely into Russian hands.

Thanks to his eloquence, the Assembly passed the draft without amendment, the President ending his speech with the pathetic phrase: 'We are born to obey and not to command'. All vestiges of liberty and autonomy had disappeared. Popular unrest again increased, one clause that aroused special resentment being that which ordained that the head of government in each island must be a foreigner, or at least from one of the other islands. For this idea, so successful in mediaeval Italian city states, seemed to Ionian minds the culminating insult to their integrity. The English, having no wish to see a permanent Russian domination of the area, encouraged the agitation, and Capodistrias was branded a Tsarist agent for all time. The sycophantic Assembly even passed a vote of thanks to Alexander, and erected a statue to him which he had the good sense to decline.

By 1807 England and Russia were at war with France and the Ottoman Empire. When the Sultan asked for assistance from his nominal vassals, Mocenigo ignored the request. Ali Pasha promptly exploited this breach of faith by demanding that the islands should expel their Russian garrisons. He prepared to invest Levkas with a force of 5,000 men with French officers and artillery. Capodistrias who had resigned his post as Secretary of State was despatched on a reconnaissance mission and then gazetted Governor and Commissioner Extraordinary to organize the defence. Hostilities had begun in February, but had made little progress by the time he arrived in June with an enthusiastic band of followers. He immediately decreed the island should be divided into four zones and the capital into two more, while all able-bodied men between sixteen and sixty were to be conscripted. The *Yiro,* or narrow isthmus projecting into the channel, was hastily fortified. Soon he had the whole population plus his 200 Russian soldiers, 100 volunteers each from Ithaca and Zante, and 300 from Cephalonia, all digging ditches. Nor did he lack for able lieutenants. The mainland *kapetanioi,* many of them Suliotes like Marco Botzaris, had been driven from their homes by Ali, and Capodistrias encountered them for the first time along with Theodore Kolokotronis and other future heroes of the Greek War of Independence.

Despite a sporadic bombardment, work on the fortifications continued, and when a general attack was rumoured to be imminent everyone calmly went to their allotted posts. Nothing happened, however, and by mid-July Capodistrias could report that Levkas was secured. A great banquet was held to celebrate this and all the defenders foregathered in a mossy field, 'where they had toasted the liberation of Greece, and had embraced each other with tears in their eyes,' as one later account described it. Capodistrias had proved himself as an energetic and redoubtable leader, and had become the symbol of Ionian patriotism. He was unfortunately one of the few bright stars in an increasingly gloomy firmament. Neither Mocenigo himself nor his deputies in the other islands left behind good reputations. Coercion and mass corruption in the political and social spheres clouded the last days of the Septinsular Republic. However benevolent Alexander's intentions had been, he had failed to instal a government capable of winning the Ionians' affections. With his allies conquered and his armies defeated he now had to negotiate peace with France. The Treaty of Tilsit was signed on 8 July 1807, and one of the secret articles it contained stipulated: 'that the Ionian Islands would be held in absolute sovereignty by the Emperor Napoleon.' The wheel of fate had turned full circle.

C. THE FOREIGN OCCUPATIONS

'Corfu is so important to me that its loss would deal a fatal blow to my plans. The Adriatic would be closed, and your kingdom would have on its left flank a port where the enemy could assemble to attack you. You must regard it as more valuable than Sicily. Mark my words; in the current situation in Europe the worst misfortune that can happen to me is to lose Corfu.' So wrote Napoleon to his brother Joseph, whom he had placed on the throne of Naples. Bonaparte had expressed exactly the same views a decade before. If anything, he now held them even more emphatically. Thus it was hardly surprising that the cession of the Ionian Islands had been one of the provisos of the Treaty of Tilsit, although theoretically they had not been the Tsar's to cede.

The news only reached the islands in August. Meanwhile Napoleon asked his brother to send two companies of artillery, with a French and an Italian line regiment, to Otranto on the pretext of improving the defences. General César Berthier, the brother of Bonaparte's chief of staff, was given command of the force and enough provisions for six months. Secrecy was essential as the English controlled the seas, and if forewarned would not allow the crossing to go unopposed. On 20 August the first detachment of French troops landed at Corfu, and three days later Berthier arrived with the remainder, having successfully eluded the English cruisers and having lost only one transport ship on the journey. His instructions were to treat the Russians with deference, to arrange for their garrisons to be evacuated at French expense, to pay for all stores and to treat their sick and wounded as if they were his own. He must also concert a defence with them against any external aggressor. Mocenigo advanced a myriad difficulties involved in handing over control, for he still hoped for a change of policy or some support from the Russian squadron which was anchored in the harbour. None came of course and after a few days he reluctantly submitted. The garrisons were collected from all the islands and the squadron sailed away.

Albeit without marked enthusiasm, the Ionians accepted another change of masters. In a proclamation, the Senate welcomed 'the happy news that the Septinsular Republic should be placed under the protection of Napoleon the Great'. Most people had grumbled at the heavy taxation levied by the previous regime, and by the spendthrift administration fostered by Mocenigo, who had latterly seemed more concerned to further his personal interests than those of his charges. Once again many hoped that the advent of the French might herald the dawn of a Golden Age. Berthier lost no time in raising the tricouleur and declaring that the islands were French possessions, although all incumbent officials might keep their jobs. This was barely truthful, for a fortnight later a decree revised the governmental structure. The Senate was reduced to five members including the President; the censors and most of the magistrates were dismissed, and only fragments of the 1803 constitution were retained. The other islands were occupied without incident; in Levkas Capodistrias himself handed over power before returning to Corfu as a private citizen, for he would not serve under the French. He left a letter for the Regents stressing the importance of national defence, including continuing to arm and pay the mainland klephts, and begging them to maintain the standards of honesty and efficiency in the administration of finances and justice which the moral obligations of the aristocracy demanded.

Berthier might well have congratulated himself that everything had gone so smoothly. But Napoleon was far from pleased with his general, who should, he felt, have acted with more circumspection. 'I did not tell him to declare that Corfu was part of the Empire, and because I kept silence, so should he.' In fact, Bonaparte feared that the Tsar might be enraged by this public annexation of a state of which he had styled himself the Protector, and by the abolition of a constitution which he had personally designed. England was unlikely to accept such an annexation tamely either. With his strategic insight, the Emperor foresaw that the other islands, if attacked, would be no better able to put up a lengthy resistance than they had in 1798. He was determined to avoid the surrender of any French garrisons this time, so all the soldiers scattered round the various towns and forts were recalled to Corfu, and were replaced by Italians, Greeks, or Albanians. The loss of Kythera or Ithaca, even of Cephalonia or Zante, would scarcely matter provided Corfu was held. Therefore its garrison was increased to 8,000 men, 600 more were sent to occupy Parga, and a strong contingent to Levkas. The whole autumn, convoys of men, munitions, and stores were ferried from Toulon or Italy into Corfu. The wisdom of this was proved by the close blockade which the English cruisers began that winter. Not until the following March did a strong fleet manage to beat off the blockading squadron and revictual the island. By then Napoleon could justifiably boast that it contained 10,000 men, two million bullets, and provisions sufficient for two years, enough equipment for an army of 40,000–50,000, and 500 new guns or bronze mortars.

When he heard of the French gains at Tilsit, Ali affected to ignore them. His power was still growing. Not only did he control most of continental Greece, but his sons Mouktar and Veli had become joint governors of the Morea as well. Having been sent officers to train his men and gunners to work his artillery, he had used them to fortify his strongholds, Preveza in particular, and to besiege Levkas. In return he had declared himself the Tsar's mortal enemy; once more he wore a tricouleur cockade in his turban and pleaded for instruction in the cult of the Supreme Being. 'Master of every expression, his measured laugh denotes a feeling exactly opposite to that which he pretends,' noted one observer. The Pasha's duplicity was indeed limitless. He had just sent his confidante Mehemet Effendi, alias Gueri, the former Dominican representative of the Inquisition in Malta who was a convert to Islam, to Napoleon to request the cession of Parga and Levkas. The Emperor not surprisingly had no wish to weaken his new territorial acquisiton. So while he wrote effusively to Ali and sent him presents, he recalled his instructors and warned the local commanders accordingly. The Pasha was not deceived, and realizing that the French, having occupied the islands, would concede him nothing, became overtly hostile. Couriers were intercepted, bogus official seals were even made so that letters could be opened or false orders issued. To demands that he should evacuate Butrinto he propounded a thousand excuses without a precise refusal. When Berthier asked him for a loan he replied that he was no banker, but he knew plenty of Jews who were. Ali's answer was well justified for a change, for having pressed for the 80,000 francs owed him for provisions and outstanding for almost ten years, he had been told he must pay his own father's debts first. Such however was the Pasha's skill in dissimulation that Berthier believed him to be a sincere friend. So Napoleon was warned against any attempt to recapture Butrinto, and even advised to cede Parga, though this was met by a tart rejoinder that the Emperor did not expect his generals to dispose of French territory. When Corfu was revictualled in the spring of 1808, supplies suddenly began to arrive from the mainland again, and the exorbitant export taxes were lifted as their efficacy had ceased.

By then Berthier had been recalled, having seriously compromised French authority in the islands by his indiscretions. Admittedly he had always been short of money, his original funds had been spent in a few weeks, and the extravagant Mocenigo had nearly bankrupted the Corfiotes to whom he owed vast sums on his departure. But the French had recourse to loans that were forced in the literal sense of the word, which did little to enhance their popularity. Moreover their commander led a dissipated life, dressed in Turkish robes, and outraged Ionian susceptibilities. He had also installed in the palace a lady 'famed for her beauty and the uses to which she put it'. Her behaviour further scandalized local society, for she did not lack for other suitors, to whom it was rumoured she gave, along with her favours, the general's love letters for purposes of blackmail. She shamelessly trafficked in places and encouraged her lover to do the same. Conveniently forgetting his pledges to respect the Corfiotes' liberties and customs, Berthier turned the secretaries of the Senate into ministers, then shut his eyes to their abuses. The judges went unpaid, and likewise were urged to sell justice to the highest bidder. Learning of all this, Napoleon recalled him in January 1808 and appointed General Donzelot, who commanded on Cephalonia, in his stead.

His successor had earned golden opinions as a gallant officer in Egypt and as a chief of staff in Germany. A born diplomat, he was to need his talents to persuade the islanders to accept the annexation that had been imposed upon them, for an imperial decree had at last regularized the position. The

Governor-General, as Donzelot was to be styled, had vested in him the supreme military authority and overall charge of the civil government. All internal administration was the responsibility of the Imperial Commissioner, Bessières, who had the power of a colonial prefect and would attend the Senate's meetings in a consultative capacity. The Senate's functions were drastically reduced, although its numbers were raised to eight. Membership, albeit a sinecure, was to be well paid at 6,000 francs per annum, which should ensure a suitably compliant body. The Imperial Commissioner had to regulate the budget each year, the local authorities being allowed merely to raise or lower the customs duties. Indeed the financial problem was acute, for the annual deficit exceeded 400,000 francs, and provisions must be bought and the fortifications repaired if Corfu was to be enabled to stand a six-month siege. Thus Donzelot suggested to the municipality that they should grant a subsidy of the staggering sum of two or preferably three million francs. It was unreasonable of Napoleon to complain that these estimates were absurd and grossly inflated; his policies had occasioned them.

To reduce the costs of occupation, three infantry regiments were transferred to the Army of Italy, which was in need of reinforcements, and the entire naval force was ordered to regroup at Ancona. As all the garrisons had been recalled there were only two French officers plus a few men on Zante and on Cephalonia to instruct some 1,200 Albanians and the pitifully small number of friendly Greeks that had been enlisted. Even at Parga the detachment was withdrawn, to the protests of the inhabitants who knew their town was now indefensible. Despite its value as a toehold into Epirus, Napoleon remained adamant. Naturally Ali had not been slow to exploit this change of tactics. Again he closed his harbours to French shipping, harassed the posts, and forbade any further provisioning of Corfu. He even had four officers who had crossed to the mainland murdered, and afforded refuge to pirates. His sons adopted a similar policy in the Morea. When added to the English blockade in the Adriatic, which hampered communications with Italy, it meant that Corfu was cut off almost completely. Donzelot felt his position was precarious; trade was at a standstill, the Barbary corsairs roved the seas unchecked, and discontent within the islands was mounting. The arbitrary exchange rates for converting sequins into francs had infuriated the Ionians; so did fresh taxation including the levy on timber which hit the poor particularly hard. On Cephalonia and Zante several villages were in almost open revolt.

The time was ripe for the British counterstroke. The Cabinet had been alarmed by the French occupation of the islands, but had so far chosen to concentrate their efforts in Malta and Sicily. Forresti had consistently advocated an expedition, especially after hearing of the popular discontent. In a despatch to London he had warned: 'Corfu, once in the hands of the enemy, would become in every respect a position of equal importance to Malta to His Majesty's Government', but so far he had gone unheeded. Admiral Lord Collingwood, the Commander-in-Chief, was eventually convinced, after a deputation of Cephalonian and Zantiote merchants had assured him they wished to regain their independence. In September 1809 Brigadier Oswald sailed from Sicily with sealed orders and 1,700 men. The English squadron appeared off Zante on 2 October and summoned the town. As the garrison prepared to oppose a landing, a force of 1,200 men disembarked down the coast, and that same day a capitulation was duly signed. The Septinsular Republic's flag was raised anew and a provisional government appointed.

Oswald sailed next to Argostoli. On 5 October his troops landed and the minute garrison retreated to the Castle of St George. However, they could not have been contemplating any serious resistance, for when their surrender was demanded they immediately complied. In Ithaca the battery consisting of only two guns and seventy men were handed over as soon as an English ship arrived there on 8 October. 'The Kingdom of Ulysses was surrendered into the hands of a sergeant and seven men.' A frigate reduced Kythera after a brief engagement on 9 October. Oswald established his head-quarters at Zante, and in each island a British officer was appointed to act as chief of the government. To assist him there was a four-man council of presidency and an administrative body of forty, but their authority was nominal and he was in reality omnipotent. The English had come, as their proclamation claimed, 'only to re-establish an independent government and to assure the Ionians the free exercise of their religion and their political and commercial rights'. Colonel Hudson Lowe, Napoleon's future gaoler on St Helena, was appointed commandant of these southern islands, which he ruled efficiently if autocratically. He was also fortunate in his subordinates. His deputy in Cephalonia, Major de Bosset, a Swiss, was, to quote Kirkwall's description, 'an excellent person, of great abilities and fairness, animated by a love of the strictest justice'. During the four years (1809–13) he spent in Argostoli, he laboured for his charges and left behind him a reputation surpassed only by Napier's. He built a causeway across the Koutavos Lagoon behind the town, in the middle of which he erected an obelisk with the vaunting inscription 'To the glory of the British nation'. He also started the excellent network of roads and tried to introduce the potato into Cephalonia, although he was opposed by two priests who declared that this was the very apple used by the serpent to seduce Adam and Eve in Paradise. Lastly, he was the first to undertake some excavations of the ancient sites; the numerous antiquities he collected are now in the museum of his native town, Neuchâtel.

It soon became apparent that the British government had no desire to express the political implications of their presence. Content to appear as the restorer of Ionian liberty, Oswald had always emphasized that the occupation was only temporary. As soon as was practicable, the councils 'of the most respectable and powerful proprietors' would run the islands themselves. Lowe became increasingly sceptical of the merits of this, and gradually the English came to believe that outright annexation would be in everybody's interest. If the islanders really were 'incapable of self-government in any shape or modification', a British regime with untrammeled authority must be the best solution. The Ionians too wanted their status clarified. Count Foscardi, a Zantiote noble, travelled to London in 1811 to express the popular wish for England's protection and assistance in commercial affairs. The southern islands' vessels were still flying the tricouleur, as the Septinsular flag had no standing at sea. The cabinet did agree to their use of British ensigns for the duration of the war. Otherwise they prevaricated for eighteen months. Finally they decided to appoint a Commissioner to the islands with overall civil and military authority. General Sir James Campbell, who was chosen for the task, had instructions to leave the political status quo, to win Ionian goodwill, and cultivate Ali Pasha and the Moreote Greeks. This was hardly implementing the grandiose promises of 1809.

A military stalemate had also been reached. Major Richard Church, who had served with distinction with the Corsican Rangers, had raised a regiment of Greek light infantry known as the Duke of York's, which included Kolokotronis and others of the kapetanioi. Helped by English regulars, they had captured Levkas in the spring of 1810, after a fierce engagement in which Church had been wounded. But nothing more could be achieved. Corfu with Paxos might be all that remained of Bonaparte's Ionian dominions, but it was too strong to be attacked, with its large garrison and ample munitions and provisions. The British blockade was supposed to be effective with two frigates, yet the French brought in supplies from the mainland with impunity. Napoleon was designing new fortifications for Corfu: a line of advanced bastions radiating from Fort San Rocco, a second line from Fort San Salvator, and two massive redoubts between here, the saltpans, and the sea. He forwarded the plans to Donzelot with renewed exhortations to hold out until the last extremity, and was soon reproaching him for his tardiness in completing the work.

The Governor-General was, however, in firm control of Corfu, and had succeeded in gaining the affections of its population. This time the French did not repeat the errors of the past. St Spyridon's processions were celebrated with great splendour. Intellectual life was stimulated, and the educational reforms sponsored by Capodistrias were continued. After presses and letter-types had been imported from Paris, the authorities began to publish the *Moniteur Ionien* while the Corfiotes produced the *Gazetta Urbana,* the *Anno* and literary periodicals like *L'Ape* and the *Mercurio Letterario,* founded by Emmanuel Theotokis under the pseudonym of Pheakas. The main achievement, however, was the foundation in 1808 of the Ionian Academy, to encourage the arts and sciences. A six-monthly journal was envisaged, with annual grants for travel and research. A library, a natural history museum, and a botanical garden were to be attached to it. The island's intelligentsia certainly showed interest, and many, like the Capodistrias brothers, Pieri, and the architect Prosalendis, belonged to it, while other luminaries like Ugo Foscolo were corresponding members. Historical studies similarly flourished, and chroniclers of local events such as Antonios Rodostamas were joined by more sophisticated and intellectual writers such as Stylianos Vassopoulos (or Biagio Colonna, to give him his pen-name).

The French administration had a more practical side too. Agriculture was vastly improved by extending the land under cultivation, and importing new olive presses and fertilizers from Italy. Those landlords who refused to co-operate had their holdings confiscated and distributed among the garrison. Donzelot himself acquired some land near the town, which he tended with great care, reclaiming much of it at his own expense and introducing the use of ploughs, which, amazingly, had hitherto been unknown. It was unfortunate that the exigencies of the war prevented him from using his energies to revive Corfu's declining commerce. But his government was certainly mild, justice was equable, and large French subsidies brought some amelioration in the financial situation. In the years up to 1814, the French spent sixty million francs on their Ionian dominions; in 1812, for instance, of a total of thirteen and a half million francs for budgetary expenses, over eleven million were provided directly by France and most of the rest by her tributary Italian Kingdoms. The construction of roads and defence works brought relative prosperity to the island.

A thorough overhaul of the entire governmental system, which still depended on mediaeval Venetian laws, was called for, and Donzelot tackled the task enthusiastically. He was on excellent terms with the Corfiote politicians, and indeed strongly criticized Bessières, who wished to disgrace Spyridon Theotokis for his chameleon behaviour in serving every regime. In August 1808 the Senate requested in the name of the people a formal deed of annexation by the French Empire. A deputation waited on Napoleon at Saint Cloud, headed by the indestructible Theotokis, praised the Governor-General's solicitude for his charges, and proceeded to flatter the Emperor in fulsome fashion. 'If ever the enemy dares to appear before our walls, we shall eagerly seize the opportunity to prove to Your Majesty and the world the value we attach to the ever-glorious title of subjects of Napoleon the Great'. Although not vouchsafed a particularly cordial reply, they returned overwhelmed with their reception. The needed constitutional and legal reforms were never introduced, but most Corfiotes remained reasonably satisfied with their lot.

Thus affairs continued until 1814. The English showed no urgency in their blockade and efforts to break the military stalemate. But by the turn of that year it was obvious that Napoleon's days as master of Europe were numbered, and a decision was taken to resume the offensive. In February a detachment of troops under Church took Paxos and met with no resistance. The naval patrols round Corfu were reinforced and communications across the Straits of Otranto were severed almost completely. So news of the Emperor's abdication in April did not filter through, although the French authorities could hardly fail to realize that the situation had deteriorated. Matthieu Lesseps (father of Ferdinand, the future builder of the Suez Canal), who had succeeded Bessières as Imperial Commissioner, could write by early May: 'We are reduced to our own resources, and these, already enfeebled in a blockaded and unproductive island will soon be entirely exhausted, and all services, despite our efforts, totally paralysed.' Prices rose daily, and for the first time shortages occurred in the shops. To complete the fortifications, Donzelot had had to cut down many olive trees, whose owners were awaiting compensation from a now empty treasury. A recent measure abolishing all the honorary offices and sinecures created under the Septinsular Republic had annoyed a people who set much store by such distinctions. Sinister rumours circulated. A letter was intercepted in which Ali Pasha's physician refused to carry out an order from his master, which it was said involved the poisoning of all the high officials on Corfu. Discontent spread, and a Francophobe party began to emerge.

Nevertheless, when an emissary from Vice-Admiral Gore, who commanded the British Squadron, arrived to announce that peace was concluded and to summon the garrison to surrender, as this would facilitate any pacification, he was greeted with incredulity. Donzelot's latest information had been that

Napoleon was about to push the allies back across the Rhine, and he refused to believe that France had in fact sued for peace. Moreover, Gore rejected his request to send a ship to Toulon to receive any new orders, and the next day, becoming impatient, he threatened a renewal of hostilities. The garrison was offered definite terms: if the town were handed over unconditionally, they would not be interned but repatriated, while Donzelot, with anyone he wished to accompany him, would be granted a safe-conduct in one of his own vessels. The Governor-General replied, however, that both duty and honour forbade him agreeing to any surrender except on direct instructions from his government.

The more vehemently Gore insisted, the more Donzelot prevaricated The six weeks it would take to get an answer from France seemed to the English an intolerable delay. But in the meantime the garrison refused even to replace the tricouleur with the fleur-de-lys, and Gore, enraged, threatened to treat any ship flying the flag as a pirate. In fact the French position was now critical. The population evinced a decided reluctance to undergo the rigours of another siege, and the Corfiote militia was nearly mutinous. Yet the Governor-General remained obdurate. He would not go to an interview intended to prove that he alone in Europe continued to serve a regime that no longer existed. When presented with a new ultimatum he replied that if a state of war existed the English could hardly be surprised by his refusal of their summons to surrender, and if they were at peace, no ultimatum could reasonably be presented in default of a treaty signed by the sovereign of the place summoned. When he could no longer deny the evidence, he argued that it still did not follow that he should yield Corfu to the English without the express authorization of the French supreme commander. He simply ignored the deadline to evacuate by 8 a.m. the following morning, and eight days passed without further negotiations.

On 18 May Donzelot summoned the Senate and demanded they should recognize the new sovereign of France, while Lesseps drew up an oath of allegiance to be taken by all officials, French or Greek. He asked the Senate to stay in session and to ensure the courts did the same. The members received the news with detachment. On 21 May they voted a resolution that the Septinsular Republic was freed from any vassalage whatever, and should have its four mainland dependencies restored. The 1803 constitution was to be retained until the people decided otherwise. Campbell had arrived in the channel with a sizeable fleet but his 'final' evacuation date of 1 June was ignored once again. Only when a French general arrived from Toulon on 7 June, with a formal order from Louis XVIII, did Donzelot at last give way. A week was taken up with the formalities of evacuation and a joint tour of the fortifications; not until 21 June was Corfu handed over to the English troops. Emotional farewells were composed, and the Governor-General's speech ended with these words: 'Already the prows of our ships are turned towards home. Because of the war I leave you without having accomplished all the good I would have wished to do; others will come and have the honour of achieving this. You have given me the name of father, and this memory will be my only consolation in my departure.' As he embarked the Senate presented him with a gold sword. The Bourbon regime in Paris showed far less gratitude, for they refused to compensate him for the expenses he had incurred by paying officials out of his own pocket, which amounted to 90,000 francs. Such was the melancholy end to a career that had given Corfu one of its finest and most disinterested rulers.

The Ionian Islands had finally been reunited under one master. Yet Campbell felt his position was invidious. He was now administering six islands as British Commissioner, and Corfu as the Commissioner for the allies. Once more he urged the Cabinet to make a policy declaration, while recommending annexation: 'There is not a possession in Europe so admirably adapted and formed to uphold British power'. His idea of an orthodox colonial relationship differed from Richard Church's suggestion of a vague British protectorate over an independent republic. But everyone agreed that if no action was taken in regard to islands of such strategic importance, and so close to the Morea and the Ottoman Empire, Russia, who had many partisans on the spot, would certainly intervene. Meanwhile, Campbell determined to curb Ionian pretensions. The Senate, which was claiming authority over all the islands, had its competence further restricted and the printing presses were closed down. The Ionian Academy shut its doors. Most significantly, he refused to allow the Senate 'or anyone else whatsoever' to send a delegation to argue their case for independence before the monarchs and statesmen assembled at the Congress of Vienna. It was fortunate that there was someone there already to do it for them.

Capodistrias had left Corfu in 1808 after being offered a post in the Tsar's service. Gradually he had risen to become one of Alexander's most trusted advisers and had just completed an arduous mission as his representative in settling the affairs of Switzerland, before arriving at Vienna as one of the chief Russian diplomats. Nor had he forgotten his native people. In 1812 he had compiled a *Memoire sur les Iles Ioniennes*, a largely factual document. But he besought his patron 'not to reach any decisions on my home land without permitting me to expound my views on the subject'. Alexander replied:

'Nothing could be more just and advantageous for the Greeks than having you near me as their advocate.' The Tsar was undoubtedly sincere in his wish to reassert the right of the Septinsular Republic to autonomy under the guarantee of the Powers, and with the constitution of 1803. All the noblest sentiments in the world had, however, first to recognize the fait accompli of a British military occupation.

Initially, the plan to create a principality of the Ionian Islands, and place Prince Gustavus Vasa, the Tsarina's fifteen-year-old cousin, on the throne, seemed feasible. But the united opposition of the other powers soon put an end to this scheme. By October Capodistrias had reluctantly accepted the status quo, and was agreeing that a British protectorate might be necessary 'given suitable conditions to which Russia can and must contribute'. He also presented the Tsar with a memorandum on the state of Greece and Turkey. The arrival of a deputation in Vienna, despite all Campbell's precuations, led by Andreas Moustoxidis and Count Valsamakis, enabled him to develop the theme: 'it is through the Ionian Islands that the prospects of a better future should be opened up for Greece.' The deputation simply asked for the islands to be granted their independence, for the restoration of the mainland dependencies, and for all those who had transferred to the French service in 1807 to be allowed to re-enter the Russian. Notwithstanding this, the list of possible solutions continued to grow. The idea of giving the Ionian Islands to some foreign prince as 'compensation' appealed to some of the diplomats. Suggestions included Ferdinand of Sicily, the Bourbon monarch then in exile, and even two Bonapartist figures, the Empress Marie Louise and Napoleon's stepson, Eugene de Beauharnais, although they were not seriously considered. Capodistrias countered by claiming that no minor power could afford the cost of developing the resources and ensuring the prosperity of the impoverished islands. The idea of granting them to the Knights of St John, whom Napoleon had expelled from Malta, seemed equally preposterous. By nineteenth-century standards the Order was an anachronism: being militantly Catholic it would provoke the Greeks, as a relic of the Crusades it would annoy the Turks. Rivalry between the great powers was too acute to contemplate an outright annexation by any of them. Surely it was obvious to everyone that the re-establishment of the Septinsular Republic, with its mainland dependencies as a neutral and autonomous state guaranteed by the five powers who would subsidize the Ionian armed forces and advance a loan repayable over an agreed period, was the only conceivable settlement? But Capodistrias' conviction was not shared by the British government.

By the beginning of 1815 Castlereagh had told the Cabinet of his intention to open negotiations on the fate of the islands. Bathurst at the Colonial Office might want to retain them, yet the Foreign Secretary was more concerned to exclude Russia from this sphere of influence. So he and Wellington proposed to the Congress that the protectorate should devolve upon Austria, which had already absorbed most of the former Venetian dominions. Capodistrias was appalled; if there was to be a sole guarantor it must be England, both as the greatest maritime power, able to secure the advantages of their flag and the freedom of commerce, and as the nation with the most liberal institutions in Europe. The Tsar was anyway opposed to further extension of Austria's influence in the Balkans, and his wishes were paramount in rejecting the scheme. The Congress adjourned with the Ionian issue still undecided.

In May 1815 Count Valsamakis, encouraged by Capodistrias, presented a memorandum to the Powers proposing the restoration of the Septinsular Republic, with a single unspecified power as guarantor, which would not enjoy the right to interfere in the islands' internal affairs. Either the constitutions of 1803 and 1806 could be readopted, or a new one drafted. Bathurst and Castlereagh utterly repudiated this: 'a complete sovereignty, and consequently a full legislative discretion' was essential. In August the British proposals were produced, and Capodistrias was shocked by the claim to 'a full and entire sovereignty in perpetuity'. Concessions were limited to assuring the Ionians 'the free exercise of their religion, a just degree of civil liberty, and freedom of trade.' His protest was prompt and vehement, but the counter proposal he made in September was equally unacceptable to Wellington and Castlereagh. This consisted of a stipulation that the British protectorate should be exercised under an allied guarantee through a minister plenipotentiary, who would merely supervise legislation and administration. The 1806 Constitution was to be restored, and not amended for ten years without the minister's consent, while for that period he could nominate members to the executive. Deadlock had been reached, and it was evident that both sides would have to compromise.

'I am inclined to think we may get more substantial control from the people of these islands with good humour, than if we were to act under the more authorative appellation of a direct sovereignty', wrote Castlereagh that autumn. He had come to feel that some gesture towards Ionian independence must be made, if only to save the Tsar's face. With this decidedly empirical attitude, negotiations were recommenced. On 5 November 1815 the treaty was signed in Paris whereby the Ionian Islands became 'a single, free, and independent state under the exclusive protection of His Britannic Majesty', the other contracting powers renouncing their rights. The British government would appoint a Lord High Commissioner to convoke a legislative assembly which would in turn draft a constitutional charter for the King to ratify. The protecting Power could garrison the fortresses. Although the Ionian flag was accorded international recognition, only consuls could be appointed to Corfu. Thus after many vicissitudes the destiny of the islands appeared settled to the satisfaction of most of the interested parties. Yet the Treaty of Paris had raised more questions than it answered, and time would show that the desire to find a solution had blurred the fact that Capodistrias and Castlereagh had very different aims.

50 *Opposite, top*—Detail from the central door to the sanctuary of the mid 17th iconostasis at Exochora, Zante.

51 *Opposite, bottom*—Bucolic angels are used as Caryatids to support the second row of icon arches on the iconostasis at Exokhora.

52 *Above*—Detail of the lectern in the church of Ayia Maura at Makheradon.

53 *Overleaf*—The icon of Ayia Maura, (the Black Madonna) at Makheradon.

54 Interior of the church at Makheradon, Zante. The sumptuous decor shows the influence of the Italian Baroque in Zante in the 17th and 18th century.

ΥΠΕΡ ΑΠΟΠΕΡΑΤΩΣΕΩΣ
ΤΟΥ ΘΕΙΟΥ ΚΑΙ
ΙΕΡΟΥ ΝΑΟΥ ΤΟΥΤΟΥ

55 *Above*—The coffin of Ayios Gerasimos in his monastery church in the Omala Valley, Cephalonia. Like the patron saints of Corfu and Zante he has two homes. The coffin and a glass-fronted palanquin used in processions.

56 *Opposite*—Votive offerings in the church at Ayios Nikolaos, Zante.

57 *Opposite* — The icon of Chryssopighi in the church at Bokhali, Zante. Brought from Crete it is reputed to have been painted by a 9th century Byzantine artist. The miraculous icon is decorated with silver leaf and precious stones.

58 *Above* — Detail of angels carved by George Baffas on the top of the silver frame of the icon of Chryssopighi.

59 *Overleaf* — Iconostasis in the church of Ayios Minas, Levkas.

60 Detail of gilt carving on iconostasis at Kaligata, Cephalonia.

61 *Above* — The Archangels Michael and Gabriel from the iconostasis in the church of Ayia Ekaterini, Zante, probably painted by Nicholas Doxaras.

62 *Opposite* — Doors of the Sanctuary at the church of Ayia Ekaterini, Zante. They depict St. Peter (left) and St. Paul (right) painted by Michael Damaskinos in 1665.

64 *Above*—Illumination from a 15th century Bible in the Jakovatos Library at Lixouri, Cephalonia.

65 *Opposite*—Icon of St. Jason, one of the two patron saints of the Byzantine church in Corfu (Door of the Sanctuary) painted by Emmanuel Tzanes in the mid 17th century.

66 *Above*—Top of the iconostasis at Isodia tis Theotokou, Levkas, depicting the Last Judgement.

67 *Opposite*—Ceiling painting by Nicholas Doxaras in Ayios Minas, Zante.

68 Icon of Our Lord surrounded by the four Evangelists, painted by Emmanuel Tzanes in the mid 17th century and now in the Bishop's Palace, Corfu.

69 Detail of the Tzanes Icon showing head of Christ.

Chapter V
The British Protectorate

A. THE MODEL CONSTITUTION

'The Ionians must retain no wild speculative notions respecting government, nor imagine they can make a constitution as they would a pudding upon a British or French recipe', wrote Bathurst in 1816. The previous year his colleagues had shrunk from accepting responsibility without sovereignty; now they believed they were substantially to enjoy both. British supremacy in the islands was to be limited by the use of some indirect methods and by discretion, not by explicit exclusion from any sphere of Ionian affairs. Bathurst had already decided the system of government should resemble Malta's. Thus he ignored most of the clauses of the Treaty, for Article I was quite specific about the islands' independence, while Article III concerning the Crown's authority over them remained extremely vague, as was Article IV on the commissioner's relationship to the constitutional assembly. The conviction 'not to part with an atom of power for the sake of revenue' meant that British control of all strongpoints and forts, and of Ionian foreign, political and commercial affairs was essential. The Lord High Commissioner must exercise a check on all legislation, in short he must indeed be *suprema potestas*. The heads of the local government in all the islands shoud be his nominees and British subjects, as should some office-holders in the central administration, especially in the treasury. The guide-lines for the new constitution were already drawn; a suitable figure was needed to follow them.

Sir Thomas Maitland had been born in 1759, the second son of Lord Lauderdale. He had gained colonial and military experience in India and the Caribbean, had been a radical MP, a notable governor of Ceylon, and in 1813 was placed in charge of Malta. Now he was made Lord High Commissioner of the Ionian Islands and Commander-in-Chief for the whole Mediterranean except Gibraltar as well. His critics, and they were to be many, described him as 'insufferably rude and abrupt', 'particularly dirty in his person', and 'constantly drunk and surrounded by sycophants'. But 'King

Tom', as he was nicknamed by his staff, was the right man for the job. For he was a convinced autocrat, whose regard for the material welfare of his charges was equalled by his contempt for their political capacity. 'Any man who has seen much of them would agree with me that colonial assemblies are injurious to the people, and disadvantageous to good government', he said. The past history of the Ionian Islands, with six different masters in twenty years, and three constitutions under the Russian aegis, did not impress him. To Maitland the people were either illiterate peasants or nobles 'whose only object is the possession of power for corrupt ends'. He once sneered: 'To the nobility liberty and independence mean liberty to plunder the country and independence of all judicial proceedings.' Therefore they could not be granted a free constitution. Yet concerned as he was to keep all effective power in the hands of the Lord High Commissioner, he was also far too shrewd not to win acceptance of this by the Ionian Constituent Assembly, as stipulated in the Treaty, by conciliating as many people as possible. So he toured all the islands during 1816, redressing minor grievances and meeting the prominent men in each. He celebrated his return to Corfu by dismissing the seven senators from office, on the grounds they were too Russophile.

Originally Maitland had contemplated nominating the entire Assembly, although he admitted this might be stretching his rights a little too far. His scheme now was to nominate some well-affected persons to agree the exact format with him first. They themselves would be members of the Assembly, and would help to nominate their remaining colleagues. In winter 1816 Maitland selected his Primary Council of eleven, with Count Spyridon Theotokis' son as its President, and arranged for the election of the remaining twenty-nine. This was done by compiling a list of fifty-eight names, from which the electorate, based on a narrow franchise, could choose half. Eight of his council were from leading island families; several had expressed anti-British sentiments before, so this was a triumph for his diplomacy. In April 1817, the Constituent Assembly duly met, unanimously approved the constitution within a fortnight, and appointed a delegation to go to England to get the Prince Regent's ratification. This was obtained in August, officially promulgated by the British government in December, and by January 1818 the new institutions it had created were in being.

For the next thirty years Maitland's constitution, practical and cynical as it was, remained the basis of British rule, and once its consistency had been destroyed by the reforms of 1849, the administration was irreparably crippled. By clever manoeuvring, both Parliamentary criticism and Russian intervention were avoided. But Capodistrias, when he visited Corfu in 1819, was shocked by what he found. He roundly accused Britain of installing a despotism in the islands and infringing the Treaty of Paris by regarding its clauses '*comme des inconvénients à éviter, et non comme des stipulations à etre exécutés*'. Bathurst and Castlereagh defended themselves on the vague wording of the Treaty, and Capodistrias, although he took his complaints to London in person, received no satisfaction. Russia as a signatory to the 1815 treaty could legitimately take action, but the British government chose to treat his complaints, as had Maitland, as his personal observations, being enraged by the comment that it was counter-productive to treat the Greeks like Indians. His influence with Tsar Alexander was anyway on the wane, and when he ceased to be chief Foreign Minister in 1822 and retired to Switzerland, he was no longer in a position to see that his views were heeded. Similarly the organizers of a protest petition to the Powers were exiled from the islands, and the document was confiscated.

From an Ionian standpoint their concern was well merited. The Constitution had vested all effective power in the hands of the Lord High Commissioner. He retained exclusive control of the police, posts, and sanitation, and enjoyed the powers of High Police which enabled him to declare an emergency or arrest, imprison, and exile individuals without trial. The conduct of foreign relations, and all military establishments, came directly under the British governments, while most of the important posts—the Treasurer-General, the Principal Secretaries, the Residents in the islands and the members of the Supreme Judicial Bench, were held by Englishmen. The elaborate superstructure of independence was a façade which scarcely interfered with these arrangements at all. Nevertheless, an Ionian Senate with some executive and much legislative power did exist, as did an Ionian Assembly which was supposed to represent the democratic aspirations of its electorate.

The Senate had five members and a President. It could amend or veto the Assembly's bills, it could introduce its own into the Lower House, and during the latter's recess, which lasted for twenty-one months out of twenty-four, it could issue regulations with the force of law—*Atti di Governo*, which could only be repealed subsequently by a two-thirds majority. In addition, the Senate prepared the Civil List, exclusively controlled all other expenditure, nominated local functionaries like the Regents in the islands, a part of the Judicial Bench, and other minor appointments which were not purely municipal. It was divided into three departments—general, political, and financial. Each senator was only allowed to propose a project once per session, and if the President disapproved, he had to submit it in writing. If rejected, it could only be introduced once again. The Assembly had forty members and a President, of which twenty-nine were elected (each island returning a specified number), and eleven were ex officio, comprising the Senators and Regents from the previous quinquennium, that being the life of an Ionian Parliament. When it did meet, for three months every second year, the Assembly elected the Senate from its own ranks and was supposed to initiate all legislation. Under this central government the plan was for each island (except Paxos, which was treated as part of Corfu) to have its own local administration headed by a Regent, who was appointed by and answerable to the Senate. He was assisted by a Municipal Council of five, elected on the same franchise and nominated by him from the ten most successful candidates at the polls. These bodies could make local regulations, and appoint or suspend local magistrates and other petty officials.

The subtlety of the system was that it always left the initiative with the Lord High Commissioner. It was he who nominated the President of the Senate to hold office for only half the quinquennium, and then decided whether to reappoint him. He had to approve all other Senators elected by the Assembly, and after the second refusal he could present them with two names, one of which they must accept. No legislation, including Atti di Governo was valid without his consent, nor were any Senate appointments, including those made by the Regents. A daily record of the Senate's proceedings was submitted to him by the Secretary, another nominee of his. Similarly the appointment of the President and Principal Secretary of the Assembly was subject to his veto, and he could prorogue, or with the British government's consent, dissolve the Assembly. He virtually controlled its composition in any case, as the Primary Council of eleven drew up the Double List of Candidates, from whom half, the remaining twenty-nine, could be elected. Furthermore he appointed the Residents in the islands, usually military officers, who could suspend the power of the local authorities, and who had to approve the proceedings of the Regents and their municipal councils.

Is it surprising that in their despatches home, the polite fictions of independence were often abandoned? 'Elsewhere history is the biography of Societies, here it is the biography of Lord High Commissioners' wrote Charles Napier, and again of the President of the Senate: 'His Highness is an animal of very nondescript kind, a sort of shadow who puts a very large salary in his pocket; in short he is brother-in-law to a very magnificent three-tailed Bashaw.' The justice of his comment on his superiors is proved by the variety of subjects on which they concerned themselves, even in appointments where they were supposed to have only a negative voice. In 1845 Seaton could write of the Senators he intended to have, before the Assembly elections had taken place. Residents too were instructed to look out for suitable candidates, particularly for the post of Regent. In 1820 a Cephalonian senator's relative was among the possible choices—'Veja's conduct is excellent, and on that account his uncle ought to be elected.'

Maitland had only ever intended a minor role for the Assembly, but in the early years the role it played was almost non-existent. Often there were insufficient members present to form a quorum, so it never met at all. It was estimated in the 1850s that two-thirds of all Ionian legislation had originated as Atti di Governo. Only twice in thirty years did the Assembly even attempt to modify the Civil List as presented to it by the Senate. Relations with the latter were always smooth. Only once, in 1842, was the appointment of the President for the remainder of the quinquennium refused for non-cooperation. The Lord High Commissioner's relations with the Assembly were somewhat less easy. In 1837 Douglas twice dissolved it for its factious spirit, although this was the only real clash until the late 1840s. For on the whole successive British administrators used their power tactfully and well. On one celebrated occasion Maitland, clad only in a brief nightshirt, a red nightcap, and a pair of slippers did tell the assembled Senate to go to hell, but such incidents were rare, and the Residents behaved in general with equal rectitude. Moreover the Lord High Commissioners provided positive incentives to good conduct, for their patronage was the path to prestige, influence—and salary. The Ionian administration was certainly well paid. The President of the Senate received £1,400 per annum, a Senator £700, a Regent £400, and the Assembly members £108 for three months' work out of twenty-four. All carried resounding titles of which the Ionians were notoriously fond, the most blatant example being Maitland's creation of the Order of SS Michael and George. Some local patronage was also fostered, although the practice was sometimes abused. As Napier protested: 'A man should not be made Regent three times if his whole cargo of poor relations are to be brought in with him.' But trusted friends did tend to be reappointed. In these thirty years, forty-eight Senate places were filled by thirty-two individuals, and forty-five Regencies by thirty-six. This applied in all the islands: the Petritsopoulos of Levkas, the Zavos of Ithaca, the Gangadis, Theotokis, and Khalikiopoulos families in Corfu, the Foscardis of Zante, the Kondoleos of Kythera, and the Vejas and Karidis of Cephalonia being notable examples.

Advocates of a British protectorate had always stressed how much this would benefit the Ionian Islands. Therefore the record for the thirty years that Maitland's Constitution lasted should be examined in broad terms. After 1849 the Lord High Commissioners no longer enjoyed the same tremendous powers of positive action, and the political opposition they encountered was far more bitter. One salient fact soon emerges. In the earlier period it was the attitudes of these proconsuls and the policies they followed which mattered far more than those of the London government. Ultimately of course the Secretary of State could recall a Lord High Commissioner, as happened to Mackenzie in 1842, but the British Parliament had no authority recognized under the Treaty of Paris. Thus Adam in 1828 objected to the Financial Committee of both Houses scrutinizing Ionian revenue and expenditure, while Douglas in 1840 successfully resisted the proposal to send a Commission of Inquiry to the islands. The paramountcy of the Crown was acknowledged, and its ability to change the constitution with the consent of the Ionian Senate and Assembly, but Ionian legislation did not require confirmation in England. Hence the Colonial Office seldom disagreed with its representative's actions, even when, as occasionally happened, he disobeyed instructions and behaved almost like an independent sovereign. The islands had to pay an annual sum to London towards the military costs of protection, otherwise the Treasury's competence to interfere was extremely circumscribed.

During the British occupation, the Ionians were secured from external attack, a fact seldom paralleled in their history. Otherwise they might have felt the armed might of Ibrahim and his Egyptian army, which invaded the Morea to crush the Greek revolt in 1824–5. After the Treaty of Paris their own volunteer cadres were not reconstituted. Instead, a garrison of 3,000 British troops, mainly in Corfu, but with detachments in the other islands, manned the fortifications. They also supplemented the police force, which, although a paid body in the towns, relied on the unpaid and often unreliable village primates in the countryside. Certainly internal order was maintained, as it had not been in the eighteenth century, and Maitland largely succeeded in disarming a naturally warlike people. Justice was similarly improved. At the end of Venetian rule, the nobility had constantly perverted the course of the law, while the bureaucracy had been totally corrupt. Now the new constitution overhauled the judicature, and established a Supreme Council of Justice with four judges: two English, two Ionian, and the Lord High Commissioner with the President of the Senate ex officio, which served as a High Court of Appeal. Every island had its own courts, civil, criminal and commercial, also petty sessions with local magistrates. In 1843 Seaton instituted district courts as well to administer justice in remoter areas. The character and salary of the judges was accordingly supervised; on average, the pay scale quadrupled between 1814 and 1820. Judicial expenses amounted to between ten per cent and twenty per cent of the total budget, and when Adam decreed that justices should not sit in their own islands, the costs rose again. Their selection was carefully made; seldom indeed did a Resident have to upbraid his entire bench as Napier did in Cephalonia in 1823.

There was an equal enthusiasm for improving the law itself. The British rigidly adhered to the principles of no direct interference by the executive and no favouritism for the rich, although the entail on fiefs was broken, thus facilitating the sale of estates. When the Senate tried to commute part of the sentence passed on a Theotokis, they were severely censured by Adam. The intention to replace bad old Venetian laws by new codes was sincere enough. Unfortunately Maitland's desire to make the law incorruptible had enshrined the whole corpus within the constitution, so any amendment however small had to be ratified by the Crown, which was absurd. This frustrated all attempts to introduce new codes of law, and not until the 1840s did Douglas manage to devise new civil, commercial and criminal codes for the Colonial Office's approval. This was not forthcoming, so the Lord High Commissioner introduced some proposals as ordinary bills to the Assembly in 1841. His successor Mackenzie was soon demanding a proper codification. The only solution was to abrogate the offending Article VI of the Ionian Constitution, which was duly done. Now the local government could amend the law as it wanted without reference to the Crown, and in the ensuing twenty years much solid work was done on improvements to the old Venetian legal system.

It was the same with education. The Republic's complete neglect of it in the islands had been a sorry legacy. The reforms introduced during the Napoleonic Wars had not struck any deep roots, and the upper classes still sent their children to be educated abroad. Maitland showed scant interest in the subject, and it was thanks to the efforts of the Philhellene Lord Guilford that the Ionian Academy was founded at Corfu in 1824. Its central role in the cultural life of the islands will be described later, but its educational importance was very real too. Frederick North, fifth Earl of Guilford, was an accomplished classical scholar, who had been Maitland's predecessor as Governor of Ceylon, and whose self-proclaimed mission in life was to revive the spirit of ancient Greece. To this end he had been received into the Orthodox Church, and with Capodistrias had founded the Philomuse Society at Athens. Benevolent, generous, and dedicated, his eccentricities endeared him to everybody. As Napier wrote: 'Lord Guilford is here again. He goes about dressed up like Plato with a gold band round his mad pate and flowing drapery of a purple hue. His students' dress is very pretty and said to be taken from ancient statues.' Actually it consisted of a tunic and chlamys, with hair bound like Hermes, and red leather buskins reaching to the knee.

Originally Guilford had intended Ithaca for the site of his university. Local enthusiasm was enormous, the land was given free, and gifts of money and materials poured in, including 9,500 tiles from the ladies of Ithaca. Maitland however, an unrepentant sceptic about the whole project, persuaded the Assembly that the site should be transferred to Corfu. In fact, he was probably right. As Jervis-White-Jervis later wrote: 'Visionary ideals of academical groves and the birthplace of Ulysses do not form young men to be useful citizens, and for one real student sent forth, there would have been a hundred turned out upon the world with their ideas confined to a barren rock and a few goats.' Indeed only after Maitland's death did the project proceed. On 29 May 1824 the Ionian Academy was formally inaugurated with Guilford as Chancellor, and four faculties, of theology, jurisprudence, medicine, and philosophy. At the end of the first academic year there were 211 students enrolled and fourteen professors. The latter frequently complained of their pay and conditions. Mr Joss, the German lecturer, claimed: 'I have suffered in these islands every kind of privation and every degree of mental suffering. When first I met Your Lordship I thought I had found a refuge from my misfortunes.' But on the whole, the Academy flourished. By 1827 its library contained 21,000 volumes, mainly donated by Guilford and by a host of distinguished benefactors. Housed in the former palace of the Provveditore Generale in the Old Fortress, the Academy had become a famous and much-loved institution, although Adam was not amenable to pleas for increased grants, remarking privately 'the whole thing is pure humbug'. When Guilford died that same year, the youth of Greece had indeed lost 'their most loving father', and the unedifying behaviour of his heirs in demanding the return of the library provided a sad postscript. Eventually Adam agreed to a much reduced scheme for the Academy, which moved in 1837 to the former Grimani barracks at the southern end of the Spianada, a fine seventeenth-century building, now, alas, a shell.

On each island a secondary school was founded, teaching classics, languages, and mathematics, while in the capital of each there was a central elementary school to teach reading, writing, and arithmetic. These were entirely financed by the government, while in country districts schools were set up on the Lancastrian model, whereby the parents paid the master's salary, the older pupils helped teach the younger ones, and the buildings and books were provided by the authorities. By 1832 the islands had sixty schools with more than 2,500 pupils, as opposed to twenty-nine in 1827, and only twelve in

1823. Douglas founded another hundred Lancastrian schools in the villages in 1836, and fixed the masters' salaries at ten dollars a month, half to be paid for by the state. That there were over 6,000 pupils in almost two hundred schools by 1850 must rank as one of the proudest achievements of the Protectorate. In his *Address to the British Parliament,* Count Viaro Capodistrias, although bitterly critical of other aspects of the regime, contrasts English enlightenment with the obscurantism practised by the Venetians.

The British record in the matter of public works is also good. All the Lord High Commissioners realized the importance of new roads, prisons, hospitals, piers, and swamp clearance, and this dominated their correspondence. Expenditure rose from around eleven per cent of the total budget in the 1820s and 1830s to twenty-eight per cent in 1844, for Seaton for one never considered postponing a project through shortage of money. The memorials of this work are still evident today. In Kythera, which had an extremely energetic Resident in John MacPhail during the 1820s and 1830s, there are many buildings, roads, and bridges, and the Katouni viaduct, built to carry the never-completed road down to Avlemona, with a total length of 120 yards and twelve tall arches, is one of the finest, if most pointless triumphs of engineering in all Greece. It is in this context, too, that we shall consider one of the most remarkable men ever associated with the Ionian Islands—Charles Napier.

Born the eldest son of an impoverished Irish soldier and Lady Sarah Lennox, daughter of the Duke of Richmond and the celebrated beauty to whom George III had once proposed, he had spent all his adult life in the army, and was an outstanding soldier and military theorist. His impeccably Whig sentiments were infused with Victorian ideals of progress and imperial expansion. Hence he believed with Gibbon that free government is irrecoverably lost when the legislative power is nominated by the executive, and that the sine qua non of both good government and morality is a free press, a nobility made to live part of the year on their estates, a vigorous execution of the laws, and the encouragement of colonizing and military aspirations. Yet he was always an iconoclast, with a social conscience that suffered for the starving poor in England after Waterloo. Although his views were unlikely to commend themselves to Maitland, he was made Inspecting Field Officer for the islands in 1819, and both men came to appreciate the other's qualities. So, without preconditions, Napier was appointed Resident of Cephalonia in March 1822. His task was enormous. As he wrote to his mother: 'My kingdom is of 60,000 souls and martial law exists. My predecessor is going home half dead from the labour, but to me it is health, spirit, everything. I live for some use now.' Within three months he had put in hand a mass of improvements and had abolished martial law. He instituted a corvée, one day's unpaid labour a week for every able-bodied man; objections were overridden, for Napier understood that if roads could be built through the bleak Cephalonian mountains, local enmities would disappear. The peasant's lot could be improved by loans, by a model farm for instruction, by easier access to markets, and by exciting the landlord's pride in his land. With the aid of Captain Kennedy, his subordinate and architect, who was to become his best friend, he threw himself into the task, personally supervising much of it, while his affection for Cephalonia grew. 'The people are very much to my liking, but the greatest liars in the world.' Marshes were drained, slums cleared, streets widened, prisons built. Kennedy designed two market places, one for Argostoli, one for Lixouri, at a cost of less than £50,000, also the charming neo-classical Lighthouse of Ayios Theodoros at the end of the promontory.

How much all this depended on Napier is proved by his depression on returning from leave in England in 1825. The work on the roads had slowed down, more expense and superintendence of twelve parties instead of five had produced fewer results without him. Usury was rampant, with the peasants being charged interest at between fifty per cent and 300 per cent, and a new bishop had been appointed, 'an excellent, pious man, who used to live by sheep stealing, which he now calls his pastoral life, and he believes that Justinian wrote the Code Napoléon.' He reasserted his authority by sacking two of the judges, who were conspiring to imprison a man unfairly for debt, and as one was a Metaxas, the people were suitably impressed. But, irrepressibly outspoken, he had made an enemy in Adam, whose roads over level ground in Corfu had necessitated borrowing 80,000 dollars from the public chest, while Napier's were to save an estimated 50,000. The Lord High Commissioner avenged himself by ordering his Resident to shave off his moustaches; 'the order was obeyed to a hair', and the results sent back to Corfu. He also enraged the Duke of York, then Commander-in-Chief, by forcing visiting regimental officers to take on garrison duty, and by court-martialling with total justification two subalterns who had seduced a girl of thirteen.

In 1827 Napier was still as active as ever. An agricultural colony of 300 Maltese had been founded at Pronnoi in southern Cephalonia, under a Scotsman, Edward Curling. When he drew up a list of twenty improvements effected under his supervision, he left out the new fisheries and expanded port facilities and his projected pier at Lixouri, which would have doubled the revenue from the shops. He also devised an elaborate plan to drain the Krane swamp, which made Argostoli such a malarial and unhealthy place. As more of his revenue was taken to support the extravagances of the central administration in Corfu, difficulties increased. In July 1828 they came to a head. Adam, endeavouring to appease Greek public opinion, suddenly decreed that the direction of roads and other public works be removed from the Resident's control and vested in the Regent and Municipality. Napier was furious, both at the implication of a guilty conscience over past policy, and at the stupidity of the measure. 'The Cephalonian peasant is idle, fond of shooting, gambling, and law-suits, for these he will sacrifice tillage, family, and substance.' As he had already reduced the corvée to one day a fortnight, and had levied assessments which were hardly onerous on those who preferred to pay rather than work, the system's worth was tested. Of the six categories listed, the highest paid only £5 per annum, and the lowest £1, the Resident had voluntarily paid more than the richest gentleman, while the indigent priests had been excused altogether. Even the peasants could remit a day's labour for 10d. Without this interference, Napier reckoned he could finish his roads and abolish the corvée within two years. As it was, the Regent and his colleagues were unlikely to agree what should be undertaken; they would obviously never tax themselves or fairly assess their own property. Although he lingered on in office for another two years, his disillusionment with the central government grew. 'Take the Sanita. All that touches the public health depends on the local officers in each island, they cannot wait for orders from Corfu, which are anyway incredibly foolish. Two men die of plague. Long after they are buried comes an order, directing a peculiar treatment for cure! Answer—dead. Some weeks later come full instructions for burying them. Answer—bodies of plague victims are not kept as curiosities; they are buried at once. This office costs enormous sums, as do the others; the names serve as an excuse for high pay.'

The end came in 1830. Napier's wife became ill, and as she had to return to England, he decided to accompany her. En route they stopped at Corfu, where Adam received them cordially, saying as they embarked, 'Good-bye, Napier. Stay as long as you please, but remember the longer you stay, the worse for us.' As soon as they had sailed, Adam stopped all public works in Cephalonia, removing the Maltese colony, despite Curling's offer to keep it on for £100 per annum, and the guarantee of a good return in four years. Five months later, the Lord High Commissioner visited the island, as the people, prompted by Russian agents, had refused an address to the new King, William IV. The reason was that they believed the British would regulate their religion, and in public Adam assuaged their fears, while claiming to the

Secretary of State that Napier's oppressive rule was to blame. He professed his surprise that charges had not been made against the absent Resident before, seized Napier's public papers, and, but for Kennedy's foresight, he would have taken the private ones too. He stated that seventy serious charges had been represented to him. When challenged, this diminished to nineteen, mostly too ludicrous to require an answer. Nevertheless, Adam refused to permit his return on the pretext that it would occasion revolt. Napier's scornful comment was that 'the howling of the wolves had been mistaken for the bleating of the sheep'.

The Colonial Office offered him the Residency of Zante instead, a theoretical promotion which was refused, and for ten years he remained unemployed. Yet his love for Cephalonia never left him, and in 1845, after his Indian campaigns had won him fame and glory, he would write to his friend, Demetrius Kambitsi: 'You give me great pleasure in telling me that the colony at Poros is to be revived. I am sure it will become again a great town and port. I would give all Sind for Poros. Here in Sind I am a King, it is true, but they say first love is truest and Cephalonia is mine.' Although he never returned to the islands, Napier christened one of his daughters Emily Cephalonia, kept two properties in Argostoli, and remembered the islanders with many bequests. His statue was defaced by the Italians in the last war, and still awaits restoration, but if his likeness has to be sought in the huge monument in Trafalgar Square, his rule is best commemorated by the roads which form the bulk of the modern network—134 miles of them completed, mainly over mountains, of which only twenty-one were unfit for carriages, and at a cost of a mere £17,849. If there were twenty miles of road in the whole Protectorate in 1824, and 366 in 1842 it was thanks to Residents like Napier.

The British were less successful in promoting the Ionian economy. Agriculture was of course the main industry in all the islands, the olive in Corfu and Paxos, the currant in the others, and it was in a very backward condition. To an educated observer, there was land and labour but little else, for the farmers were lazy, knew nothing of crop rotation or manure, and possessed primitive tools. Any change was an uphill struggle against a congenial climate and the innate conservatism of the peasant. Moreover, the *colono* system, whereby the landlord was paid rent in kind instead of cash, was long established by the nineteenth century, and the tenants had become a hereditary caste of farmers, considering they had a real right to their land. The units, small at best, were further subdivided into tiny scattered parcels. Everyone readily denounced the system, but as good relations between the *signori* and *coloni* were an essential prerequisite for any reform, and were usually lacking, very little could be done. The extent of debt and the prevalence of usury exacerbated the position, for the signori often lent to the colono in anticipation of his crop, and if the harvest was bad, the rates of interest mounted.

Class hatred could assume horrifying proportions. In Cephalonia in 1849 the peasants rose from social not political grievances 'against those dogs who wish to hang us by means of pledges or promissory bonds.' As the official report commented 'this was a civil, almost a servile war; of tenants against landlords, of *contadini* against signori, of debtors against creditors.' The government did its best by forbidding the *prostichio* system of lending money in anticipation of the crop, and by fixing the legal rate of interest at ten per cent, but neither measure was really obeyed. A scheme of advancing government loans to the cultivator was no more popular than the Agricultural Savings Bank, which, although it accepted tiny deposits and guaranteed four per cent interest, was distrusted by the peasants, while the usurers went on charging twenty per cent on locally lent money. The establishment of the Ionian Bank in 1839 was of little help; it seemed too remote, and it was only effective in facilitating the repayment of debts, despite very reasonable rates of interest. By the end of the Protectorate the tenant was still oppressed and embittered against the landlord class.

Equally unsatisfactory were the prevailing laws relating to landed property. Crop failures, the fluctuations of distant markets and foreign competition could upset even the bigger estates. While the land law protected the proprietor, it also discouraged the investment of outside capital, for the artificial valuation placed on land for debt redemption meant that the creditor could only accept it in payment at seventy-five per cent of this low figure. Attempts to authorize the sale by public auction of landed property caused an outcry in all the islands, although ten years' grace to pay debts was still given, and the scheme had to be dropped. Adam did import new seeds, tools, and plants which he told the Residents to distribute, but his destruction of Napier's model farm hardly encouraged innovation. Douglas even founded a society to improve agriculture, although this achieved little, When the powers of the Lord High Commissioner were reduced after 1849, the chances of reforming agriculture vanished altogether with the Assembly so strongly representative of the impoverished landowners.

In any assessment of British rule, it must not be forgotten just how small were the resources at the disposal of any administration in Corfu. Ionian revenues averaged £146,000 per annum in the years until 1849. The best year, 1834, saw a huge olive crop and a rise to £187,000, but in three other years the revenue barely touched £120,000. Small as this was in view of the high cost of government, it probably could not have been much improved. Before British rule the average had been only £90,000, and this amelioration was due to better and more honest accounting, the abolition of tax farming and a decline in peculation. The incidence of taxation, mainly indirect, was however raised. In 1819 Maitland's tariff left the duty on currants unchanged at eight and one-third dollars per mille, and a six per cent ad valorem surcharge. On olive oil the duty rose from one and one-quarter to two dollars a barrel, and import tariffs of foreign raw and manufactured goods were raised from five to seven per cent ad valorem. But the system was hardly satisfactory; oil revenues varied from £63,000 in 1834 to £8,000 in 1846, and currant revenues anywhere between £55,000 and £22,000. Furthermore export duties could not be raised too high, as Ionian produce had to compete against foreign, often superior products—Apulian oil or Moreote currants. Several times falling prices compelled a reduction in the ad valorem rates, while the administration always tried to find alternative methods of taxation without success. The Lord High Commissioners shrank from transferring the burden from exports to imports, reasonably enough as the export duties did regularly provide more than half the total revenue, and Douglas' new tax on grain was extremely unpopular. Direct taxation was never practicable, for until the 1850s there were no reliable figures for the islands' populations, and there were justifiable fears at Ionian reaction to its introduction.

Yet if revenue could not be improved, it seemed scarcely easier to control expenditure. No government wanted to cut down on public works, education, or charitable enterprises too much. In any case far the biggest item was the cost of government itself. In his *Memoir on Ionian Finances*, which appeared in 1829, Napier was bitterly critical of the system established by Maitland. Was it not ridiculous in islands whose total population hardly equalled a smallish English city to have a senate, a legislative and judicial apparatus, with all their members receiving large salaries? His cynical conclusion was that 'our partisans are our bayonets and our people in office—we have no other', and that in each island a Resident, a Regent and a small municipal council would suffice, with the Lord High Commissioner to co-ordinate policy. 'Out of a total revenue of under £150,000, when £50,000 is regularly appropriated for ships, troops, and fortifications, and another £57,000 for a civil list, no state can long avoid ruin.' In Cephalonia he had a police force sixty-five per cent the size of Corfu's, for a population a third larger. This, of course, he attributed to the spendthrift policies which allowed the Lord High Commissioner two magnificant palaces 'within gunshot of each other'.

As usual, he had a point. But the need for efficiency and the difficulties of administering islands stretching for more than 300 miles could be cited in defence of these heavy costs in a protectorate of only 1,000 square miles with a population under 200,000. As careers open to Ionian youth were now so limited—principally medicine and the law, for they were excluded from the diplomatic or armed forces—government jobs were vital in easing the employment situation. By 1848 some reduction in salaries had been achieved compared to 1830, although the number of state employees had risen from 1,014 to 1,487. Nationalists like Dandolo might sneer: 'Why must we have genteel youths perpetually imported to lounge on our esplanades, and be plentifully paid for putting their names to papers?', but in fact the number of English on the establishment declined from sixty-nine to forty-six in the same period, and many of these were among the lower paid.

With a perpetual budget deficit the only help could come from the protecting Power, in direct or indirect financial aid. The direct aid related to the military contribution, which the Treaty of Paris had left to be defined by a convention. Maitland always managed to avoid doing so, while carrying the costs of a military staff on Malta's accounts, and postponing repairs to the fortifications. After his death these could be delayed no longer, and the Ionian Parliament agreed to provide funds of £164,000 in annual instalments of £20,000. To this was soon added another £20,000 per annum for military staff and incidentals, and by 1830 it was reckoned that a further £63,000 was needed in excess of the original estimates which the Ionians must pay. After objections had been raised to 'the monstrous miscalculations of the engineers', a military convention was demanded, and in 1836 it was agreed the islands should pay £35,000 as their contribution to the costs of protection, and a further £15,000 towards the cost of British officials' salaries. Douglas was furious and asserted that the Ionian Islands were worse treated in this respect than any other colony, but his requests for relief were refused. The Treasury was adamant and demanded a speedy payment of arrears. Only in 1844 was this arrangement modified, and the Protectorate was designated to pay one-fifth of its annual revenue as the military contribution.

The British government was no less mean-minded on the subject of trade protection. By the end of the 1820s, Ionian currant growers, who had enjoyed a virtual monopoly of the English market while the Greek War of Independence was raging, found that supply was exceeding demand and Moreote competition was reviving. With prices down by seventy-five per cent, Adam asked for some reduction in the very high English duty of 44s.4d per hundredweight. In 1828 Napier helped the Cephalonians to frame a petition to the Crown. In it they pointed out that since 1820 the currant crop had been doubled from five to ten million pounds, and much new land had been brought into cultivation. Indeed, after peace had returned the currant trade had revived rapidly, England importing £74,000 worth in 1818, £91,000 in 1820 rising to £122,000 in 1824. Interestingly this was the time of the final demise of the Levant Company, which had long been an anachronism in an era of free trade, and which no longer had a share of the Ionian market when its charter passed to the Crown in 1825. It was claimed that the high duty could not be reduced because currants were a luxury. This was all very well if the whole crop was bought—unfortunately in the last year three-quarters of it had remained unsold in the merchants' magazines. If people were not permitted to sell their currants freely, the large proprietors would be ruined and the poor would emigrate. 'We can live by, but we cannot live upon, our currants.' After repeated representations, the duty was reduced to 22s.2d in 1834, but no preference was given to Ionian currants, nor was it again in 1844, when the duty went down to 15s.0d per hundredweight, the same as on raisins. The arguments of successive Lord High Commissioners failed to soften the Treasury's heart, and anyway by 1850 it was considered more important to foster good commercial relations with Greece. It was these relations with Greece, political even more than commercial, which determined British and Ionian attitudes, and ultimately the future of the Protectorate.

The Congress of Vienna had reimposed peace and legitimacy on Europe, but in many countries revolutionary fervour still smouldered. Greece was no exception, and the accession of Sultan Mahmoud in 1808, who was determined to reverse the decay of Ottoman power, had made an eventual clash with resurgent Hellenic nationalism inevitable. Much of the impetus for this still came from the Ionian Islands, despite British attempts to discourage it. The Masonic Lodge at Zante, founded by Count Dionysios Romas in 1811, had become the Grand National Lodge of Greece, with branches in Levkas, Paris, and Moscow. Again the islands, with their cosmopolitan traditions, acted as the bridge between the mainland and the expatriate Greeks, for the Masons had close links with the *Philike Etairia*, founded at Odessa in 1814, the covert purpose of which was to organize a rising against Turkish rule. This 'Friendly Society', with its six grades, four civilian and two military, gained many Ionian recruits. Maitland regarded its activities as subversive, a view doubly justified had he known of the meeting of its branch on Zante at the little church of Ayios Yeorgios tou Latinou, where the members swore a secret oath to fight for an independent Greece, which the islands would eventually join. Moreover many of the klephts, and the kapetanioi like Botzaris and

Kolokotronis, had stayed in the islands after 1815, although the British government had refused to re-employ them, or in many cases settle their arrears of pay, and their regiments, like the Duke of York's Light Infantry, had been disbanded.

Maitland had furthermore outraged nationalist sentiment by signing a convention in May 1817 which ceded Parga to the Sultan, or in reality to Ali Pasha, who alone had sufficient power in the area to profit by its possession. From the standpoint of British government policy it made sense to get rid of a troublesome outpost and placate a useful ally. After two years of haggling about compensation for those inhabitants who preferred to emigrate, Maitland arbitrarily fixed the sum at £150,000. Moreover by pleading that the assets had depreciated, the Pasha only ever paid half of this inadequate amount. On 27 April 1819, the Orthodox Good Friday, Ali's Albanian troops moved in, and virtually the entire population was evacuated across the straits. The Lord High Commissioner even refused to give the Pargiotes a site on which to build a new town, and this so disgusted Capodistrias, then visiting Corfu, that he was moved to remonstrate. The newcomers were gradually assimilated, but the boost which this betrayal, as most Ionians saw it, of people whose only crime had been a touching, if inconvenient, attachment to their native town, gave to the nationalist cause in the islands was enormous.

Certainly British policy contained a measure of duplicity, for it involved supporting Ali Pasha against his nominal sovereign the Sultan. Napier was sent to Ioannina in 1819, and returned the next year to advise on the state of its defences. Fully realizing that Ali was hated by many of his own men for his avarice and perfidy, Napier nevertheless conceived an unwilling admiration for him and felt sure he was the logical leader round whom any revolt in Greece should form. Thus all his suggestions for strengthening the fortifications were made in good faith; all were rejected on grounds of economy, and nothing was done. When a Turkish army of 20,000 crossed the Pindus and invested Ioannina, Ali offered Napier unlimited command and money, but by then it was too late. After a long siege, he was tricked into surrendering in January 1822, was promptly decapitated, and his head washed, stuffed and exposed on a platter, was sent to the Sultan in Constantinople. So died the octogenarian Despot of Epirus, who in the past had coveted and threatened the Ionian Islands, but whose career made him one of the precursors of Greek independence.

On 25 March 1821 Archbishop Germanos raised the standard of revolt at Ayia Lavra, the monastery near Kalavryta. All over the Peloponnese the Greeks rose and began to massacre their Turkish neighbours. Within a few weeks over 20,000 had been killed, and the remainder had sought refuge in the coastal towns. At the same time Prince Alexander Ypsilantis, a Phanariote officer in the Russian army, invaded the Danubian principalities with a small force. He was disowned by the Tsar and Capodistrias, and his campaign quickly collapsed, for the local population disliked Greeks as much as Turks. But the flame of revolution was not so easily extinguished. The Porte responded by a campaign of terror. The Patriarch Gregorius, although he had condemned the rebels and was a high Ottoman official, was summarily hanged on Easter Day as were many of the leading Phanariotes. A ship from Domata in Cephalonia was passing through the Bosphorus shortly afterwards when the captain saw a coffin floating on the waters. This was found to contain the Patriarch's mortal remains, which were duly buried at Odessa, while the empty coffin is now the treasured possession of the village church.

Excitement in the Ionian Islands had risen to fever pitch. During 1821 some 2,000 or 3,000 crossed to the Morea to join the struggle, vessels were fitted out, money and arms subscribed, and public prayers offered for the success of the rising. The British government, anxious to retain friendly relations with the Porte, was however determined to pursue a course of strict neutrality, if necessary at the expense of popularity. Several proclamations that summer had no effect, and in the autumn Maitland was compelled to take drastic action. A Cephalonian contingent was serving with the insurgents, and its leaders, two of whom were from the Metaxas family, were claiming they had been sent by the British government, and were wearing English uniform. The Lord High Commissioner issued another proclamation ordering them to return within a fortnight on pain of perpetual banishment and confiscation of their property. When they ignored the order the sentence was duly enforced, while two Cephalonian ships' captains who were serving the Greek cause while flying the White Ensign were declared pirates.

Some forty Turks who fled from the Mani to Kythera were massacred by the islanders in October. They were enticed ashore, and were then ambushed among the rocks. Being unarmed, they were killed to a man, but the outrage was concealed from the Resident for three days. In Zante a direct clash occurred between the peasants and British troops sent to escort the crew of a grounded Turkish brig to safety, in which one soldier was killed and three wounded. Maitland immediately declared martial law in Zante and Cephalonia, executed five troublemakers in each island and reinforced the garrisons. By the end of the year he had declared a state of emergency successively in all seven islands, while disarming the population. The arms gathered were certainly impressive: in Corfu alone they amounted to more than 13,000 pieces. Severe penalties were enacted for illegal possession, and licenses were only granted to the most trustworthy. In October too the Lord High Commissioner published a decree closing all Ionian ports to the armed ships of both belligerents. The following April a law was passed punishing any islander who took part in the fighting on the mainland with banishment and confiscation of his property. This had the desired result, and the flood of volunteers diminished to a trickle stealing across the straits under cover of darkness. The policy had succeeded, but many Ionians were neither to forget nor to forgive.

Within the islands unrest also increased. At the request of the local population, the government had agreed to erect a mole and re-excavate the canal at Levkas, linking the lagoon and the sea, which had silted up entirely. But when demands for additional taxation to pay for the scheme were made, the peasants, who had blithely imagined a beneficient deity would provide, were incited by agitators. It was rumoured that in addition to higher duties on wine and oil, further taxes on doors, windows, births, marriages, and deaths were to be levied. On 3 October 1819 a mob invaded the town, fired on the garrison, and set fire to several buildings. Only when reinforcements arrived from Corfu was it eventually dispersed, and the ringleaders fled to the mainland. Some were hanged, but in Jervis White-Jervis' words: 'Accustomed to broils for years, it was difficult to make them understand they had committed a serious violation of the laws; the execution of a few ringleaders, amongst whom was a priest, although it successfully awed them, at the same time roused their sympathies in favour of men whom they viewed in the light of martyrs.' In 1821 a more serious conspiracy was detected on Zante, where an act sequestrating church property was exploited to foment unrest. The instigator, Martengo, wrote to the Lord High Commissioner offering to restore order if he was appointed a senator. When this impudent proposition was rejected he tried to start a general insurrection, although he only succeeded in causing a few people to pelt an Anglophile priest with stones. He was soon arrested and imprisoned.

1822 was a decisive year in the struggle for Greek independence. The massacre on Chios, where the Turks killed or enslaved eighty per cent of a population of 100,000 and entirely devastated a previously rich island, outraged the conscience of Europe. Eight shiploads of Philhellene volunteers arrived in Greece. Although they found affairs there in a state of total chaos, the enthusiasm of this motley collection of idealists, adventurers, and political exiles remained undiminished. Formed into the Philhellene Battalion, with the Regiment Tarella, which was officered by Italians and run on Western lines, and which many of the Ionian recruits had joined, they comprised all the regular troops at the disposal of Mavrocordatos, whose government was nominally the supreme authority in Greece. Unfortunately, at the battle of Peta that July, they were betrayed by the local kapetanioi and almost annihilated by the Turks. The Albanian Suliotes, who had joined the revolt and in whose support the expedition into Epirus had been made, were evacuated en masse to the Ionian Islands. On Cephalonia, Napier was given twenty-four hours notice to prepare the fortress of Assos to receive them. More than 1,400 landed, many *palikars* or old warriors among them, their faces the colour of a tea-urn. They did not deign to carry their baggage, while most of the women bore the arms of their dead menfolk as well. Firmly independent, they refused to surrender a convicted murderer to the police, and Napier was forced to blockade them in the isthmus. Eventually the man was handed over, tried, and hanged, but the Suliotes were to cause endless problems for the British authorities.

By 1823 the remaining Philhellenes, homesick and disillusioned, had left Greece, although new volunteers continued to arrive. Surprisingly, in view of his declared policy of rigid neutrality, Maitland allowed many of them to pass through the Ionian Islands en route to Italy. The British soldiers even raised subscriptions to buy them food and clothes, for most were destitute. Yet their sacrifice had not been entirely in vain, for the Turkish campaign of reconquest had outrun its supplies, and all the Peloponnese except for a few fortresses was still in the hands of the insurgents. Real power however did not reside with the politicians like Mavrocordatos at Navplion, but with the kapetanioi and klephts like Kolokotronis, whose guerrilla warfare had been primarily responsible for defeating the Turks. For the first time it seemed that an independent Greece might not be a chimera, and the British government, with Canning now Foreign Secretary, decided discreetly to adjust its policy. Through a network of agents on the mainland, and by intercepting the mails in London and the Ionian Islands, the Cabinet was well informed on the situation, and like the French, feared that the new Greece, perhaps with Capodistrias as President, would be drawn into the Russian orbit. Hence the formation of the London Greek Committee and the flotation of the first loan were permitted. The radicals like Blaquiere and Bowring often seemed more interested in devising model Benthamite constitutions than in assisting a struggle for national independence. They succeeded in deluding much of the public as well as themselves that the regenerated Greeks had a greater need of water colours and a printing press to revive painting and literature than they had of money, arms and food. But for all their shortcomings they did succeed in persuading Byron to espouse the cause. In July 1823 the poet embarked at Genoa with several volunteers including Count Gamba, the young brother of his mistress Teresa Guiccioli, nine servants, five horses, two cannon, and 50,000 Spanish dollars. Fate had ordained that his destination should be Cephalonia.

By then the mainland was in a state of virtual civil war, with the kapetanioi challenging the politicians and each other for pre-eminence. Byron sensibly decided to review the situation first in the safety of the Ionian Islands to see where he could best lend his support. He rented a house in the village of Metaxata, and had soon established friendly relations with the Resident. He was impressed by Napier's energy, confidence, and military knowledge, while the latter, who had been sending memoranda to Mavrocordatos on how to conduct his campaigns, found a listener whose views coincided with his own. Both were liberals, iconoclasts, and wits. Byron was delighted with Napier's aphorisms: 'We are hoping that the French and Spaniards will war like Kilkenny cats, and that Cadiz will be so famished that the people will eat the King and Royal Family. To behead a King is vulgar, but to eat one will render the annals of the age entertaining and instructive in two arts; freedom and cookery. Moreover it will be said that the Spaniards have had their bellies full of tyranny.' For four months Byron remained there, receiving the emissaries of the various factions. He made many friends on the island, particularly Count Delladecima, and he was so entranced by the beauty of Ithaca, that he seriously considered buying it for himself. Only after much prompting did he agree to go to Missolonghi in December. Napier, who had advised him to equip a reliable force of his own and not give the kapetanioi a penny, saw him go with regret. 'Lord B is off to Greece, but it is hard to get there, harder still to get back, and if the Turks catch him off goes his poetical nob!' Alas, the so-called Byron Brigade quarrelled ceaselessly, his Suliote bodyguard mutinied for lack of pay, and in April 1824 the poet died of an epileptic fit and over-bleeding. His famous last words were thought to be 'Poor Greece!' Six days later Blaquiere arrived in Zante with a merchant ship bearing the first instalment of the English loan, but as Byron, one of the two commissioners for administering it, was dead, the money had to be deposited in a bank there, much to the fury of everyone on the mainland.

The illusion that the war was over was soon to be rudely shattered. Sultan Mahmoud had agreed to cede Crete to his nominal vassal, Mehemet Ali, Pasha of Egypt, and to make the latter's son, Ibrahim, Pasha of the Morea, if the Greek revolt was crushed. The well-trained Egyptian troops carried all before them during 1825, and the following April Missolonghi fell after a heroic defence. Again Greece, as symbolized in Delacroix's great painting, stirred the imagination of Europe. In the Ionian Islands too, with popular feeling running higher than ever, it seemed that Britain must intervene, and the proceeds of the loan were shipped across to the mainland, where they were promptly spent. Maitland had died in January 1824, and Adam had continued his policy, although this was increasingly overtaken by events. In June 1825 the Act of Submission was sent to London, whereby various leaders like Mavrocordatos asked the British government to assume the sole protectorate over Greece. Lord Guilford and a committee of Zantiote supporters publicly endorsed this. Canning rejected the offer, but the protocol he negotiated with the Russians would have made Greece into an autonomous state, and when the French acceded to the Treaty of London in July 1827, a secret clause provided for the use of force if the Porte rejected any attempts at mediation with its rebellious subjects. The stage was set for allied intervention. Meanwhile this all lay in the future, and during 1825 Napier, who had already requested and been refused permission to accept a command in the war, was formulating his terms if he were to lead the Greek revolutionary forces, and thus sacrifice his career. As sent to the London Committee in September these were: £12,000 as some compensation for abandoning his prospects, £2,000 to pay two scientific officers, and £150,000 or a minimum of £100,000 with which to pay his soldiers at least for the first six months. He calculated that he would also need 10,000 muskets with ammunition and bayonets, plus about 500 British soldiers to act as the nucleus of his army, apart from the many Ionian gentlemen who would, he believed, accompany him. Matters were almost settled, when the Committee decided to have a fleet under Cochrane rather than an army under Napier. Judged by subsequent events, the wisdom of their decision was certainly questionable.

Throughout 1826 the fate of the Greek revolution hung in the balance. More Philhellenes passed through the Ionian Islands on their way to join the fighting, among them Richard Church, now in the service of the Bourbons of Naples, but filled with enthusiasm to join his old comrades like Kolokotronis. Despite all their efforts, Athens fell with the surrender of the Acropolis in June 1827, and many despaired of ever defeating the Turks. Only when the allied fleet under Admiral Codrington had destroyed the Turkish and Egyptian ships in the Bay of Navarino that October was the cause of Greek independence assured. When Russia declared war on the Porte in 1829 Napier wrote from Cephalonia: 'Everybody is clear Russian here except the Regent and D. Delladecima.' Capodistrias' return from his self-imposed exile in Switzerland provided fresh inspiration for the Russophile Greeks. The squabbling factions on the mainland had united in calling on him to guide the destinies of his native country, despite the misgivings of most of the politicians. As it was, he had only been offered the post of *Kyvernitis* or President for seven years, with a strikingly democratic constitution which ascribed all sovereignty to the people, and which divided power between the executive and the assembly. In Capodistrias' retinue of expatriate Greeks were several Ionians like the scholar Andreas Moustoxidis and the architect Stamatios Voulgaris. Although a British man-of-war was transporting them, Adam refused to let the party land at Corfu, so Capodistrias only arrived in Greece via Malta in January 1828. When he started to form his government, various friends were summoned from the islands, while his brother Viaro and John Gennatas with their legal knowledge began to organize a judicial system. The Lord High Commissioner was convinced that the aim was to identify the Ionian Islands with the Greek state, and remained unhelpful with loans, only advancing 500,000 francs once in several years, while the Russians and French were far more generous. In fairness to Capodistrias, he was terribly short of suitable lieutenants, and recruits like his brother Agostino from Corfu, Andreas Metaxas from Cephalonia, and Dionysios Eumorphopoulos from Ithaca were invaluably useful. By mid 1829 Adam complained that Capodistrias was employing twenty-four Ionians. The task confronting the new government was titanic, but the President laboured to show that education and a properly codified law would bring social and political cohesion. The Lancastrian school system, as used in the islands, was introduced throughout Greece. As the war petered out, Capodistrias struggled to make a satisfactory peace, to fix reasonable frontiers for his country, and in a monarchical age to find a suitable sovereign. By 1831 Greece was in turmoil again, a secession movement ruled in the Aegean islands, and the kapetanioi were disaffected. That October the President was assassinated as he entered church in Navplion, and his brothers fled back to Corfu with his body, which lies buried in the convent of the Panayia of Platytera.

With the arrival of Prince Otho of Bavaria as King of Greece in February 1833, a semblance of order was restored. The Powers recognized the new nation, and the task of reconstructing the ruined country began. At last the Ionians could rejoice that their brethren on the mainland had been freed from the Ottoman yoke. And inevitably, as the issue of future boundaries was being negotiated, rumours spread that Britain would cede the islands as a gesture of good will. This opinion was definitely not shared in London, where it was so emphatically denied by the Cabinet that Adam's secretary could write to Napier: 'You may plant a tree on Cephalonia and safely calculate on being able to repose in its shade while under the present Protectorate.' The coming to power of the Whigs made no difference, for Palmerston held strong views on the strategic importance of Corfu. Yet whatever the views of the British government, the creation of an independent Greece had fundamentally altered its position in the islands, and the effect on Ionian attitudes to the protecting Power was soon to be demonstrated.

B. THE GROWING DISCONTENT

'A sort of middle state between a colony and a perfectly independent country, without in some respects possessing the advantages of either', is how Douglas described the Ionian Constitution in 1838. After twenty years of British rule, the islands had enjoyed the blessings of peace, internal security, and a considerable advance in material welfare, yet all was far from well. The malcontents could argue with some justification that Venice had not taken twenty per cent of their revenue as military tribute, that she had paid all her own officials from the metropolis, and that almost all posts had been open to Ionians, including the armed services of the Republic. Under the British aegis they were better and more expensively governed, while the control of the elective house, the non-existence of a popular press, and the patronage system established by Maitland smothered discontent. So did the formidable barrier of 3,000 British soldiers, and the power of High Police to remove trouble-makers. Gladstone was to describe these early years as a period of silence rather than of tranquillity. The old aristrocracy resented the curtailment of their privileges, and many, like Flamburiari, who was refused office as President of the Assembly, became patriotic critics for personal reasons. Without the necessary groundswell of public opinion the interminable feuds between the families prevented much united opposition. Despite the foundation of the Ionian Academy many young men were still being educated abroad, and in a restless Italy they imbibed much revolutionary doctrine. The realization when they returned that career opportunities were so limited, that the law and medicine were both overcrowded professions, and that despite British efforts there was an inadequacy of jobs in government service, further nurtured their radicalism. By the 1830s petitions were being organized, and minor disturbances incited, particularly on Cephalonia, where lawyers like Focas and Aninos were the most vocal. As Napier wrote, 'they were too poor to be long honest'.

After twelve years of dealing with the islands, Bathurst had retired from the

Colonial Office. Maitland was dead, and in 1832 Adam departed to become Governor of Madras. Lord Nugent, the new Lord High Commissioner and a Whig, was determined to introduce some reforms. Within twenty-four hours of landing on Corfu he had published a proclamation extolling Greece as the founder of free institutions, and telling the Ionians that their faults had been the faults of their protectors, but their virtues had always been their own. For the elections to the 1833 Assembly a triple rather than the double list was issued, and Residents were ordered not to interfere in elections. In Argostoli excitement turned into disorder, there were riots on election day, and the island's representatives had to be directly nominated by the government. Nugent agreed to make Greek compulsory throughout the judicial system, to keep the Assembly's records more fully, and to open the House to the public. However, the radicals, not satisfied by these concessions, refused to vote the extra £63,000 needed for the fortifications of Corfu, and opened a war of the prerogative on the Senate for being dilatory and high-handed when sending down bills. The Assembly for the first time had exercised its powers to amend the civil list as presented by the executive. Otherwise the concrete gains of Ionian liberalism under the Nugent regime were fairly small. No constitutional changes were permitted, for the Cabinet was adamantly opposed to them, and the Lord High Commissioner himself was alarmed by the riots, and the intrigues and conspiracy which his commission of enquiry revealed. He claimed to be diverting discontent from fundamental issues, and, for instance, transferred superintendence of education to the legislature. More significantly, he kept the double lists for the next Assembly, withdrew permission for a literary magazine after four issues, as there were too many thinly-veiled political allusions, and allowed his uncontroversial press commission to collapse without making its report. Some veteran officials still thought he was too lenient, and MacPhail, now the senior Resident, wrote from Kythera to deplore the new-found pretensions of the radicals. E. J. Baynes, the Secretary to the Senate, felt that some compromise was needed, and recommended judicious changes in Maitland's system to accord with the spirit of the times. Nugent however suddenly resigned in 1835 before anything had been implemented.

His successor, General Sir Howard Douglas, was cast in the autocratic mould. Yet he was an excellent administrator, and had a very real concern for the welfare of his charges. He fought with the British government on the subject of the military contribution, and made advances in the fields of education and law. But he remained unyielding to the clamour for constitutional change, and in 1837, with the support of the Secretary of State, rejected the Assembly's demands for control of extraordinary expenditure. Similarly, the call for a free press was intolerable, 'for I have no doubt that it will become an organ of private scandal and public abuse.' Not surprisingly the liberal opposition, now led by Moustoxidis, who had returned from Greece, retaliated by sabotaging several government measures. Outside the Assembly feeling mounted too, and in September 1838 a religious procession in Corfu was the occasion of a popular demonstration against the Lord High Commissioner. Douglas obtained permission to dissolve the Assembly, although he kept it until the eve of the 1839 session, when he proclaimed new elections. Normally this would have excluded opposition candidates from the double lists, but an unprecedented revolt in the Primary Council, led by Voulgaris, the retiring President, kept many liberal names on the lists. When the Sixth Assembly met in March 1839, fifteen of its forty members, mostly from Corfu and Zante, were avowedly hostile. The civil list was attacked, then the demands for constitutional reform were presented: free elections, annual sessions, control of all finances, an unfettered press, and the right to initiate legislation. When the opposition denied that the Senate was entitled to any voice in the introduction of new codes of law, Douglas prorogued the Assembly, and again sought permission to dissolve it. That August, Moustoxidis sailed to England, and presented a memorial directly to the Colonial Office.

It was Douglas' misfortune that Lord John Russell took over the Colonial Office the following month, for it deprived him of support when he most needed it. The Secretary of State granted the Lord High Commissioner's request for a dissolution, and admitted that former policies entitled him to the British government's support. But as a good liberal he could not remain unmoved by this exposé of arbitrary power. Moreover Douglas' conduct seemed to confirm the accusations. He was using the High Police to imprison opponents, he was preventing the circulation of reform petitions, prohibiting the entry of foreign journals as subversive, and making no secret of his intention to pack the next Assembly. His querulous despatches and excessive touchiness were very irritating to London. Moustoxidis' case that Britain should introduce reforms to recapture Ionian confidence and respect was sensibly presented and his assertion 'that the Ionians are attached to Greece by origin, religion, language and nationality; that nationality is dear to every people, but to the Greeks it is a religion', was incontrovertibly true. Russell was impressed, but when Douglas, admitting the constitution was 'a very imperfect instrument for a very imperfect state of society', produced a detailed defence, the Secretary of State had to recognize his ignorance of the islands at first hand. Thus he rejected the memorial, although he reaffirmed his sympathy with Ionian desires for a free constitution. The reformers had suffered a setback, especially when coupled with Douglas' blatant management of the seventh Assembly. He had even compiled a list of ringleaders who were to be excluded from public life in perpetuity. On his retirement in June 1841, he could feel the situation was well under control, and that with such trusted Residents as Sutherland in Cephalonia and Parsons in Zante, a zealous watch was being kept on the reform movement.

Russell had had to defend Douglas in the Commons, and had refused the radicals' demand to send out a commission of enquiry. He had appointed a liberal, Stewart Mackenzie, to succeed him, but this meant little, for the instructions were 'not to introduce any change of any kind', and Douglas' Residents were confirmed in their posts. The advent of a Tory Ministry that year made the prospects for reform even bleaker, while the new Colonial Secretary, Stanley, had doubts as to Mackenzie's abilities. So those Ionians who wanted change might well have felt depressed in the early 1840s, despite a conviction that time was ultimately on their side. In 1843 Mackenzie, who had proved ineffective, was recalled for 'disobeying his orders'. Determined to introduce reforms, he had baulked at the prospect of working with a Senate wedded to the old system, and so had not reappointed its President, Petritsopoulos, for the second half of his quinquennium. This was perfectly proper constitutionally, but the latter, a staunch supporter of the Protectorate, had complained, and Stanley expressed his disapproval of the Lord High Commissioner's conduct. Count Demetrius Delladecima, the new President, then offered his resignation and although honour should have been satisfied, Mackenzie's too was given and accepted. The poor man died shortly afterwards deeply mortified. Ironically he had been the only Lord High Commissioner apart from Maitland whose revenue had exceeded his expenditure. His successor, Lord Seaton, had been another of Wellington's generals and was known to be a Tory. Could the clock really be turned back to 1817?

Interestingly Seaton described himself as a reasonable Conservative, which his behaviour soon bore out. With his vigour, charm and confidence, he was not content to allow any sphere of Ionian affairs to escape his zeal for improvement. His outstanding fair-mindedness ensured his popularity with everyone, and he disregarded Douglas' vendetta with prominent liberals like Moustoxidis. Indeed the Corfiote lawyer Damaskinos was approved as President of the eighth Assembly. Seaton had scant respect for 'the gang of patriots', yet he refused to let the Residents make arrests for political crimes.

With such ideas he became convinced that the constitution was indefensible, especially as King Otho had just been forced to grant the elements of democracy in Greece. Britain should forestall Ionian disaffection by introducing reforms, but he favoured an entirely new system rather than a modified version of Maitland's, although the primary council and double lists must be retained unaltered. His policy was twofold: to educate the people for greater responsibility by associating them more closely in administration, and to prevent unrest by removing the most vexatious restrictions.

Seaton believed that social and administrative improvements were a necessary prelude to constitutional reform. He therefore encouraged the municipal authorities in each island, and transferred the appropriation of road funds from central to local government. He propounded a novel financial theory: that only revenue accruing from sources imposed by parliamentary legislation was for the central treasury, income from any other source was for local use. Hence in 1844 all local revenue was omitted from a statement of general revenue, and lest the limitations of such funds should deter the municipal authorities from desirable but expensive schemes, they were authorized to raise loans or request subsidies from central government. He also instituted an inspectorate of *epistani* for country districts, who were to be elected by the village primates from among their own ranks. A proposal to set up district municipal councils, elected by the *sinditi* of each area was not adopted until 1849. He built an excellent prison, schools prospered under his sway, and he encouraged the islanders to educate their children to play a greater part in public life. The £28,000 spent on dredging the canal at Levkas would have much aided Ionian commerce had the Assembly voted the money needed to complete the project. Seaton further proved his progressive inclinations by appointing an Ionian to the post of Treasurer-General for the first time. Also he sanctioned presses for printing books of a non-political nature.

Any scheme for constitutional reform did, of course, need the approval of the Colonial Office. Civil servants in London remained sceptical when the Lord High Commissioner advocated giving the Assembly control over extraordinary expenditure, for they suspected that the docility of an Assembly with control of the purse could not be deduced from the docility of an Assembly without it. This new-found co-operation had in fact resulted from improved conditions within the islands. Trade and agriculture were beginning to flourish again. The olive crop, blighted for several years, was showing signs of recovery, while the currant trade was stimulated by the reduction of the English import duty in 1844. Exports and imports were increasing too; the shipping entering Ionian ports rose from 285,000 tons in 1842 to over 350,000 tons in 1848. Albanian dealers, who had previously bought from Venice or Trieste, began to come to Corfu; a reciprocal treaty with Russia was signed in 1846, allowing Ionian vessels to trade in Black Sea ports. All this surplus was ploughed back, and amid such favourable conditions Seaton's reforms flourished. The police force was overhauled and district courts set up, which dispensed cheaper and more accessible justice to the peasants. He embarked on an ambitious programme of public works, as the figures show, for average annual expenditure under this head rose from £16,500 per annum in 1839–42 to over £40,000 in 1844–7.

The tragic events of 1848 were to prove that most of the subject peoples of Europe were dissatisfied with their lot, even if it was combined with material improvement and gradual reform. Liberal doctrines gained ever wider credence, and when news of the risings reached the islands, the political temperature began to rise. Determined not to lose the initiative, Seaton argued for one bold stroke of policy to restore Britain's position and confound the extremists. Throughout 1848 and 1849 he remained an optimist, convinced that enlightened self-interest favouring the British connection still outweighed the emotional attractions of union with Greece. Thus in February 1848 he recommended granting freedom of the press and control over extraordinary expenditure to the Assembly, while guaranteeing that municipal elections would not be supervised. In July he advocated the abolition of the primary council and the double lists, thereby sacrificing the eleven 'tame' seats in the Assembly, and abandoning control of the elections. By 1849 he was proposing to extend the franchise by lowering the income qualification and to introduce the secret ballot. The Liberal government then in power received all this quite well. Grey at the Colonial Office thought that 'Ionian finance was a very loose and irregular system', and its reform should be connected with changes in the constitution. Moreover, pressed by the Treasury, he hoped to settle the vexed question of a regular military contribution at the same time. As he disliked keeping so large a British force permanently immobilized in the islands, he also wondered if an Ionian militia could be created to permit reductions in the garrisons.

As ignorant of the real situation as most of his predecessors, Grey relied on the advice of his departmental officials headed by Strachey. The latter saw merit in many of Seaton's suggestions; he also saw the flaws. 'What is wanted is to try the experiment of giving the people more power and the Lord High Commissioner less, but not to give the whole power of a sudden to the former, and this too, as far as constitutional means go, irrevocably.' For the abolition of the Primary Council and the Double Lists would remove the one effective safeguard the executive had over the extended powers of the legislative. Better to devise a new system altogether than to destroy Maitland's from within. In Strachey's opinion what was needed was 'some fixed position upon which we may fall back and take our stand in the event of the experiment working ill.' Otherwise with no power to suspend the constitution or revoke measures in an emergency, deadlock between the Lord High Commissioner and a popular assembly would be inevitable. So Grey cautiously advised Seaton to wait and see how the first reforms were working before proceeding too fast. Furthermore he pointed out the limits of the available information. For example, outside Corfu no-one knew what the likely increase in the electorate to be expected from a new franchise might be. Nothing could damp Seaton's ardour, and in April 1849 Grey authorized him to proceed. On 8 May the Assembly adopted the reforms in two resolutions. As one observer put it, 'In ten days he hurried the wandering Ionians through more political changes than England had undergone in ten generations. On 1 May 1849 the Lord High Commissioner had more power than Queen Elizabeth. On the 10th of the same month he was left with less power than Queen Victoria.' At that moment Seaton's tenure of office expired, and this remarkable, if paradoxical, man departed.

Luckily Sir Henry Ward, who succeeded him, enjoyed a staunchly liberal reputation. He also enjoyed Grey's confidence. The Secretary of State was not entirely pleased with Seaton; the distinct order for a separate agreement making the military contribution a first charge on the revenue had been disregarded. Moreover, the resolutions embodying the proposed reforms as adopted by the Assembly differed from the draft agreed by Grey, who feared that so important a matter had received insufficient consideration. Since they still needed ratification by the Crown, Ward was to remedy these omissions and defects and reconsider the proposals. The latter soon showed he disagreed with his predecessor, although admitting the necessity for reform. As regards elections to the Senate, Seaton had agreed that he should nominate the senators directly, with his choice restricted to the ranks of the Assembly. Ward saw this to be fatal, for both Senate and Assembly would be put in the hands of a new and unpredictable electorate, and if the Lord High Commissioner clashed with both, government could not be carried on. His idea to retain the right to select some senators from outside the Assembly certainly appeared more practical; at least the administrative machine could still function in a crisis. He failed to realize that a powerful and popularly based Assembly would not tolerate a powerful and non-answerable Senate for long. Here again was the dubious wisdom of keeping the old forms of government in the new circumstances.

Ward was a quick learner. By December he had acknowledged that no scheme combining a freely elected Assembly with the existing Senate could ever work. One of his most trusted advisers, Kourkoumeli, suggested doing away with the Senate altogether, and replacing it by a responsible ministry, which alone would exercise executive powers. The Lord High Commissioner was gaining an insight into the temper of the people he had come to rule. He realized far more acutely than had Seaton just how weak Ionian ties with Britain were, and how little gratitude had been earned by the reforms already instituted. As he wrote to Grey, 'Your Lordship must not imagine that I have to deal here with British colonists, bound to the mother country by ties of blood, language, and religion.' He cited the case of Sir R. Petritsopoulos from Levkas, who had held office as Regent, senator, or deputy for over twenty years, but who before his death in 1849 had made his family's peace with the future by an alliance with the Unionists. As Ward now understood this, he could see the extent of the problem, though he remained undaunted adding, 'I can only humbly repeat my conviction that to give up power altogether is to give up these islands.'

His worst fears had already been confirmed by the outbreak of revolt on Cephalonia. More mountainous, and with its population more scattered through the countryside than that of Zante or Corfu, it was living up to its reputation as the most unruly of all the islands. The decline in currant prices since the peak of the 1820s had hit the small farmers hard, and here especially the contadini were in debt to the usurers and signori. Cephalonia was the most fiercely Hellenic in its sympathies, and the least reconciled to the British régime. The accession to power of Kolettis in Athens signified a resurgence of militant Greek nationalism, and in 1847 some emigrant Ionians returned to the island and formed a Society for the Extension of Free Greece, which meant outright annexation. Since March 1848, the Resident d'Everton had reported a growing revolutionary fervour, there was a serious run on the Ionian Bank, and many overtly political meetings. That Easter there were anti-British demonstrations, and on 26 September some two hundred peasants marched on Lixouri and Argostoli and clashed with the troops. Ten agitators fled to the mainland; they were outlawed and the villages concerned were heavily fined. Seaton, who blamed d'Everton for laxness in allowing this trouble to develop, demoted him to the inferior Residency of Levkas and appointed an entirely inexperienced successor, Major Symonds.

On 8 May 1849 Captain John Parker, the officer in charge of the forest on Mount Aenos, was murdered. He was trying to prevent the peasants from burning large tracts of woodland, chopping down the trees for firewood, or letting their goats loose on the saplings, offences for which Napier had habitually jailed the owners and confiscated the livestock twenty years before. One day walking down to Argostoli from his cottage, beautifully situated 4,000 feet up on the mountainside, he was ambushed, shot, and butchered as he lay bleeding on the ground. When help arrived his little dog was found still whimpering by its master's body, as it is depicted on his tombstone. Parker had been a popular figure, and this crime outraged public opinion. Seaton's feebleness when the villagers persisted in concealing the assassins was culpable, for it encouraged the agitators to foment more discontent.

The situation was still uneasy when Ward took up his post in June 1849. He proclaimed a general amnesty, and two of the ringleaders, Zervos and Livadas, were released. Again the malcontents interpreted this as a sign of weakness, and that August a serious rising occurred near the village of Scala in the south. A brief but savage jacquerie terrorized the neighbourhood for four days, and panic reigned in Argostoli. Troops scattered the insurgents, but some, led by Vlacco, a brigand, and Nodaros, a priest, retired to the hills. When the Lord High Commissioner arrived in Cephalonia in September, he was impressed by the calls for stern measures. The rebels were avoiding the soldiers, but in scattered bands were doing much damage in the countryside. Landowners were being killed and their houses burned; Count Metaxas was incinerated in his. Attempting to take an active part in the campaign, Ward accompanied a force to Troionata, and told the village primate to ring the church bell, so that the people could gather to hear the proclamation. 'At this moment a shot was fired and the primate fell dead at the feet of His Excellency. Insurgents concealed in the houses then began to shoot at the troops, who returned their fire and advanced to attack with the bayonet; upon which the rebels fled, the soldiers pursued, and took some prisoners.' Kirkwall notes sardonically that Ward was rather shaken by his experience.

The garrison was reinforced from Corfu, and for six weeks the island suffered under martial law. Soldiers searched and often ransacked the villages, houses were burned, seventy malefactors were flogged, and by court-martial sentences twenty-one were executed and another thirty jailed. Zervos retreated to Greece, whence his journal *Phileleftheris* exhorted the Ionians to throw off the foreign yoke, while his colleague Monferrato published the inflammatory *Anagennesis,* which priests read aloud to peasants in many villages. The repression, of unprecedented severity under the Protectorate brought much odium on Ward's head and made most Cephalonians thoroughly Anglophobe. It is hard to assess the importance of the movements.

Both risings only involved small numbers in limited areas. Local or class grievances played as large a part as political aims. Agitators from the towns were mainly responsible; the Scala villagers had been assured 'that on a given day the whole island would rise and exterminate the English'.

It did finally destroy the Colonial Office's faith in Seaton's proposed reforms. Twice within twelve months, the Army had had to put down armed, if futile, revolts. The proposals, which were meant to have been a package of political surprises, could now be said to have been wrung from the British by fear. During the autumn, a dejected Ward contemplated jettisoning most of the reforms. With Grey's backing, he agreed to try out his scheme for selecting senators. Strachey again warned of the folly of adopting measures which would permanently impair the British government's powers to shape the Ionian constitution, but the Secretary of State would not be swayed; 'though deprived of all confidence in the working of the system with the proposed amendments, I yet think it absolutely impossible to keep things as they are'.

In December 1849 the Assembly accepted the May resolutions as duly revised. Its own size was to be increased from forty to forty-two members, all freely elected as the Primary Council and Double Lists had been abolished. The income qualification was lowered, thereby more than trebling the size of the electorate, and a secret ballot was introduced. To illustrate the point, there were barely 400 voters in Cephalonia in Napier's time, by 1862 there were 3,560. The military contribution, fixed at £25,000 per annum, was to be a first charge on the Ionian revenue, while the civil list was fixed at £15,000, which figure could not be altered without the Crown's assent. The Lord High Commissioner retained the right to appoint two senators from outside the Assembly. Ward now felt that the whole programme was 'a perfect lottery', and that he had devised a new system of government for a society entirely different from the English in race, culture and traditions. Obviously the arbitrary solution acceptable in 1817 was indefensible in 1849, but would the new compromise ultimately please anybody? He wondered whether anything could work, if an independent Greece drew Ionian sentiment increasingly away from the British connection. The spirit in which the reforms were adopted had once been liberalizing, it was now fatalistic and betrayed the London government's lack of faith in the whole edifice. Thus when Grey criticized Colonial Office policy a decade later, Gladstone could say: 'He is going to throw stones out of the thinnest glass in which mortals e'er dwelt.'

For the next few months the question was whether the reforms were succeeding and satisfying everybody. The Assembly was polite and co-operative, and Ward became a qualified optimist. Despite the Don Pacifico affair, when the British fleet bombarded Athens, and Palmerston was furiously denounced in the Ionian Press, the extremists stayed fairly quiescent. However the new elections only returned four of the previous members, over thirty of the newcomers had never sat in the House before, and the Cephalonian contingent was especially radical. They even adopted the insolent habit of calling in a priest to purify the House, after the 'heretic' Lord High Commissioner had departed from opening the session. A majority refused to take the oath as it referred to 'the indissoluble union' with the protecting Power, and a compromise had to be found. Worse was to come. The Assembly replied to Ward's address with a passionate indictment of thirty-five years of British rule. They complained of the decay of the mercantile marine, the decline of agriculture, the merely nominal powers of the municipal councils, and the wholesale jobbery practised by a few foreigners and favoured Ionian families. They condemned the failure to introduce Greek as the official language, and suggested that some truly radical reforms would speed the reunion with their mother country. Ward's stiff rejoinder showed the tenor of their future relationship.

The Assembly made a test case out of the election of a Corfiote, Doctor Braila. When he had stood as a candidate he lacked the documents needed to prove his eligibility, so the Regent had rejected him. Braila then impugned the elections and the Assembly decided the returns were invalid. The Senate promptly objected that the Regents were entitled to pronounce on a candidate's credentials, while the Assembly reasserted its exclusive right to decide on the validity of elections. Deadlock persisted until June 1850, when the Senate passed an atto di governo providing for annually revised lists of those eligible to be candidates, with right of appeal to the civil courts. The Assembly refused to accept this, and a compromise was only reached two years later. With the mutual hostility of both chambers, Ward's optimism began to dwindle. Ten deputies formed a cohesive radical group, 'without a shilling in the world, and fed upon the histories of Lamartine and Thiers', who joined in any protest to embarrass the administration. The majority, although they protested against a motion for immediate union with Greece, were scarcely more helpful. Even those who were privately friendly remained publicly silent. The Lord High Commissioner's aim was now to get through the first session without a prorogation. He begged Russell for time – time in which his reforms could mature and win over the wavering majority. He even agreed to a bill limiting the unpopular powers of High Police, but the radicals, set on sabotaging his best efforts, had it thrown out by the Assembly. Ward was disgusted by their hypocrisy, and enraged by the row over the Civil List. The extremists wished to reduce the salaries of all department heads, senators, and judges by half. Even Moustoxidis, leader of the liberal opposition to Douglas agreed on the futility of treating with men 'bidding for popularity under the eye of the galleries'. A new motion demanding union which seemed to have a chance of success, was impending, so in June 1850 Parliament was prorogued for six months.

Travelling round the islands, Ward found the peasantry friendly, and principally anxious for practical improvements. Cephalonia was again in a dangerously turbulent state, as the currant market had slumped, and the carrying trade had further declined. Agitators, abetted by many of the clergy, were hard at work, and the garrison once more had to be reinforced. Otherwise the situation could have been worse, although this had little bearing on the conduct of the Assembly members. This they proved at the start of the new session in December by declaring, on grounds of principle, that all atti di governo enacted by the Senate during the recess were invalid, a decision in which the Senate naturally refused to concur. Fresh motions for union were only thwarted by a further prorogation for twelve months. It was during this next year that Ward showed his real determination to make his reforms work. He attacked the extremists, allowing the Residents to close down radical clubs in Zante and Cephalonia, suppressing agitation in the countryside, and forcing the Regents to suspend firebrand members of the district councils. Prominent unionists were banished under the High Police power. Simultaneously the Lord High Commissioner tried to heal the breach between his supporters and the moderate opposition, mainly Corfiote and known because of their journal as the *Patris* party. By the following summer the moderates had agreed to support him in return for some concessions — annual sessions, some internal reorganization of the Senate, an extension of the powers of the municipal governments and the abandonment of the executive's role in the Supreme Court of Justice. In the absence of any more promising alternatives, Grey reluctantly agreed this was the best policy.

The ninth Assembly was dissolved in December 1851 and more elections were proclaimed. This time the Residents were encouraged to interfere, a decision which seemed justified when the new parliament met the next February. All ten Corfiote deputies were government men; so were the Cephalonian contingent thanks to the Regent Caruso's purge of the electoral register. From all the other islands the members seemed friendly, except from Zante, where the weakness of the coalition had been rapidly exposed as Solomos, the Senate President, showed small desire to share the spoils of office with Romas, the moderates' leader. Thanks to this feud, all ten members returned had been radicals. Yet again Ward was to be disillusioned. His majority evaporated through resignations, the nomination of half-a-dozen loyal members to the Senate and the thwarted aspirations to office of others of his erstwhile supporters. The opposition avoided replying to the address by staying away from the House, so that the needed quorum of twenty-two was lacking. Ward again prorogued parliament, and was equally gloomy when he reconvened it in June. 'I beg to be distinctly understood not to guarantee the success of the measures that I have indicated. I merely point out what I think is possible.' So ran his despatch to the Colonial Office. Events were to show that his pessimism was well merited.

At first the Assembly seemed determined to be propitiatory. A vote of thanks to the Queen was passed for the first time since 1849; atti di governo were discussed on their merits rather than rejected on principle. Even the Lord High Commissioner's refusal to approve a bill forbidding the public sale of debtors' lands in payment of debts did not produce a breach. This had been designed to protect the impoverished agriculturists, particularly on Cephalonia, but he had had to safeguard the position of the Ionian Bank, in which £250,000 of British capital was invested. By August 1852 Ward felt sufficiently confident to introduce the reforms agreed on in 1851, including a new press law stipulating a £100 Deposit before starting a newspaper. In return he offered to surrender his High Police powers of banishment. The Assembly was not satisfied. They passed a motion demanding a Senate answerable to the electorate, and concurrent powers with the executive in a state of emergency. Knowing that the basic objection was to his press law, Ward would not compromise. After a debate the Assembly then rejected his reform proposals by one vote.

In effect this marked the end of British attempts to revise the constitution. A coalition had been laboriously constructed, only to see the *retrogradi* (i.e. the die-hard conservatives) side with the radicals to defeat the government. Fortunately a generous civil list and a loan of £40,000 had already been sanctioned. It was manifestly impossible to govern Greeks like Anglo-Saxons, but a genuine attempt had been made to conciliate them. The mistake in the 1849 reforms was to give the unionists clear access to the public platforms of the press and Assembly to advocate a policy which Ward, without any definite instructions from London, regarded as totally inimical to his main function of preserving the Protectorate. Radical reform would not divert the Unionists from their political aims. Even the granting of a pure democracy would not do this, nor was there any reason to believe that it would swing the mass of non-unionist opinion squarely behind the protectorate. So after 1852 the British attitude was one of complete disillusionment. Ward now believed that it had been a fatal error ever to abandon Maitland's constitution, and until his departure in 1855 the government's role became increasingly passive. In 1852 he had encouraged the Residents to interfere against Unionist candidates; as 'the reforms have thrown all political power into the hands of those who can get elected', he intended to ignore a hostile Assembly by meeting it as seldom as possible. Yet the High Police power was sparingly used after 1852, and the extremist press was left unmolested, although the *Panhellenion*, a unionist club on Corfu, was closed. The government functioned through atti di governo, and in the three years until July 1855 the Assembly was only summoned once, then prorogued after three weeks. Their exclusive control of the Civil List had to be recognized, but Ward avoided executing their financial projects on the pretext that they had not been sent to the Senate before his decision to prorogue.

The tragedy was that the English were making a mockery of the very constitutional system they had created, and of the representative government which the islands ostensibly enjoyed. The dubious conduct of some of their Ionian associates was hardly an advantage; Caruso flagrantly rigged the electoral lists in Cephalonia to secure his own advancement, and things were no better if less efficiently managed in Zante. The Senate and the Lord High Commissioner were ever more closely identified. Senators had to be ceaselessly placated, both because they comprised the one amenable legislative body and as some compensation for the unpopularity they incurred with their compatriots for collaborating with the occupying power. More and more patronage, central and municipal, came into their hands to be used for personal or local interests. In 1858 Gladstone could report: 'The notion that office is a property to be enjoyed is widespread and deeply rooted.' Paid places increased by twenty-five per cent during this decade, but the administration had to turn a blind eye to these abuses for fear of offending its friends. Party divisions had now sharpened. On the one side stood the conservatives, the heirs spiritually and often literally of the oligarchic faction which had coalesced during the days of the French Revolution. They accepted the Protectorate as a necessity and a good, but while some advocated a return to Maitland's methods, others favoured a measure of reform. The opposition was similarly divided. Many of the older liberals saw the Protectorate as a fact, and merely demanded a guarantee of their liberties and some concessions to national sentiment. The unionists of course claimed it was all a hoax and an evil to be destroyed, although few were prepared to pursue resistance by violent means. If not the most numerous, they were undoubtedly the most vocal and cohesive of all the parties.

There were other reasons why their strength grew during the 1850s. Many old grievances in the social and economic spheres remained unalleviated. The educated youth of the islands found career opportunities as limited as ever, although by an act passed in 1857 Ionians were permitted to hold commissions in the British armed forces. Social intercourse between the two communities had never been prevalent, and now steeply declined. Trade did increase; imports, which had stood at £708,000 in 1850, had risen to £1,306,000 in 1859, while exports rose from £380,000 to £649,000 over the same period. This boom in commerce did not, however, reflect prosperity in the Ionian economy; most of the goods were British in transit to the mainland. Indeed, though British shipping to the islands rose from 12,600 to 22,000 tons over these years, shipping entering Britain from them fell from 10,200 to 7,700 tons. The currant crop failed frequently. The thirty-one million pounds produced in 1850 had dwindled to five million in 1854, and seven million in 1855. The amount imported to Britain fell less drastically—from 138,000 hundredweight in 1850 to 37,000 in 1855, and back up to 106,000 in 1859 as fresh markets were tapped. Nevertheless, the distress in the southern islands was very real; in 1855 almost everyone in Cephalonia, Ithaca, and Zante was said to be ruined. Ward got permission to use £5,000 per annum of the military contribution to mitigate the worst of the poverty, but far more funds were needed to solve the problem. Greek nationalism received a further boost from the Crimean War, when Britain, by supporting its ally Turkey, forfeited Ionian sympathies. The Lord High Commissioner was particularly tactless, supplying the Albanian authorities with ammunition and trying to arrange Anglo-French intervention at Ioannina, when Greek troops invaded Epirus in 1854. Placards appeared in the streets demanding war against the Porte, the Archbishop of Corfu introduced a prayer for the Tsar into the liturgy, and despite vigilant patrols along the straits enough men, arms, and money were smuggled across the mainland for an Ionian Corps to join the Greek army in Albania.

When Ward's successor, Sir John Young, arrived and requested information on public feeling in the islands, it was hardly encouraging. In Cephalonia and Zante opinion was 'rife in favour of union with Greece', in Ithaca at least three-quarters of the population favoured it. Only in Corfu could a majority be said to be neutral or opposed to the idea. Discontent in Levkas was attributed primarily to the prevalence of usury, and any reduction in the garrison would merely enhearten the agitators, while in Kythera, unrest among the peasantry was fanned by unionists, who ironically had been exiled there to silence them. The municipalities were being equally refractory, and their officers, elected from 'free' constituencies, were continually trying to extend their powers at the expense of the Residents'. Furthermore, they neglected their duties; roads were left unrepaired, marshes undrained, and the schools allowed to decay. Only among the upper reaches of Ionian society, and primarily among the landed proprietors, did sentiment favour the Protectorate. This was anyway tempered by an interest in the distribution of the spoils of office, so that a Kaloutsis in Kythera or a Solomos in Zante, if dispossessed, could be as obstructive as any unionist. Moreover, an attitude of moral cowardice ensured that they persistently failed to stand up and be counted. The vicious hounding of Kourkoumeli, one of the most distinguished figures in public life, who had dared to propose that Corfu should become a British colony, showed what could happen to those who openly disavowed unionism.

Despite the infrequent meetings of the Assembly, power could be seen to reside with the electorate. In 1850 Ward had estimated there were six unionist deputies, in 1852 ten, usually abetted by five more, while in 1855 the hard core had swelled to twelve with six supporters. In 1850 almost all the radicals had come from Cephalonia. Thanks to Caruso's manipulations this was no longer true after 1851, and most of the extremists were returned from Zante, but except for the ballot-rigging the unionist bloc would have been much larger. The press and the clergy were rabidly unionist. Apart from the official Government Gazette, every paper, and there were four in 1856 and seven a year later, supported the opposition. The sole attempt to apply the law by prosecuting a violently abusive editor on Zante had resulted in his triumphant acquittal. In the countryside the priests played the chief part. Although the British had enshrined the position of the Orthodox Church, and had forbidden any proselytizing by Catholics or Protestants, it had done them little good. Only once had the government interfered in religious affairs, and after a lengthy dispute with the Patriarch of Constantinople about 1840, that intractable cleric had been deposed. Initially they had taken part in the St Spyridon processions just as the Venetians had done; indeed the relics had been carried by four colonels, but with relations at such a low ebb the British had taken to ignoring the occasion. Most of the clergy still distrusted the heretics, who seemed temporarily to have been entrusted with the government, and emphasized their congregations' links with their co-religionists in Greece.

The one brief session of the tenth Assembly in 1854 was characterized by attacks on Britain as the defender of the Turks and the betrayer of Hellenism.

When it resumed in 1855, all the interim legislation presented by the executive was rejected, and a petition was prepared to annul the powers of the High Police. No wonder Young shrank from meeting this body, promptly dissolved it, and sent out writs for another election. The eleventh Assembly, when it convened in 1857, seemed slightly more reasonable, although the Lord High Commissioner had to ignore its more obstreperous measures, for he was determined not to prorogue. But he was eventually forced to do so, when the Assembly unanimously passed a motion by the Zantiote deputy Lombardos protesting against an alleged plan to offer Ionians some seats in the British Parliament, thus making the islands a Crown Colony. He gloomily anticipated a worse session in 1858, culminating probably in an appeal to the European powers. Complete deadlock had been reached; as he wrote 'they do nothing themselves and will not suffer others to do anything'. Actually, the 1857 session had seen the passing of twenty-two bills, a larger number than had been passed in all the other sessions together since 1849, and these included two important ones reorganizing the pensions and education schemes. The sad deterioration in administration was no less marked in local governments. These were naturally in continuous session, and since Greek had at last superseded English and Italian as the official language in 1852, the Residents had had to depend more on their Greek-speaking subordinates. Like the Assembly, the municipal councillors tried to curry favour with the new electorate, and again the result had been that the machine no longer ran smoothly. As d'Everton, one of the most experienced Residents, had pointed out, in the eleven years before 1851 the veto had never been used at all in Argostoli, in the next nine years it had to be employed sixty times. Corruption flourished here too; in Young's view it was rifer among the municipal officials than among an Irish Grand Jury. It was reckoned that up to thirty per cent of local revenues were not being collected, and in consequence the roads were far worse in 1859 than 1849. What a far cry from the noble ideals and achievements of men like Napier, and how soon had their legacy of high-minded, albeit autocratic, government been dissipated!

C. 'THE BENEFICENCE OF EMPIRE'

'The joint production of a pupil of Machiavelli and The Man in the Moon' was how Bulwer Lytton, Colonial Secretary in 1858, described the suggestion to reimpose British authority in the islands by a coup d'état. Nevertheless, the Cabinet had finally come to realize that drastic measures, political or constitutional, would have to be taken, and that the initiative for this could only come from London. Both Ward and Young had acknowledged that nothing within their competence was adequate. The Crimean War had brought this home to the British government, which was annoyed by the judgement given by Lushington in the Supreme Court at Corfu, that Ionian shipping was neutral although England was at war. When the Cabinet considered a definite declaration of Ionian belligerency, Ward advised against it. The Assembly would refuse assent to any bill, while the Senate was nervous of passing an atto di governo on this contentious topic; so nothing was done. Further irritation was occasioned in 1857 by an argument as to whether the British consular court at Constantinople had jurisdiction over Ionian subjects. The only practical way of ending their virtual immunity in civil cases was for the Ionian Parliament to pass an act declaring Ionians in the Levant subject to the same laws as British citizens. Because of the political situation, this had not been possible either.

Irksome though these constraints were, the Ionian question was not sufficiently urgent or vital to attract the prolonged attention of the Cabinet. In the same way it had never appealed to humanitarians or colonial and commercial theorists, involving merely a small military outpost with no native problem and no outstanding economic potentialities. Rude remarks might be made in the French Chamber; the Austrian ambassador even cited the islands as a useful retort to a Palmerstonian lecture on liberty, but nothing drastic was likely to come of all this. The press, Parliament, and public in England paid scant attention to Ionian affairs, and the ministry wished to remain equally aloof. For the alternatives were not attractive. To extend the reforms granted to the Ionians in 1849 was to invite them to exploit their increased power to make the administration of the Protectorate wholly unworkable. A return to Maitland's system, or the imposition of a new one narrowly restricting popular rights, was out of the question by legal means. As Newcastle remarked, only a mild despotism would suit such people, but as a constitution had been given, to remove it again 'will merely please every tyrant from Louis Napoleon to Bomba.'

The best hope, so it seemed, was to change the relationship established by the Treaty of Paris. As no-one then in power was prepared to contemplate ceding all the islands to Greece, an ingenious scheme was propounded: Corfu with Paxos should be annexed by Britain, while the other islands would be handed over to Greece. Young welcomed the proposal, but the idea was not new. Russell and Grey had briefly considered it in 1849; some Corfiote politicians like Kourkoumeli wanted it. Both the Foreign and Colonial Offices recognized the obvious advantages. The ambiguous relationship which had bedevilled the Anglo-Ionian connection from the start would be ended. Corfu was the only island of real importance to them, it alone was fortified and supposedly defensible against an outside attack. Moreover, it alone contained the moderate reform party like Damaskinos and the Zambelli brothers, who were prepared to co-operate; it did not lie off Greek territory, its population had the largest non-Greek element of all the islands, and its aristocracy was strongly Italianate. As the headquarters of the Ionian government and garrison, Corfu had benefited more directly from British expenditure than anywhere else. The scheme, thought Young, was bound to suit the Corfiotes, for 'the island would become a garden, and its port the centre of commerce for the adjacent countries.' He was delighted by the prospect of disposing of those hotbeds of unionist clamour, the strategically worthless and now impoverished southern islands.

Although the plan appeared to offer a viable solution, it was not without its critics. Such a fundamental change in the status of all the islands could not be effected by Britain alone. The other signatories of the Treaty of Paris in 1815 would have to give their consent, and Palmerston had already expressed doubts as to their readiness to sanction Britain's annexation of the desirable Corfu. When a Tory ministry returned to power in 1858 under Lord Derby (who, as Stanley, had been Colonial Secretary in the 1840s), further objections were raised. Lytton disliked European congresses, he deplored the virtual confession of her inability to rule the Ionians which Britain would have to make, and felt that to give anything to Greece was tantamount to giving it to Russia. Moreover would not the English press and public resent such a policy of surrender? Yet the new Secretary of State, with his profound veneration for the classics, his romantic imagination and concept of the civilizing mission of Empire, was certainly keen to do something. Difficult and dangerous as every policy seemed, he needed some impetus to action.

The affair of the Corfu municipal officers provided the match to light the fuse. In July 1858 Turkish ships had called at the harbour to buy bread. The municipal official in charge of the market had prevented its sale, on the grounds that it might leave the island short, and had called in the police to enforce his edict. Young was incensed at what he regarded as a slight on Britain's ally, and a cheap attempt to play to the nationalist gallery. Furthermore, the official had exceeded his authority by using the police, who came directly under the command of the Lord High Commissioner. Accordingly, he instructed the Director of Police to refuse constabulary assistance in such cases. The entire corporation then sent in a memorandum disputing Young's right to subordinate the highest local elected authority to an executive official. They made their feelings plain by falling out of the August St Spyridon procession as it stopped outside the Palace of SS Michael and George to offer prayers for the Sovereign. Convinced that they were merely demonstrating their hostility in the most offensive manner, Young asked the Secretary of State for permission to dismiss all five of them. Lytton wavered. The Crown could of course dismiss them all, but it could not prevent their re-election, which was likely. To dismiss them again would be to start a farce. In such circumstances, where the British Protectorate was so clearly unpopular, where it might even have to be defended by physical force, 'I doubt that it would be advisable for authority to strike the first blow at all.' Conciliation not punishment was surely the needed remedy. Such was the direct origin of the Gladstone mission.

By October Lytton had conceived the idea of sending out a special commissioner to investigate grievances and suggest remedies. He needed someone well-known as a philhellene, a liberal, and a statesman able to inspire confidence. Gladstone, then chafing in opposition, was pleased to be offered such a mission in an area famous for its Homeric associations. First he demanded that his work for a Tory government bear no political connotations, and that the municipal officers must go unpunished. After this had been agreed Gladstone accepted, and in late November landed in Corfu. Within several weeks he had concluded that the situation was discreditable to Britain and disagreeable to most Ionians. The benefits had outweighed the drawbacks of protection, but 'no method of dealing with a civilized community can be satisfactory which does not make provision for its political action as well as its social state.' Maitland's system had been effective, albeit illiberal. 'The misshapen reforms' of 1849 had by contrast lit the fire while stopping up the chimney. A popularly elected representative assembly could not be reconciled with the existence of a non-responsible executive. The Lord High Commissioner in tandem with an unpopular Senate could no longer control the machine of government, but was blamed nevertheless for its discordant operation. As he wrote to Lytton, 'nothing less than an army of Cherubim and Seraphim can make anything tolerable out of the present system'. Both were adamant that a retreat to absolutism and cession of the islands to Greece were equally inconceivable. So the only solution was to extend the sphere of popular liberties until a parliamentary democracy existed. Gladstone refuted the notion that the Ionians were unfitted for free institutions; in any case, the royal veto imposed a check on any really objectionable legislation. He did not believe that the Assembly would continue to press for union regardless, as it was a slogan covering a multitude of grievances. Anyway, the Assembly had a perfect constitutional right to request it of the protecting power, and indeed had no reason to regard the arrangements made by the Treaty of Paris, to which it had not been a signatory, as definitive. If this recurred, a petition to the Crown could properly be allowed, and would be answered not with a rebuke but by an explicit declaration from the highest authority.

His constitutional proposals would then be seen as the answer to Ionian problems. These had two objectives: to increase the influence of the Assembly over the executive and to restrict the British element in government. The Senate was to be replaced by a Council of Ministers, which would wield executive power. They would be appointed by the Lord High Commissioner, and would be removable on address from the legislature. The latter would consist of two Houses. The Upper House would have most of its members elected on a narrow franchise, with a minority nominated by the executive. Lacking any power or initiative of its own, it would possess a veto on money bills and concurrent control over other legislation. The Lower House, composed entirely of members elected on the extended franchise, would alone levy taxation and authorize expenditure, while officials could be impeached before the Upper House. The Lord High Commissioner's approval need no longer be cited in the preamble to acts; where he now held sole authority, this would be shared with a minister, where his authority was held jointly with the Senate, it would in future belong solely to a minister. The High Police power was to be abolished. Either chamber could petition the Crown against a Lord High Commissioner for malversation, and could send an envoy to London to argue the case. Far-reaching these proposals certainly were. Unfortunately they presupposed an Ionian concern with constitutional reform that simply did not exist. To admit that a political campaign for union with Greece was the paramount problem, and then to ignore it, was not constructive. Even without the misgivings of the Colonial Office, this programme, if implemented, would have worked little better than Seaton's.

The mission was also dogged by bad luck. As Gladstone was en route to Corfu, the *Daily News* published a despatch from Young to the Secretary of State recommending the annexation of two islands and the cession of the other five. This leak naturally led the Ionians to assume that Gladstone had come to implement this policy, and no amount of denials on his part could repair the damage. Corfu's Deputies and municipal officers affirmed their unquenchable desire for union with Greece, so did the representatives from Paxos. As he travelled round the islands, nationalist fervour ran high. On his arrival in Argostoli a turbulent crowd, at least a thousand strong, surrounded him as he crossed the causeway over the lagoon, and when he tried to make a speech, shouted him down with unionist and anti-British slogans. In Zante over eight thousand people did the same, and in both places the bishops and clergy presented petitions against the Protectorate. Gladstone journeyed on to Athens, where King Otho received him politely. He thought he detected no great desire to acquire the islands, but the fact that the leading unionist journal on Corfu, *New Era*, was subsidized by the Greek government scarcely substantiated this.

Luckily the trip did not lack a humorous side. In Gaio he called upon the Bishop of Paxos, as Kirkwall recounts: 'At Paxos as everywhere else he showed the most unbounded veneration for the dignitaries of the Greek Church. In Corfu he had excited the perhaps illiberal disgust of the English by publicly kissing the hand of the Archbishop and duly receiving his blessing . . . The simple Bishop of Paxos appears to have been ignorant of the etiquette which the High Commissioner Extraordinary practised with ecclesiastical dignitaries. Mr Gladstone, having taken and respectfully kissed the Bishop's hand, leaned forward to receive the Orthodox blessing. The Bishop hesitated, not knowing what was expected of him, and not imagining perhaps that a member of the Anglican Church could require his benediction. At last he perceived the truth, and, bending forward, he hastened to comply with the flattering desire of the representative of the British Crown. But at this moment, unfortunately, Mr Gladstone imagining that the deferred blessing was not forthcoming suddenly raised his head and struck the episcopal chin. The Resident and other spectators of the scene had considerable difficulty in maintaining the gravity befitting so solemn an occasion.'

If Gladstone still persisted in trying to find a settlement, it was no longer with any real confidence that his proposals would be accepted, but because he believed the offer must be made to vindicate government policy. 'England's first interest is that her honour should be cleared.' Thereafter any breakdown in the system could justly be ascribed to Ionian intransigence. In January 1859 Gladstone had Young recalled, and himself appointed as Lord High Commissioner. He then met the Assembly in extraordinary session. They unanimously carried a resolution that all seven islands only desired union with Greece, and a petition embodying this was forwarded to the Queen. After its prompt rejection, the reform proposals were presented to them. Nine days passed with no signs of progress, then in mid-February another resolution was carried declaring the reforms unacceptable. Only the President voted against it, six members abstained and thirty-one supported the motion. Gladstone returned to England, 'thoroughly disgusted with the Greeks in general, and the Ionians in particular'. His successor, Sir Henry Storks, received the Assembly's formal reply. In it they stated that their declaration of 27 January and the subsequent petition, as well as prevailing public sentiment, made them view the reforms as irrelevant. But if Lytton and Gladstone had failed, they had the consolation of having accomplished something; the honour of England was vindicated. The stark truth had emerged in the process; only one solution to the Ionian problem, union, was feasible.

The British now fell back on a long-term policy: the conciliation of reasonable material grievances, tolerance towards orderly Ionian political life, combined with firmness towards extravagant demands. Most ministers in London were still not prepared to contemplate cession. Newcastle indeed believed that an improvement in economic conditions might blunt the unionist campaign. Although an autocrat of Maitland's stamp, Storks was able and energetic, and quite determined that the regime should remain non-partisan. Residents were told to stay aloof from local factions, while cultivating the goodwill of the municipal authorities. Use of the veto was discouraged, and interference in elections made punishable by dismissal. The Lord High Commissioner himself refused to discuss tactics with the notorious Cephalonian politician Caruso, disdained to use the powers of High Police, and amnestied the 1849 rebels who had fled the island. He travelled frequently and held weekly audiences to which any Ionian might come. Examinations for admission to and promotion in the government civil service were introduced; this was long overdue but caused much grumbling among incumbent officials.

These conciliatory tactics involved some material concessions. In July 1859 Storks urged that Ionian currants be granted a preferential duty on entering England or at least that the present duty might be reduced. Similarly, attempts were made to gain the same preferential treatment for Ionian as for Cape wine. All foundered on the Treasury's obstinacy and 'the high fiction of state' which persisted in classifying the islands as a foreign country for commercial purposes. The Colonial Office got a ruling from the Law Officers to reverse this decision, but it came too late, as Gladstone's 1860 budget abolished the whole system of colonial preference, and reduced all duties on wine and currants. Arguing that if the islands were denied the privileges of a colony, they should not have to bear the burdens of one, Storks then stopped the practice of allowing the garrison to import certain goods free of duty. He also brought forward applications for commissions in the British armed services under the hitherto uninvoked act of 1857, and improved Anglo-Ionian social relations by sponsoring the formation of an Ionian association for promoting science, literature, and the arts. His secretary, Wolff, was the moving spirit in it, and the veteran scholar Moustoxidis its first president. An exhibition of products from the islands was staged in London and was a great success. In all this Newcastle, now at the Colonial Office, loyally supported the policy, although as sceptical about its chances as anyone.

Most Ionians, however, convinced that Britain's resolve was weakening, refused to compromise. Relations between the Lord High Commissioner and Assembly fell into the familiar pattern. In March 1859 Storks opened the new session; within a fortnight he had had to prorogue it. The next session was postponed until the winter and actually ran its course, despite being full of recriminations and 'extravagant vote-getting proposals', while his carefully prepared legislative programme was ignored. By March 1861 the position had further deteriorated. Propagandists like the Corfiote Dandolo were producing open letters and pamphlets; many Assembly members wondered whether to absent themselves from sessions altogether, and to urge the electorate to abstain from voting. The unionists were enheartened by the British government's support for the Italian *Risorgimento*, and they received information that public and official opinion in England would soon accede to their demands. Storks' address from the throne was met by 'a bill of indictment against the Protectorate which was offensive and insulting'. Two unionists, Lombardos and Baccomi, suggested respectively a plebiscite to demonstrate the islands' desire for union, and 'an appeal to Christian Europe' to aid them in their legitimate aspirations. After a request to withdraw the motion had been refused, Storks prorogued the session after ten days, and despite widespread complaints continued it until the dissolution at the end of 1861. Little was to be expected from fresh elections, as he well knew. 'The *Rhizopasti*', (a new and scornful nickname for them), 'are in possession of the field, and no other candidates have the moral courage to come forward and contest the elections with them.'

Indeed the results of the poll of February 1862 represented a triumph for the radicals, for almost every member returned was of their persuasion. However the unionist ranks now split; a minority under the 1848 stalwarts, Zervos and Monferrato, regarded union as eventually certain, and were prepared to attend to necessary legislation in the meantime, a majority under Lombardos believed that any consideration of constitutional reform was 'an act of national treason', and the session ended with another petition for union to the Crown, which was, as usual, rejected. Relations had reached an all-time low. As Kirkwall acidly commented: 'One of the propositions made was the assertion of the rights of the Assembly to be addressed in Greek instead of in

English by the Lord High Commissioner. Undoubtedly this was conceived as a mere insult to the executive, for the Assembly was well aware that His Excellency could as easily have addressed them in Chinese or Hebrew.'

Suddenly, in October, an event of great significance for the Ionians as well as for the mainland Greeks occurred. A coup d'état in Athens deposed King Otho. He had never been trusted by the British government, which disliked his absolutist tendencies and feared that he would start another war in the Balkans by attacking the Ottoman Empire to distract attention from his misrule at home. If a more reasonable regime with a suitable sovereign were installed, perhaps a settlement of the Ionian question could safely be negotiated. Prince Alfred, the second son of Queen Victoria, had visited Corfu in December 1859, and had made an excellent impression. In Kirkwall's words: 'Long before the fall of Otho, the hope that the Prince might one day reign in Greece, bringing with him the Ionian Islands, had become the general sentiment of the Hellenic race'. Unfortunately the Russians, who were pushing the candidature of the Tsar's nephew, the Duke of Leuchtenburg, would never have accepted this. In December 1862 the Greeks held a plebiscite which elected Alfred almost unanimously, but by then his candidature had been withdrawn by the British government, and another scheduled trip to the islands was cancelled. Palmerston had, however, realized that the Ionian card was the trump in his hand; he had already offered it to Otho if the latter refrained from attacking Turkey, and had been rejected; now he prepared to use it again when the time was ripe.

Public opinion in England, in so far as it was interested in the Protectorate at all, was growing increasingly sceptical of its advantages, and aware of its disadvantages. Abraham Hayward wrote: 'They may or may not be really important, but they may go to the Devil for aught we care.' Their commercial potentialities had never been exploited, and neither as a market nor as a distributing centre had they been valuable to Britain. Both Gibraltar and Malta imported far more goods, and as the *Economist* commented, 'the loss of a dependency does not mean the loss of a customer'. Their strategic worth had similarly declined, provided they passed to an established minor power not to a rival Great Power, while their proximity to the trouble spots in the Ottoman Empire had diminished with the advent of an independent Greece. Malta was better placed for a crisis in the Near East or the Bosphorus, and the proposals to annex Cyprus or Acre seemed far more practical. Furthermore Malta's naval facilities en route to Egypt and India were far better than Corfu's, which possessed a good roadstead, but no large harbour, dockyard, or naval commissariat. Proof of all this was provided by the Admiralty's suggestion just before cession that a part of Corfu should be retained as a coaling station; but when the Colonial Office offered to open negotiations, their Lordships did not think it worthwhile to press the point.

In truth the military value of Corfu was crippled by its vulnerability. British strategy in the event of war had always been to abandon the other islands, and concentrate on holding it, just as Napoleon had done. But expert opinion remained dubious about the fortifications. In 1849 the Inspector General had reported they were hopelessly inadequate, and doubted they could hold out for three weeks against a determined attack. When the War Office undertook a thorough survey in 1859, it was even more discouraging: despite all the expenditure, the fortifications were less strong than the Franco-Venetian ones had been in 1815. As Storks noted: 'Despite an expenditure of £350,000, this is in fact an open town.' By 1863 the annual charge for the garrison was higher than for either Gibraltar or Malta, while the Ionians were £90,000 in arrears with their military contributions. Further improvements would cost at least £200,000 and would anyway necessitate a larger garrison. Thus the current annual outlay of £100,000 seemed a case of throwing good money after bad.

The nuisance value of the Protectorate had also become a serious factor. With a total constitutional deadlock, British governments, especially Liberal ones, were increasingly embarrassed by the charge of ignoring here the principles they were so busy advocating elsewhere. As Sidney Herbert wrote: 'It is Lombardy all over again', and most of his party had agreed with him. So when they returned to power in 1859, many Whigs were ready to contemplate cession. Grey was now advocating it, Russell concurred on conditions, as did most of the Cabinet. Some, however, still supported Palmerston's argument that the islands were strategically important and that Otho's regime was too unreliable to be entrusted with them, while others agreed with Gladstone that cession would stimulate Greek irredentism and inflame the Eastern Question. The October Revolution satisfied these objectors, provided a reliable monarchy could be installed at Athens to stabilize the local situation. Unfortunately the Self-Denying Ordinance of 1830 finally prevented the nomination of the English Prince Alfred. Another suitable candidate seemed lacking. Frightened of being outmanoeuvred by Russia and France, Palmerston now urged Russell to agree to cede the islands, 'if our man is chosen'. On 8 December the Cabinet, virtually unanimous, made the decision. The Greeks were informed that if they maintained a constitutional monarchy, refrained from any aggressive policies, and chose a suitable King, the British government would be prepared to relinquish its Ionian Protectorate. In March 1863 the right man was at last found in the Danish Prince William of

Glücksburg, whom the Greeks duly accepted as King George I of the Hellenes. If the Ionian Parliament consented, an issue that could hardly have been in doubt, along with the other four signatory powers to the Treaty of Paris — Russia, France, Austria and Prussia — the British conditions for cession had now been met. Moreover, it was agreed the islands would provide £10,000 per annum, a fifth of the new King's civil list.

The Opposition denounced the whole idea. Power was the safeguard of wealth, stated Disraeli, and a maritime nation must control the strong places of the world. But the Tories did not press the motion to a division, and other speakers, like Derby, emphasized the bad timing of the move, not the wrongheadedness of the policy. Public opinion was even more docile. Among the leading journals, only the *Quarterly Review* denounced a reduction of Empire from motives of parsimony. As *The Times* put it: 'For several months the cession had been announced . . . yet no alarm for the consequences has seized the English people. Although jealous of everything that may tend to weaken the naval power of England, the public has heard with perfect contentment that the islands are to be ceded.' The ghosts of Maitland and indeed of Napier might well have been turning in their graves!

The news was received in the islands with almost universal rejoicing. Many of the proprietors might secretly fear peasant risings once the garrisons had left, just as the peasants might fear a new tyranny of the signori once the restraining hand of British justice had been removed. Many public employees might worry about their jobs, some of the more prescient unionists might privately wonder if their parliamentary talents would receive due recognition on the wider stage of Athens. For the moment, however, such doubts would scarcely be voiced. In every island there were celebrations. A solemn Te Deum was celebrated in Corfu in June, and Storks's aides, like Wolff and the young Evelyn Baring, were pelted with flowers in the streets. British soldiers were given free drinks in the cafés, and the local bands played the National Anthem at an excruciating tempo. When elections were held in September all the candidates as well as all the members returned had stood on a unionist ticket; and anyone urging caution did so in extremely muted tones. Storks convened the thirteenth Assembly which immediately voted for 'a perfect union with Greece', and sent an address of gratitude to the Queen.

The euphoria and the new-found goodwill did not, of course, last. The treaty which Britain had signed with the four other guarantor Powers on 14 November 1863 was largely responsible for this revived hostility. The islands were declared to be perpetually neutral. Austria had, indeed, insisted on this as a condition of acceding to the treaty, and Russell found it a perfectly reasonable stipulation. He was quite unprepared for the storm of protests that broke from the Ionian and mainland Greeks, although it was eventually conceded that only Corfu, Paxos, and their dependencies must be neutralized. But in consequence of this, the fortifications, the Corfiotes' pride and joy, were to be demolished. The decision in January 1864 to make the demolition only partial scarcely alleviated public indignation. For Storks had never mentioned either of these possibilities when he laid the conditions of cession before the Assembly the preceding October. Even deducting the unpaid military contributions, the Ionians had paid nearly £1 million for their defences during the Protectorate, and at least half of this had been spent on the fortifications, without considering the substantial sums the English and the French before them had provided. Now everything except the Old Fortress and the landward side of the New Fortress was to be destroyed.

In February 1864 the work of demolition began, and lasted some weeks. Tactless English comments about going to watch 'the beautiful blow-up' did little to help. Crowds gathered on the Spianada to watch the spectacular explosions on Vido islet, and Kirkwall noted remarks like 'I wish that Lord Roosel were on the top of it,' although most Ionians seemed sad and resigned. The local press condemned 'this act of spite', and from his deathbed Dandolo issued a last bitter pamphlet: 'We Ionians thank you that you have left us our hands and tongues; with the one to write your infamy, with the other to heap threefold curses on your head'. The Anglo-Greek Convention signed in March exacerbated these grievances, for the continued payment of pensions to former British and Ionian officials in the administration was made a principal charge on the national revenue. Englishmen were equally disgusted by this petty meanness; only fifty-three people were affected for a sum barely in excess of £10,000. 'Millionaire Britain has foisted this injustice on bankrupt Greece.' Although complete responsibility for the demoliton could plausibly be disclaimed, in this matter the blame belonged entirely to the protecting Power. Remonstrances poured in, but the Treasury remained adamant.

Storks had prorogued the Assembly's sole short session in October 1863, after forbidding it to discuss the conditions of cession. It never met again. Only three members had voted against the resolution, requesting some modification of the terms. All three, including the poet Aristotelis Valaoritis, although confirmed unionists, desired to prove their confidence in English generosity. Their colleagues had been less trusting and their scepticism now seemed well justified. In the last months of the Protectorate, the ill-feeling between the two races was a sad postscript to British rule. In Kirkwall's eyes 'Our isolation had become complete, and for much of this result we had no-one to blame but ourselves, for our ignorance of, and indifference to, all matters not exclusively of domestic interest'. The local papers carried scurrilous articles abusing the English with such epithets as 'villains, robbers, thieves, and monsters', even for removing the guns and stores that in fact belonged to them. In April the Greek representatives arrived to arrange the details of cession, but the diplomatic formalities were as protracted as usual, and not until 21 May was the final document signed. On 2 June large crowds assembled to watch the evacuation of the last British troops. By midday all was completed, and with undisguised joy they witnessed the embarkation of the Lord High Commissioner. Four days later King George landed in Corfu and proceeded to the church of St Spyridon to celebrate a Te Deum.

As the Anglo-Ionian connection had never been really happy or intimate, it was perhaps fitting that it was terminated in the same vein. In so vague and anomalous a relationship, the arbitrary arrangements of the Protectorate could only have been counterbalanced by the practical benefits stemming from it. Many British officials had worked hard to improve the material condition of the islands, and it was certainly true that they were better off in 1864 than they had been in 1815, and richer than the other provinces of the Kingdom of Greece. Yet Britain could hardly be lauded for her generosity. Most of the revenue had gone to pay the costs of protection, and although the Ionians had provided the salaries for their officials, they had never been sufficiently encouraged to enter government service. Nor had their protectors offered careers to them in the mother country, as the Venetians had always done. Even a career in the British armed services was only opened to them after forty years of the Protectorate. The grudging response to requests for financial or trading concessions had only made the islanders more aware of their peculiar status. Time could perhaps have reconciled them to an arrangement to which there seemed no practical alternative. Freer political institutions, perhaps a restricted independence under British tutelage, might then have had some appeal. But as soon as Greece had been liberated from foreign domination, the protecting Power appeared not as the guardian but as the frustrator of national aspirations. Reform, which seemed to English liberal minds to offer a panacea to all grievances, served in reality to emphasize how weak the connection was. Once the unionists were permitted access to the benches of the Assembly and the columns of the press, although not initially in a majority, they were bound to prevail in the end, for they had a virulence and cohesion that was entirely lacking among their opponents. In a long and bitter struggle they had proved that Britain had no fundamental roots in Ionian sentiment, which was firmly orientated towards Greece, and

Greece alone.

Despite many faults, the English had behaved with magnanimity. As Kirkwall put it, 'Our country has certainly performed a great and generous act in ceding the islands to Greece, although it is to be regretted the boon has been but little calculated to arouse the gratitude of those for whose benefit the sacrifice was supposed to have been voluntarily made.' Yet in the mid-nineteenth century the voluntary cession of territory anywhere by a great power was an unusual occurrence. To have done so in accordance with the wishes of a small population was equally remarkable. The islands had certainly posed problems, but so have other colonial situations before and since, and even in 1864 the British position was not untenable. Admittedly the government was glad in many ways to be rid of an expensive and troublesome responsibility—'one useless dependency is taken from our burden of Empire'. And cession was shrewd politics, for the Ionians have come to remember the Protectorate almost with nostalgia, while Britain thereby consolidated its influence and interests in an area where they had seemed in question. In retrospect, many thinking men were glad that expediency had forced them in this instance to bring their practice into line with their principles. As Russell said, 'there is something in the Ionian wish for union with Greece, which must obtain the respect of the British nation', and the relationship between both peoples has been cordial ever since. Yet it is an interesting reflection how different the subsequent history of the islands might have been if they had remained part of an Empire that was moving from an eighteenth-century dilettantist approach to the stern improving spirit of the Victorian age.

D. THE CULTURAL RENAISSANCE

We know thee of old,
Oh divinely restored,
By the light of thine eyes,
And the light of thy sword!

From the grave of our slain
Shall thy valour prevail,
As we greet thee again—
Hail, Liberty! Hail!

The Hymn to Liberty by Dionysios Solomos, one of the greatest of Ionian and indeed of modern Greek poets, was to become the country's national anthem after 1864. Fittingly, it was to be set to music by Nicholas Mantzaros, a Corfiote who had trained at the Philharmonic Society in his native town. For the islands had become the cradle of the culture and learning of the new Greece. The Ionians were fortunate that they could develop their artistic and literary talents in the stability and security provided by the British Protectorate, conditions which were certainly lacking for their compatriots on the mainland.

The French had sown the seeds of this intellectual revival, and although their Academy had been closed when Campbell occupied Corfu in 1814, the enthusiasm it had generated was less easily quelled. The next year Pavlos Prosalendis, an able pupil of the sculptor Canova, refounded the School of Fine Arts, which he had first set up in 1805 to teach sculpture, painting, and bronze-working. His statues of Capodistrias, Adam, and Guilford still stand on the Spianada. Two musical societies, whose fame was to spread throughout Greece, were founded simultaneously. And the Ionian Academy which opened its doors in 1824, gave the necessary impetus, both official and financial, to the renaissance of learning. The fine library which Guilford collected contained manuscripts, scientific equipment, and sulphur casts of antique medallions, as well as many books, and could be consulted by any interested member of the public. With professors like the priest Idromenos (his real name was Athanasius Politis), who became Metropolitan of Corfu in 1848, and the poet and philologist Andreas Kalvos, lectures were well attended and of a high standard. Moreover, a fifth faculty, of chemistry, was added after 1841, plus various subsidiary courses, so that the Academy catered for almost every branch of scholarship. Gradually the practice of sending the sons of the aristocracy to be educated in Italian universities declined. Despite the government's scepticism and much reduced patronage after Guilford's death, the Academy continued to flourish. Sir George Bowen, who became Rector in 1847, soon after leaving Oxford, introduced reforms in the curriculum, and being both persuasive and bilingual attracted much local support for his schemes, before being appointed to the thankless post of Secretary to the Lord High Commissioner. Only in the latter days of the Protectorate did the Academy begin to decay. By 1863 one observer noted that each faculty rarely had more than twenty students. And sadly, after the islands had been ceded to Greece, it was closed for ever.

In 1836 the Philological Society of Corfu was founded under the auspices of Doctor Gonaimis to debate current literary and linguistic questions. Transformed into the Reading Club it still survives today. The Society of the Friends of Learning came into being in 1845 to encourage discussion of artistic and scientific topics, while the Ionian Association was founded in 1851, particularly to foster agricultural and industrial developments. With a relatively small and scattered population this all attests to a remarkable and genuine desire for education. It stands in marked contrast to mainland Greece, whose first university was not founded in Athens until 1837. So it is hardly surprising that the islands provided the setting in which the issue between the *Katharevousa* or 'purist' and 'demotic' idioms of the language emerged.

The anomaly of having two languages dated from the conquests of Alexander the Great, which had introduced a vast number of aliens to Hellenistic culture. A reversion to the 'pure classical' idiom of Plato and Demosthenes had ensued, and in the Byzantine era had successfully monopolized the written although not the spoken word, as used by Church and State. But by the nineteenth century it seemed increasingly difficult to express modern thought and terminology through an archaic language. The demotic on the other hand, after such a long exclusion from educated usage, lacked an adequate vocabulary or abstract expression. An effort obviously had to be made to weld judiciously the spoken language with classical vocabulary subject to modern grammatical forms. Unfortunately, in Othonian Greece the purist ideal remained paramount, and demotic all too often became synonymous with demagogue. The coexistence of both idioms inevitably led to conflict, especially after they had acquired the political connotations of liberal and conservative; yet the fact that a reasonably acceptable compromise was eventually formulated was due in large measure to Ionian literary genius, and in particular to one outstanding man—Dionysios Solomos.

Born in 1798 of an old Venetian family, whose name Salomon occurs throughout the Levant, Solomos' ancestors had emigrated to Candia, thence, after the fall of Crete, to Zante. His father, Count Nicholas, was a typical Ionian noble, who was nicknamed 'Old Tobacco' from his monopoly on importing that commodity into the island. Although already married and with children, he started living with Angela Nikli, a servant girl who bore him two sons, Dionysios and Demetrius, three years later. Dionysios was educated at Cremona in the care of a clever priest, Santo Rossi, and then went on to the University of Padua, where he acquired a thorough grounding in the classics and a love of Virgil and Dante. Thanks to fellow Ionians like Andreas Moustoxidis he joined a literary circle whose luminaries included Manti and Manzoni. While aged only seventeen he had begun to write poetry under their inspiration. When he returned to Zante in 1818 he embarked upon life there with gusto, frequenting salons such as Count Mercati's where everyone had to complete the lines of a poem in *rime obbligate,* given by their host. He was also influenced by advocates of the demotic like John Vilaras, formerly Ali Pasha's physician, who came from Kythera. Finally he acquired the habit of heavy drinking which was to prove so disastrous later on, but which he now treated with levity, throwing bottles off the end of the jetty while delivering a farewell oration solemnly abjuring the evils of alcohol.

In 1822 Spyridon Trikoupis, writer and historian, passed through Zante on his way to take up a professorial chair at the Ionian Academy, and he succeeded in firing the young man's patriotic zeal. Solomos, although he remained cautious and did not even join the Philike Etairia, decided to do something for the cause of Greece. At this point he could only write in Italian, but when Trikoupis challenged him to produce a poem in Greek he began to consider the matter. Inspiration was provided by the Cretan demotic poetry of the sixteenth and seventeenth centuries and the immense corpus of folk songs which had arisen spontaneously from popular culture. In his native island the *kantades,* sung to the guitar or mandolin, were a unique and popular genre of poetry. His first composition in the new language was mediocre, but with his second he was acclaimed as a national poet, whose fame spread throughout Europe. *The Hymn to Liberty* was a second Marseillaise. In Italy Manzoni applauded his pupil, in Germany Goethe hailed him as 'the Byron of the East'. Its influence as the heart-cry of suffering Greece was incalculable; Canning is said to have read it just before signing the Treaty of London. Any translation is bound to be inadequate, yet Rudyard Kipling's does transmit the message Solomos gave in 158 stirring stanzas to the sovereigns of Europe:

Instruments of God most high
See ye not her agonies?
Never silent is her cry
Down the endless centuries.

How then can ye leave alone
Those who strive for liberty,
Or destroy it when 'tis won
From the needs of policy?

Ah not so! for turn your eyes
Where our Grecian heroes fell.
Rise, ye Christian monarchs, rise
Arm and strike the infidel!

For all its faults of over-hasty composition, plagiarism from other poets, and an undeniably theatrical quality, no other poem so exactly accorded with the spirit of the times, as the Turkish guns battered down the walls of Missolonghi.

Solomos now began to study hard. *The Death of the Shepherd* and *The Mad Mother* are typically romantic narrative poems, beautifully written and extremely expressive. His passionate nationalism set him at odds with his conservative brother, Demetrius, and Solomos was often profoundly unhappy. He produced some savagely satirical work like *The Dream,* which recounts the sins of a notoriously corrupt and brutal local worthy who had just died. *The Woman of Zante* is a satire on the British Protectorate, the woman being the British government, the Ionian Islands being the daughter whom she keeps in close confinement, while Greece is represented as her beautiful and destitute sister, whom she envies but will not help. Luckily the authorities missed the point, so censorship was averted.

Disillusioned with Zante, Solomos moved to Corfu in 1828. Ionian society received him ecstatically, Sir Frederick Adam and his wife delighted in entertaining him, and during the next few years the poet ceased to be an enragé and gradually found a measure of peace within himself. Epigrams, sonnets, and longer pieces poured from his pen. *Lambros*, an epic work, was his finest to date, and in his lyric poetry, such as *The Cretan*, he showed a deep interest in human nature and emotions. When Nugent asked him to contribute to the *Ionian Anthology*, the newly founded periodical, Solomos readily agreed. However, a protracted lawsuit, in which an illegitimate half-brother tried to prove he was the rightful heir of the old Count, and his adored mother conspired to seize his inheritance, again depressed and embittered him. He began to wonder if she really had married his father on his deathbed, as she claimed. His bouts of heavy drinking grew more frequent, and when creativity returned in the 1840s, he had changed. Solomos had reached intellectual maturity, but his growing mania for perfection resulted in short and endlessly rewritten works. Increasingly out of sympathy both with contemporary politics and the mother country he had never visited, he now stigmatized union with Greece as 'difficult and premature'. He identified with his brother Demetrius, who had become President of the Senate, and was also a close friend of Ward's. Indeed he even reverted to composing in Italian, inspired by his love for Adelaide Grasetti, wife of the Professor of Latin Literature at the Ionian Academy. Yet his greatest poems, *The Free Besieged* and *The Porphyras*, were composed then too; although unfinished, they contain passages of genius. In 1850 Solomos suffered his first cerebral stroke. Thereafter he became ever more irritable and eccentric, and after his death in

February 1857, his literary affairs were found to be in chaos. In many ways Solomos was a sad and lonely figure, but few would dispute his title of the father of modern Greek poetry.

The mausoleum in Zante which houses his remains has since 1960 also contained those of another outstanding poet, Andreas Kalvos. He was born in 1792, and his father was a Corfiote from Mandouki, a soldier in the Venetian service who married a Zantiote girl while stationed on that island. Kalvos' father moved to Leghorn, where his uncle was consul for the Septinsular Republic, and like Solomos, he was educated in Florence. In the course of his studies he met another compatriot and poet, Ugo Foscolo, fourteen years his senior, who had already won fame with epic works like *Jacob Ortis* and *Didimi*. Although half Greek, and a fervent nationalist, Foscolo's writing and his outlook were Italian, and he had not lived in the Ionian Islands for many years. He liked Kalvos, whom he engaged as tutor for his Zantiote nephew, Stephen Voultsos. The tutor soon became the pupil, and learned the technique of writing tragedy. This he applied in works like *Danaïde* and *Theramenis,* as well as a spate of short poems to earn a little money. In 1816 both men moved to Zurich, thence to London. Kalvos acted as secretary and companion to Foscolo, whom he admired enormously. But the latter's success in London society turned his head, and the next year they quarrelled bitterly and parted. Foscolo was to remain in England until his death in 1827, but they never associated again.

Kalvos' output was prodigious. As he had to support himself he gave private tuition in Greek, Italian, and French and published grammars in his native tongue. With his interest in linguistics he embarked on a Greek-English lexicon and a translation of the Book of Common Prayer, while he gave lectures on all aspects of Greek life and literature. He even started a new edition of the Bible. Saddened by the death of his first wife in childbirth, and a subsequent unhappy love affair, Kalvos left London in 1820 and eventually settled in Geneva, where his pen aided the supporters of the Greek struggle for independence. In a volume entitled *The Patriotic Lyre*, he published ten poems, all Pindaric odes, telling of four centuries of war against the Turk. And when Lord Guilford, his friend and patron, invited him to take up the Chair of Philosophy at the Ionian Academy, he accepted with pleasure. Unfortunately, after Guilford's death, Adam refused to confirm the appointment, so he had to become an assistant teacher at the Lyceum, the secondary school, instead. Acknowledged as one of the best teachers of general philology in Corfu, he was reappointed to the Academy in 1836, although the machinations of the physics professor again deprived him of his post. For a time he edited the official *Gazette*, he became Director of the Lyceum, and with his friend Petros Vrailas-Armenis he founded the Cultural Society of Corfu in 1848. And during the twenty-six years he spent on the island he continued to write an unabated stream of poetry. Kalvos remained a fiery patriot as well. With the Zambelli brothers he produced a new journal, *Patris*, which advocated freedom for the Ionian Islands and union with Greece. In 1852 he married, as his second wife, an English woman, and the couple returned to London, where they set up a school for young ladies. This continued until 1865, when Kalvos retired to Louth in Lincolnshire, where he died in 1869. But although far removed from his native land for much of his life, his influence was considerable both in the Ionian renaissance of learning and in the development of Greek into a great language once more. If there is truth in the maxim that 'idea identifies with language, and form is the servant of the idea', as they believed, Kalvos like Solomos is entitled to a generous share of his country's gratitude.

Amid a host of lesser luminaries, one other very different figure in the intellectual movement should be considered. Andreas Lascaratos, 'the Greek Voltaire', was born in Lixouri, and educated at the college in the castle of St George, which Guilford had founded to supplement his Academy. He was a small landowner, deriving his income from the sale of his currants, but Lascaratos was first and foremost a scholar. Born into the aristocracy, for Count Delladecima was his uncle, he instinctively adopted the Count's attitude of rationalist scepticism towards the world. In 1856 he published *The Mysteries of Cephalonia*, in which he depicted all classes of society in his native island in the darkest colours, although, apart from a vitriolic attack on the Archbishop, he refrained from describing personalities. His compatriots, particularly the radicals, were enraged, and on the Resident's advice he fled to Zante, thence to England, which he had already visited. The Archbishop, of course, excommunicated him. Nevertheless Lascaratos returned twelve months later, and lived in Zante, persecuted by the rabble, and denounced as an atheist by the priests, whose gross ignorance and pretended miracles he had denounced as fiercely as the abject superstitition of the masses and the apathy and debauchery of the nobility.

Lascaratos was particularly disliked by demagogues like Lombardos, and when he denounced the latter as an arrant rogue and a political impostor, he was sued for libel. In 1859 he was sentenced to four months' jail, which he served in the jail at Argostoli. Here he was brutally treated by the governor, who hated him for his iconoclasm and for the anglophile sentiments he expressed. When a petition reached the Lord High Commissioner he was released, although the Rhizopasto governor went unpunished. His *Sufferings in Prison* is a powerful book, and his gratitude to Storks turned him into a supporter of the Protectorate. Interestingly, Lascaratos' views on nationalism were anyway those of a universalist: 'He who sacrifices the rest of humanity to his nation is as egotistical and mean as he who sacrifices his nation to his individuality.' Until his death in 1901, Lascaratos continued to live on Cephalonia, continuing his researches and publishing several learned works, while accorded a belated but growing measure of respect by his fellow-countrymen.

Of all the arts, literature and poetry flourished most under the Protectorate. The musical tradition in the islands reached its apogee at a later date, while the visual arts were only to revive at the end of the century. Nicholas Kandounis did not die until 1834, and George Baffas, the silversmith, until twenty years after that, but the artistic ideals they represented belonged to the eighteenth century not the nineteenth. However, the same cannot be said of architecture. This had already received a fillip from the French, for in 1809, Matthieu Lesseps had supervised the construction of the Liston, the arcades along the side of the Spianada, so-called from the 'list' of families entitled to walk underneath them, although the story is probably apocryphal. The Liston was built in frank imitation of the Rue de Rivoli in Paris, in a style considered suitably imperial. Donzelot had had many other ideas, but the exigencies of war had prevented their implementation.

The British showed equal enthusiasm. Maitland wanted an official residence and a meeting-place for the Ionian Senate, so he commissioned an engineer officer, Colonel George Whitmore, to design a building along the north end of the Spianada. Whitmore was an able if thoroughly neo-classical architect, and the legend that Nash drew a preliminary sketch for him on the back of an envelope lacks any authority, although the palace is undoubtedly reminiscent of Carlton House Terrace. Built of Malta sandstone, it has retained the original pale gold colour on its sheltered western façade. A Doric colonnade fronts its southern side, and the palace projects to form a curving screen, pierced by triumphal arches and terminated by balancing pavilions. Crowning the façade is an ornamental parapet, on which the emblems of the seven islands are sculpted in stone. Demeter the goddess of fertility sitting holding a cornucopia for Corfu, Bellerophon holding Pegasus for Levkas, Cephalus the hunter lance in hand, with his dog for Cephalonia, Zakynthos, a mythical figure seated for Zante, a head of Ulysses for Ithaca, a trident for Paxos, Aphrodite and a dolphin for Kythera. Britannia in her barque formed the focal point on the skyline, but after the union with Greece that lady withdrew; now only the barque remains. The Palace of St Michael and St George was also intended to be the Treasury of the Order which the Lord High Commissioner had founded. The insignia of the Order - an imperial crown over two winged lions, each of which holds a book and seven arrows in his forepaw, may still be seen on the ceiling of the state dining room, symbolizing Britain, Venice and the islands. Considering the lack of funds which bedevilled the project, and the necessity of using a comparatively unskilled work force, the completion of the palace in five years (1818-23) was no mean achievement.

Adam continued Maitland's work. Indeed he commissioned Whitmore to build the Ionic rotunda at the south end of the Spianada in his predecessor's memory. Moreover, feeling that he needed an official country residence as well, he had Whitmore design the *casino* for him, the villa now known as Mon Repos, just south of the town on the Kanoni peninsula. Napier's sarcastic comment that it hardly seemed necessary to have two splendid palaces 'within gunshot of each other' was well justified, but Adam was notoriously extravagant; 'while Corfu kept the Lord High Commissioner, Cephalonia paid his tailor, and Zante his coachmaker'. In fairness, he also constructed many excellent if expensive roads like that to Palaeokastritsa, and the aqueduct stretching eight miles from the hills behind Benitses, which for the first time ensured an abundant supply of fresh water for the town, 'a fact which in a southern climate speaks volumes for the want of energy or cleanliness in the people', as Jervis-White-Jervis disapprovingly noted, although the British always found it hard to tolerate 'the frequent use of garlic and the infrequent use of soap'.

Even after Adam's departure, the building programme was not abandoned. His successor, Nugent, did offer Mon Repos to the municipality for a museum, which they accepted, although nothing was done about it for the remainder of the Protectorate. Douglas was also interested in architectural improvements, as the obelisk erected to him on the Spianada testifies. In the 1840s the British built the Doric garrison church of St George inside the Old Fortress, 'the model of a heathen temple', as it was described, while at great cost they added the baronial keep, which still surmounts the New Fortress. They also swept away the Venetian wall and bastion above Garitsa Bay and laid out the avenue along the sea which extended on to Kanoni, for the walk to 'the one-gun', as the battery was known, became a fashionable promenade for the beau-monde.

In the other islands, similarly, official buildings were constructed. On Paxos the former British Residency at Gaio is a delightful example of Regency taste adapted to its environment. At Levkas the twin Residency and Court House, in a pleasant style, date from 1825. Napier's achievements on Cephalonia have already been mentioned, although, as almost everything in Argostoli and Lixouri was destroyed in the disastrous earthquake of 1953, few traces remain. In Zante it was less easy to change the appearance of a town remarkable since the eighteenth century for the splendour of its architecture. Here improvements were of a more practical nature, like the new harbour mole, or the aqueduct built by an energetic Resident, Lord Charles Fitzroy, which served as the model for the one on Corfu. Nevertheless, Adam did build a fine country house at Akrotiri, much to the fury of Napier, who considered a third palace for the Lord High Commissioner altogether too much. Later the Solomos family bought the property, which is still standing although, alas, shorn of its top storey. Even remote Kythera was not neglected. MacPhail built a market-place in Khora, and, in a neo-Gothic style, schools at Fatsadika and Kato Khora, as well as the magnificent bridge at Katouni.

However, architecture did not depend solely on English initiative. Under the Protectorate the standard of private buildings, particularly on Corfu, was higher than during the Venetian era, both in design and execution, as shown by examples like the Flamburiari family's residence, now the Cavalieri Hotel. John Khronis, a local architect, was entrusted with many important projects, of which the Ionian Bank, the former Ionian Parliament and the old Prefecture are the most notable. Nor was only secular architecture influenced by the new trends. In Levkas the Church of Isodia tis Theotokou (the Presentation of the Virgin) is a charming exercise in the neo-classical adapted to the needs of the Orthodox faith. With the growth of prosperity, and indeed of population, there was a permanent requirement for new buildings, both for individual and public use.

In many ways, of course, life in the islands had changed little, if at all, from the pattern of previous centuries, to which the evidence of many travellers bears witness. Lord Kirkwall, who spent four years in them at the end of the Protectorate, was an acute and intelligent observer, even if his attitudes reflect most of the prejudices of mid-Victorian England. He complained of the difficulties of getting any sleep, with people sitting in the cafés, singing, or perambulating under his window until the early hours of the morning. 'Under these torments the hapless Briton, tossing on his bed, with the thermometer perhaps at ninety degrees, writhes with mingled anguish and despair. He has work to do by day, so if he sleeps at all he must do so by night. His tormentors however sleep for half the day, and walk or sing during the greater part of the night.' Above all, he loathed the bells, especially after being stationed in

Argostoli: 'I can give no idea of the demoniacal sounds which proceed from a Cephalonian bell. To compare them with the harmony that can be extracted from poker and tongs is a gross calumny upon those useful articles of domestic architecture.' On Zante orders had been given that they were not to be rung for more than five minutes, but here, 'twenty was reckoned a trifle, and two hours a frequent dose.'

Religious customs remained entirely unchanged. In all the islands the festivals of the patron saints continued to be celebrated with unabated fervour. On Corfu the British copied the Venetians in participating in the St Spyridon processions. Four colonels carried the coffin on their shoulders, and the cortège stopped in front of the palace while a band played 'God save the King' and the batteries fired off a royal salute. As relations between the two races deteriorated, the British pretended to ignore the festivals, while the Saint only paused for a second in front of the palace to receive a perfunctory nod from the Lord High Commissioner. But to outsiders the enthusiasm St Spyridon generated was usually incomprehensible. Private Wheeler, who served in the islands from 1823 to 1828, and many of whose letters are concerned with life on them, viewed the proceedings with a jaundiced eye. 'After the whole of the town had been perambulated, and half the sick had received their death stroke from the powerful rays of the sun, the Saint is once more stood up by the altar, when the old trade of kissing his boots, and dropping money in the dish again begins, and is continued until late the next day, when the holy person is again entombed.'

The Orthodox Church did not escape criticism either. With more than 2,000 churches in the islands, public, private, and conventual, and with 900 priests salaried by the government, the intellectual and often the moral state of the clergy left much to be desired, while many churches and monasteries practised such shameless abuses that state intervention was fully justified. As Kirkwall wrote: 'In spite of their degenerate condition, the Greek clergy have deserved respect and gratitude for their past services in the national cause. But they must not be permitted by their ignorance and supersitition to clog the progress of the resurgent nation on the path of Christian civilisation and national development.' Yet even he admitted that one British Resident, who after catching a priest with arms in his possession, had had him shaved and flogged, had gone too far. Wheeler echoed these sentiments: 'It is an astonishing fact that not one papa on this island can preach a sermon. Their churches are always open, the people go in, cross themselves, go round and kiss several pictures, then cross themselves again and go out. On Sundays there is service twice when the papa goes through a deal of ceremony at the altar, while repeating the prayers and litany which he has learned by heart like a parrot.'

Obviously much of the scepticism sprang from a failure of imagination. The belief in miracles was basic to a profoundly superstitious people, yet to Kirkwall 'the bishops should discourage this cult, which cannot impress any educated person. Although the miracle is a recognised imposture among sensible people, the gentry are generally of the opinion that it is advisable for the peasants to continue to credit such fables.' Similarly Wheeler scoffed at the burial customs, 'with the body all dressed in its finery, ornamented with gold chains and jewellery, with a new pair of shoes as if going off to a ball'. But this was merely obeying time-honoured tradition. Perhaps his description of the Archbishop of Zante's funeral would not appeal to modern taste: 'After the parade they returned to the church, where he was lowered into his vault, a book placed in his hand, a candle lit and placed before him. I got a glimpse at the old fellow before he was walled up. There he sat in the same posture as I saw him in the church. I could not get his smell out of my nose for several days after.' Again unfamiliarity with local custom had bred contempt.

Many English commentators similarly remarked on Ionian attitudes towards marriage. It was indeed true that the necessity of providing a dowry made the birth of a daughter almost a misfortune. When she reached the right age a young man would come and enquire about her prospects. He would then go from father to father getting them to outbid each other. If the Greek ideal of a wife was a well dowered good housekeeper, it was hardly in accordance with the spirit of the Romantic Age. Wheeler's comment is as apt and acid as usual: 'the poor girl is betrothed to an ugly squint-eyed gentleman, upwards of thirty years older than herself. The law of marriage is very hard, particularly so far as the female is concerned. A Greek gentleman seldom if ever thinks of wedding until he has passed the prime of life. The girl says the man she is to be married to, (like all other Greek bachelors), keeps a woman. This woman will continue to live with him until his wedding. He will then, according to the laws, have to allow her a separate maintenance . . . All the children he has had by this woman are taken to the asylum, a place supported by the public.'

It is interesting too how little the treatment of the Jews by their fellow-citizens had changed either. In Corfu the community flourished, although the old Judas legend persisted, as did the ritual stoning at 11 a.m. on the morning before Easter Sunday, when a barrage of crockery was hurled into the street. Wheeler detected a closer affinity between the Jews and Greeks than the latter would have cared to admit: 'There is a great deal of Jewish ceremony in the Greek church. For instance they kill the paschal lamb at their doors, and sprinkle the posts and lintel with its blood. After the doors are daubed they throw out into the streets all the old cracked pitchers and pans that have been kept through the year for the purpose. At the same time they utter horrid curses on the Jews, who are obliged to keep out of the way until Easter is over, or they would be murdered. The part of the town the Jews occupy is barricaded, and they go in and out at two gates.' In 1860 the records show that there were 5,000–6,000 of them in Corfu, but only 274 in Zante, 34 in Cephalonia, and virtually none in the other islands. The Protectorate was definitely a happy interlude in long centuries of degradation and persecution, for it was the British who abolished the ghettos, and demolished the gates to them, while protecting the communities. In this context it is worth noting that the racial purity of much of the Greek population was not above reproach either; it was generally believed by 1860 that only one-third of the inhabitants of Corfu town were of pure Hellenic stock.

The Ionians certainly enjoyed a cosmopolitan life under the Protectorate. A constant stream of visitors passed through the islands, which most found very picturesque, with the Paxiotes catching swallows off the cliffs with a rod and fly or the Zantiotes living in branch houses above their vineyards. Turnock's Royal Hotel became extremely fashionable, while an 'English house' came to mean one with a bath. The Saxon Philhellene Christian Müller wrote of Argostoli in 1821: 'In the private houses of wealthy merchants and the nobility, everything is in European style. The luxuries of the West have entirely supplanted the customs of the Levant . . . Here we met with looking-glasses, lustres, elegantly bound libraries of books with French and Italian classics.' He found a complete mixture of nationalities in the port at Zante, and considered Corfu totally Italianate: 'Italian manners prevail inside the houses, in the public amusements, and in the language; in fact they have been adopted by all, except the lower orders of the people . . . If you go into the interior of the families, you find as little relish for society and domestic pleasures as in Italy. All their affections are turned abroad towards public assemblies, the theatre, promenades, and coffee houses.'

In the 1830s that ubiquitous traveller Prince Pückler-Muskau visited Cephalonia, Ithaca, and Zante in the course of a Balkan tour. His first experience was distinctly inauspicious: 'I left my pistol to be repaired by the gunsmith, where his small son tampered with it and managed to shoot dead an old man of seventy-two in a window across the street.' But claiming with Voltaire to like people of every kind except the boring ones, he enjoyed himself. He found the company at the Lunzis mansion at Sarakina most entertaining, while 'the house shone like glass in the sun amidst its wide terraces and gardens.' The Romas family's picture collection equally impressed him. In the countryside he observed the grapes being laid in the sun to dry for ten days or so 'like a delicious carpet.' However he was horrified to see one heavy storm ruining most of the currant crop, for only the richest growers had wooden shelters. The farmer he met appealed to him greatly: 'I have seldom seen a more practical way of life, or a happier more carefree person, than this man who virtually never leaves his rural solitude.'

All foreigners were, of course, fascinated by the trade in currants. When Kirkwall arrived in Zante he found the recently harvested crop lying about the plain in heaps, and was delighted to be given a barrel: 'what greater attention could be paid to a John Bull than thus to supply his family with the means of making an unlimited number of plum-puddings?' The list of products he gave for each island is corroborated by other writers—Corfu and Paxos specializing in oil, Zante, Cephalonia, and Ithaca in currants, while Levkas exported a little oil, less currants, salt and flax, and Kythera mainly wine made from imported Candian grapes; all of which shows how little the Ionian economy had changed through the ages. The minor products still persisted, like valonia made from acorn cups and used in the currant casks, or the lace-like material derived from aloe fibres and worked by a few villagers in Cephalonia. Yet improving Victorians such as Professor Ansted, who predicted a boom in the export of Ionian wine if the industry were properly organized, or suggested utilizing the land half-reclaimed from the sea to grow cotton, merely displayed their ignorance of the local customs and character.

One temporary visitor who acquired a definite understanding of his environment was Edward Lear. Persuaded by his friend Sir George Bowen, Lear first came to Corfu in April 1848 and was immediately entranced, as a letter to his sister Anne shows: 'I wish I could give you any idea of this island; it is really a Paradise. The extreme gardeny verdure, the fine olives, cypresses, almonds, and oranges make the landscape so rich, and the Albanian mountains are wonderfully fine. All the villages appear clean and white, with here and there a palm-tree overtopping them. The women wear duck, black and blue with a red handkerchief about the head; the men—the lower orders that is—mostly red capes and full Turkish trousers. Here and there you see an Albanian, all red and white, with a full white petticoat like a doll's, and a sheepskin over his shoulder. Then you meet some of the priests, with beards and flowing black robes. Mixed with them are the English soldiers and naval officers, and the upper class of Corfiotes who dress as we do; so the result is most attractive.' This time he only stayed three weeks, but in 1855 with failing health and his art much developed, he returned. Franklin Lushington, for whom he had formed a deep, if unrequited, homosexual attachment, had accepted a post as judge in the Ionian Supreme Court, and Lear decided to go out and spend the winter with him. The feeling of being a big fish 'in this very little fish-pond of a place' reassured him, although the incessant social round of a garrison town could become very irritating. With his inherent melancholia it began to depress him: 'What a good place this might be, if there were the people to give it a twist. As it is a more disorganized fiddle-faddle, Poodly Pumpkin place never was. At the Palace they are active rushing about pauselessly and continuously. I suspect Lady Young would not be happy in heaven if she could not get up an immense ball, or land and water picnics among the angels. It is sadly frivolous work – this life for "amusement" and that alone.'

He was, however, so well received that he was soon offered a job as the first director of a new art department at the Ionian Academy. An annual salary of £100, a free house and four months' holiday went with it, with some responsibilities for administration, for giving drawing lessons and lectures in Italian. But Lear valued his independence too much and declined. Instead he set to work on some large canvases, especially the views from above Palaeopolis, and he explored the coast with Lushington by boat. He also engaged a Suliote servant, Giorgio Kokali, who was to be his faithful companion for many years thereafter. Until 1858 he returned intermittently, although sometimes the place infuriated him: 'It is but right you should know the important life concerns of the Island, and therefore I shall not hesitate to insert the following facts – Madame Vitalis, the Greek consul's wife has purchased a large red macaw, Mrs MacFarlane's female domestic has fallen downstairs by which precipitate act Mrs M's baby has been killed. Sir Gorgeous Figginson Blowing has had an attack of fever, Captain R. has purchased a cornopeon and practises on it, (Mrs G. invariably calls it a cornucopean). Anyway it is seldom heard, on account of the superior row made by Mme Vitalis' macaw, Captain P's howling dogs and about 400 turkeys, who live at ease on the terrace, and adopt a remarkable gobble at certain periods.' That year Lushington resigned his post, and Lear accompanied him back to England.

By 1861 Lear's paintings were not selling, and his adored sister had died. His thoughts reverted to Corfu as a sort of home, and he determined to try another winter there. He spent several quiet months sketching and revising his *Book of Nonsense*, while making new friends, like the young Evelyn Baring. The bustle of garrison life now amused him: 'Just a minute ago I looked out of the window at the moment the 2nd were marching by – I having a full palate of brushes in my hand; whereat Colonel Bruce saw me and saluted. Not liking to make a formillier nod in the presence of the hole harmy I put up my hand to salute, and thereby transferred all my colours into my hair and whiskers, which I must wash in turpentine or shave off.' Gradually the island had come to represent security and an agreeable climate: 'the more I see of this place, so the more I feel that no other spot on earth can be fuller of beauty and variety of beauty.' That spring he was sketching at Palaeokastritsa, whose charm captivated him: 'On my left is the convent, and happily as the monkery has functions at 2 a.m. they are all asleep now, and to my left is one of many peacock-tail-hued bays here, reflecting the vast red cliffs and their crowning roofs of *lentisk prinari*, myrtle and sage—far above them, higher and higher, the immense rock of Angelokastro rising into the air, on whose summit the old castle is seen as a ruin, just 1400 feet above the water. It half seems to me that such life as this must be wholly another from the drumbeating bothery frivolity of the town of Corfu, and I seem to grow a year younger every hour. Not that it will last. Accursed picnic parties with miserable scores of asses, male and female, are coming tomorrow, and peace flies—as I shall too.'

In March 1863 Lear travelled round all the islands, to record a last glimpse of them under British rule, for he felt convinced that in no other part of Europe could an Englishman find such a combination of three different characteristics: the beauty of the scenery, the associations of poetical and historical antiquity, and the hospitable welcome of his compatriots. His *Views in the Seven Ionian Islands* was published that autumn. It contained twenty plates—eight of Corfu, three each of Zante, Cephalonia, and Levkas, and one each of Kythera, Paxos, and Ithaca, plus a short descriptive text. When the Protectorate ended, he hoped that King George of the Hellenes would give him a place at Court as '*Archanoediphluariapoios*' (Lord High Bosh and Nonsense Maker), but although he travelled to Athens with Evelyn Baring, the new monarch did not seem disposed to agree to Lear's terms: a fool's cap, three pounds of butter yearly, a small pig, and a donkey for transport. He visited Corfu twice more before his death in 1885, but the Anglo-Italian atmosphere of the place which he had treasured was vanishing for ever.

It is a sad reflection that the Ionian cultural renaissance took place despite as well as because of the British. Müller, who was a hostile critic, found their manners did not compare with those of the Venetians, French, and Russians, and assumed this stemmed from some superiority complex. Certainly the two races never mixed very happily, with some outstanding exceptions. Guilford was an entirely wholehearted philhellene, so was Napier, who kept a Cephalonian mistress, christened one of his daughters Emily Cephalonia, and left them each a property in Argostoli. Adam was also at home with the Greeks, as Wheeler acidly describes: 'Sir Frederick is appointed Lord High

Commissioner, nothing could have pleased the Greeks better. He is a great favourite, his lady is a Corfiote, her husband and brother are living here. The story is that he was caught in such a situation with the lady that left no doubt on the mind of her Greek lord that Sir F. had just been measuring him for an outsize pair or horns, which everyone knows is a disagreeable appendage to one's brows, particularly in a warm climate.' To be fair, Adam, with his wife, the Palatianos lady 'the beard on whose upper lip would ornament an Hussar', was at pains to become the focal point of Ionian cultural and social life, and was personally more popular than any of his successors. For all too many of them and their subordinates kept to their own compatriots' company, and ignored the attitudes and tastes of the populations they had come to govern.

The gulf was almost unbridgeable by the 1850s. Kirkwall regretted that in Storks' time 'it was a matter of general remark that the English were asked to dinner at the Palace only to meet each other, the Ionians made a similar observation as regarded themselves.' But he likewise lamented the reserve of the Greeks, who seldom gave dinner parties or other evening entertainments, and, however friendly they were, equally seldom introduced Englishmen to their wives and daughters, 'for the Ionians are naturally an agreeable, generous, quick, and hospitable people.' He also considered them instinctively charitable and loyal, even over-loyal on occasions, to all degrees of their relations. These good qualities could still have promoted a better understanding to the end of the Protectorate. But when the perfect opportunity for a grand reconciliation presented itself with the Prince of Wales' visit to the islands in 1862 en route to the East, the authorities discouraged any spontaneous display of enthusiasm by describing it as purely private. Thus the British departed in 1864 leaving behind many memories, some fond and some bitter, with the realization that they had never identified with or assimilated their Ionian protégés as the Venetians had done.

Yet without the security and the prosperity which the Protectorate had provided, the islands would not have formed the richest and most civilized part of their motherland, when at long last they rejoined it. Their political importance would of course rapildy diminish now that their Greek destiny had been fulfilled, but culturally they were to remain one of the cradles of Hellensim. Lear had written about Corfu: 'and so the aspect spiritual of this little piggy wiggy island is very much like a small village in Ireland—peopled by Orangemen and papists and having all the extra fuss and ill-will produced by a court and petty officials'; but, like most discerning judges, he acknowledged that the little piggy wiggy island and its six neighbours had a spiritual ethos which was both precious and unique.

70 The Royal Coat of Arms in the British Cemetery, in Zante. Visitors will find that earthquakes have dislodged it from its place over the gate, and now it lies neglected on the ground. Nevertheless it symbolises the long English connection with the Ionian Islands, a connection antedating the Protectorate and harking back to the 17th century, the era of the Currant Trade.

71 *Above*—A view of the British Cemetery in Zante which includes the grotto-like tomb of Sir Clement Harby, for many years the English consul. In the left background the inscription reads: 'The 90th Light Infantry to their esteemed and lamented adjutant, lieutenant Hector Monroe, who died on the 3rd August, 1828, aged 34'.

72 *Opposite*—Another gravestone from the British Cemetery.

PERINSIGNIS
COMITIS BASILII FILII
TUMULATUS
IN SIGNUM OBSEQUII
ET PERPETUÆ GRATITUDINIS
PATER ET FILIUS
EREXERUNT
D·O·M·F
ANNO A D
MDCCCLX

73 The Obelisk erected in 1813 'to the glory of the British Nation' by de Bosset on the causeway across the Koutavos Lagoon, Cephalonia.

74 The neo-classical lighthouse built by Napier on the Ayios Theodoros peninsula, Cephalonia, designed by his friend Kennedy, in the form of a Doric rotunda.

IONIAN AND POPULAR BANK OF GREECE

75 *Opposite, top*—The Ionian Bank building in Corfu. An early work by the island's distinguished 19th century architect, John Khronis.

76 *Opposite, bottom*—The former Prefecture, Corfu, also built in neo-classical style by Khronis.

77 *Above*—The Ionic rotunda on the Spianada, Corfu, erected by local wellwishers in memory of Sir Thomas Maitland, the first Lord High Commissioner.

78 *Overleaf, top*—Statue of Sir Frederic Adam by Prosalendis.

79 *Overleaf, bottom*—Façade of Palace of S.S. Michael and George, Corfu.

80 *Above* — Colonnade of Palace of S.S. Michael and George, Corfu.

81 Bellerophon holding Pegasus for Levkas — and a Head of Ulysses from Ithaca on the frieze of the Palace of S.S. Michael and George, Corfu.

82 The Goddess Demeter holding a cornucopia with a ship in the background for Corfu.

83 Cephalus the hunter with his dog for Cephalonia.

84 A mythical male figure seated, for Zante—A trident for Paxos.

85 Aphrodite with Dolphin for Kythera.

86 *Opposite, top*—The former British Residency at Gaio, Paxos, the finest building on the island.

87 *Opposite, bottom*—Another Former British Residency at Levkas, (constructed in 1826?)

ΛΙΜΕΝΙΚΟΣ ΣΤΑΘΜΟΣ

88 *Opposite, top*—The Viaduct at Katouni, Kythera, built by MacPhail in 1826 to carry a never-completed road down to Avlemona.

89 *Opposite, bottom*—Lancastrian School, built by MacPhail in 1826 in Kato Khora, Mylopotamos—Kythera.

90 *Above*—Garrison church and British cannons in the castle at Khora, Kythera.

91 Stele at Vathy—Ithaca commemorating Byron's visit to the island in August 1823 with the inscription 'if this island belonged to me, I would bury all my books here and never go away'.

Chapter IV

THE ISLES OF GREECE

'There was no Union of the Ionian Islands with Greece, but the Union of Greece with the Ionian Islands', in the words of Ilias Zervos, formerly one of the bitterest foes of the Protectorate, who had been deeply implicated in the risings in Cephalonia in 1848–9. It was ironical that those who had shouted loudest for the dissolution of the British connection were now so concerned to safeguard the privileged position which the islands enjoyed. In July 1864, sixty-six Ionian deputies took their seats in the National Assembly. Some, like Lombardos, supported the radicals, but most, especially those from the once disaffected southern islands, joined the conservatives. They were at pains to explain to their colleagues that the islands had long been under civilized rule, with an established society governed by good laws and ancient custom. Thus any Greek policy of assimilation must be extremely cautious and gradual.

The new constitution had specifically provided for the Ionians to keep their own taxation system and civil laws. So when, on 11 August 1864, a group of eighteen deputies proposed a resolution that as from the beginning of September Ionian civil law should be abolished and the legal codes used in the rest of Greece introduced, uproar ensued. Thanks to the good sense of Pavlos Kalligas, the Minister of Justice, and of Lombardos who acted as a spokesman for the islanders, the crisis was averted and the resolution quietly squashed. Many Greeks, however, muttered that although their country had gained 1813 square miles and a population of 236,000, the national revenue had only been augmented by some four and a half million drachma per annum, which barely covered the administrative costs. Moreover, the neutralization of Corfu and Paxos stipulated by the Treaty of London negated their value as forward bases, even if they were protected against external aggression by the Powers' guarantee.

It was to be the same story with the unification of the churches. In July 1866 the Holy Synod for all Greece met, and sent its proposals for unification to the Ionian prelates, with a copy to Constantinople. But negotiations soon broke down altogether, owing to the adamant opposition of Bishop Nicholas of Zante and Archbishop Spyridon of Cephalonia The latter wrote a blistering reply to Athens, refuting any form of compromise or the suggestion that he should take his seat in the synod. Unfortunately his colleague was less strong-minded, and after much vacillation agreed to submit. As the Corfiote hierarchy had already done so, the Archbishop ultimately had no choice except to follow suit. In fact few changes occurred, for religious life remained as decentralized and conservative as ever. In January 1900 a law abolished the Archdiocese of Cephalonia and enacted that in future no Ionian prelate should hold a title above that of bishop, while all would be subject to the Metropolitan of Athens. By then, anyway, the Greek church had repudiated the Patriarch's authority, and was an autocephalous and Erastian institution within an anti-monastic state, although Ionian religion still retained its own peculiarities.

The Great Powers feared that the acquisition of the islands would whet Greek appetites for expansion, and would promote 'the Great Idea', the eternal chimera of expelling the Turks from Europe and establishing a second Byzantium on the shores of the Bosphorus. The constitution had created a 'royal republic', giving King George no powers of veto, merely the right to summon and dismiss ministers, so he was ill-placed to restrain the extremists. The Cretans, seeing the Ionian example of *enosis*, and with the Christians in a three to one majority, now clamoured for union. Tacitly encouraged by the Russians and by many politicians in Athens, they rose in 1866 and continued a guerrilla war for some years.

By 1870 peace was re-established more or less, and a healthy suspicion grew that Russian policy was more concerned to promote Pan-Slavism than Pan-Hellenism. The Greek government refused to join the coalition against the Porte in 1876, and only reluctantly changed its mind when Russia had declared war. Even so, Greece gained no territory from the Congress of Berlin, although pressure from the Powers forced Turkey to cede Thessaly and Arta in 1881. Many Ionians remained belligerent, like Rovertos Romas, who constantly demanded the invasion of Epirus as well as the liberation of Crete. But an allied blockade of the Greek coastline in 1885 led to a swift climb-down and the demobilization of the army.

Greek politics had polarized by the 1880s. Charilaos Trikoupis had formed a quasi-Liberal party, which drew most of its support from the islands and the big towns. However, with the economy in a parlous state, his consistent failure to balance the budget led to a near-bankruptcy in 1893. Trikoupis retired, and his mantle descended on the Corfiote, George Theotokis, famed both for his honesty and his indolence. In all, he formed four administrations, during the last of which, 1905–9, the navy and the army were greatly expanded.

Another war had already been fought on Crete in 1896, after which the island became an autonomous province within the Ottoman Empire, ruled by King George's younger son. During hostilities all parties respected the neutrality of the Corfu channel for the free passage of shipping.

The advent of Venizelos to power in 1910 brought in a whole new range of laws, reforms, sound budgetary policies which permitted further increases in the armed forces, and eventually led to a parliamentary dictatorship. Two years later the First Balkan War broke out, in which the allies carried everything before them against the demoralized Turks; but soon the victors were quarrelling over the spoils. After more fighting, Bulgaria ceded part of Macedonia to Greece, while Venizelos gained territory in northern Epirus opposite Corfu. Its status remained ill-defined, and skirmishes between the Albanians and irregular levies continued. Still, with her territory increased by sixty-eight per cent and her population by seventy-seven per cent, Greece had done very well indeed, even if the cost had been tremendous and most of her new subjects were neither Orthodox nor Hellenic.

On the outbreak of the First World War Greece stayed neutral, although the Kaiser besought his brother-in-law, King Constantine, to side with the Central Powers. Venizelos supported the Ententes, and disputes raged throughout 1914 and 1915, with the King flatly refusing to provoke Turkish and Bulgarian hostility without firm allied support. In October 1915, a Franco-British force landed at Salonika, ostensibly to help the hard-pressed Serbs. Constantine dismissed Venizelos for permitting such an infringement of national sovereignty and, as the latter had a valid majority in Parliament, irreconcilable differences formed on both sides.

Suddenly Entente troops occupied Corfu in January 1916, in clear violation of the Treaty of London. The Serbian army had collapsed in the face of an overwhelming Austro-Bulgarian advance, and the remnants of their forces were evacuated to the island. Within a few weeks there were 80,000 soldiers encamped, plus the government-in-exile and the heir to the throne, Alexander. The cemetery on Vido island is evidence of the scale and misery of the operation. 5,000 French troops also landed, proceeded to fortify the strategic points, send detachments to the other islands, and imposed censorship, while Italy announced her readiness to send a force to her ally's aid. The Greek government flatly refused to let the Serbs be transported by land to the Salonika front, and after much wrangling they went by sea. The Serbian government, however, remained; the so-called Pact of Corfu brought into existence a new nation of Serbs, Croats, and Slovenes, and in 1918 the Kingdom of Yugoslavia was proclaimed from the steps of the Town Hall.

Relations between the allies and the Athens administration worsened steadily, while Venizelos proposed to set up a rival regime in Macedonia. Another Ionian played a prominent part in events, the King's chamberlain, the Zantiote Count Mercati, who was sent to the French admiral in November to persuade him not to order allied troops to land if war material was not forthcoming. Despite his efforts, Greece was blockaded and Constantine agreed to abdicate. At the Peace Conference and by the Treaty of Sevres, Venizelos made further territorial gains. However, the Greek army was unable to maintain its position in Asia Minor, suffering a major defeat at the hands of Ataturk, while another coup finally deposed the King. Many politicians, including Theotokis, were shot.

The danger in the Adriatic was now Italy, which had been given the Dodecanese Islands at Versailles, and was pressing for an enlarged Albania. A commission for determining the boundaries of the latter was duly appointed. On 27 August 1923 the Italian General Tellini, the president of the commission, with his adjutant and chauffeur, were ambushed on the road to Ioannina and murdered. Although the crime had taken place on Greek soil, the assassins were unknown. The Athens government expressed its deepest regrets, but Italy, where Mussolini had been in power for under a year, refused to be mollified. An ultimatum was presented, demanding, among other conditions, the payment of an indemnity of eighty million lire within five days. Greece denied any responsibility for the crime and appealed to the League of Nations.

On 31 August, after their navy had bombarded the unfortified island, the Italians occupied Corfu. Athenagoras, then its Bishop, and later Patriarch, offered himself as hostage to stop the shelling, in which sixteen civilians were killed. Italy's representative at the League, Salandra, claimed the bombardment was no act of war but a justified warning, although Lord Grey retorted that if this did not constitute an act of war the phrase had lost its meaning. The League's council reported a few days later that the Greeks should accept almost all the Italian conditions, although the indemnity was reduced to fifty million lire. The decision was manifestly unfair, but Greece had no option; the money was paid, and soon afterwards the Italian troops left Corfu.

Greek politics throughout the 1920s and 1930s could scarcely be described as settled, yet the Ionians were not directly affected by Venizelos' retirement, his return to politics, and the restoration of the monarchy. In 1936 John Metaxas, a member of the distinguished Cephalonian family, came to power and soon established a virtual dictatorship. His statue, strangely out of proportion, stands in the main square in Argostoli, for he redeemed his failings by his heroic stand against Mussolini's aggression in 1940. Greece was overrun when overwhelmingly superior German forces came to the aid of their ally Italy. That autumn, when heavy fighting was in progress in Epirus and Albania, Axis aircraft bombed the Ionian Islands, making their most damaging raid on Christmas Day. Lacking any proper defences. Corfu, the main supply base for the army, was hardest hit. Some 200 people died in the bombing and many buildings were damaged. The population bore it stoically, but after the electricity and water supplies were put out of action, the authorities gave orders to evacuate the town for fear of epidemics.

When Greece capitulated in April 1941, most Ionians wished to surrender to the Germans and appeal to their generosity. However, there was some secret agreement between the allies, for it was Italian forces which occupied the islands. The Italian occupation lasted from 28 April 1941 until 25 September 1943. There can be no doubt that if the Axis had won the war, the islands would have been annexed. The Italians suspended the executive functions of all the local authorities and installed their own administration. They tried to attract Ionian students by offering them free scholarships to their universities, but only two accepted. Even the postmen refused to deliver letters bearing a stamp marked with Victor Emmanuel's head and words *Isole Ionie,* a refusal punished by exile en masse. Attempts to revive memories of Venice by installing a lion's mouth in pillars on the façades of buildings for anonymous denunciations were no more successful.

Under the aegis of a military governor, General Pyrene, the islands were treated more and more like a province of Italy. Fascist slogans were daubed everywhere: '*Cretere, Obbedire, Combattere*', '*O l'amicizia preciosa o l'Ostilità durissima*', and '*Il Nemico e uno solo egli parla inglese*'. A government journal, the *San Marco,* was published, and streets suitably renamed. In Zante, Platia Solomou became Piazza Benito Mussolini, while the Italians tried to grab the poet's manuscripts. More islanders were removed to concentration camps, eleven Zantiotes being drowned when their prison ship was sunk by a British destroyer.

When Italy collapsed in 1943, and the Armistice was signed, the Germans moved swiftly. They had no wish to see the islands used as forward bases by the British, and did not trust their erstwhile allies. Relations between the two armies grew worse. On 13 September the Italians shot down two low-flying German aircraft on Corfu, and appealed for help to the Ionian opposition groups, promising to evacuate the island as soon as hostilities had ended. That night the Luftwaffe staged a major air raid. Incendiaries rained down on the town. Soon the Opera House, the Public Library in the Grimani Building, with its 80,000 volumes, the Post Office, the Market Place and the Church of St Nicholas were on fire. Then the Venetian barracks on the Spianada, the district down by the old port and along Zambelli Street, where Lear's old lodgings stood, were caught in the blaze. In a few hours the Germans had done more damage to the town than centuries of invaders had managed to do; it would never be quite the same again, for a third of it was destroyed.

Their occupation of the other islands was effective within a few days. In Cephalonia the commander of the Acqui Division hesitated to oppose the Germans, as he had no air cover and had received contradictory orders from Rome and Athens. His troops were anyway unpopular in the island, which they had vainly tried to Italianize, pulling down and defacing Napier's statue while Maitland's was carried away, although the boat transporting it was torpedoed and it ended at the bottom of the sea. While the general dithered, the Germans rounded up the far more numerous Italians and massacred them. Some 5,100 were killed in all, a contingent of 1,500 being marched over a sheer cliff near Assos.

Resistance stiffened. In Ipapandi cave on the west coast of Paxos, a Greek submarine, the *Papanikolis*, lay hidden in daytime, venturing out to torpedo enemy shipping by night. At the end of 1943 the Royal Navy landed an agent, Theophilus Sankhas, alias 'Captain Fly', to organize the partisans on Zante. As 1944 wore on, German defeat in the area was obviously inevitable, and headquarters in Cairo directed that the garrisons be permitted to keep their positions, supplies, and in particular weapons, lest these fell into the hands of the EAM guerillas, largely Communist inspired. On 9 October the Germans surrendered, and the islands were run by the partisans until British troops and elements of the regular Greek army arrived in March 1945 and re-established lawful authority. Even then absurd situations occurred: for instance, the Germans had seized all the telephones; when liberation came the local administrations reinstated them, except for those people who had had telephones before.

While the Second World War was still raging, civil war had broken out in Greece. Luckily this internecine strife seldom involved the Ionian Islands, although General Zervas and his EDES supporters were evacuated to Corfu because of the overwhelming Communist forces on the mainland, which briefly occupied Levkas. When stable government at last returned to Greece in 1952, it seemed that the Ionians, like the rest of their compatriots, could belatedly begin to recreate their vanished prosperity. The tragedy was that three of the islands were about to be struck by a natural disaster more awful than any human conflict.

It had only really been in the last quarter of the nineteenth century that the economic expansion of Western Europe had begun to impinge on the Balkans. Road and rail networks in Greece expanded enormously, and in the forty years preceding 1920 industrial concerns increased tenfold in number and quintupled in the manpower employed, while the population had tripled in a century. Thus land was in relatively short supply, especially as the agricultural economy had changed from being self-sufficient to being profit-orientated. This of course, was nothing new to the Ionians, who had been concentrating on olives and currants for centuries, and initially they benefited. Currant exports for all Greece trebled in money terms during the decade after the annexation of the islands, and doubled again in the following ten years. This was due to vastly increased demand from French growers, who found it hard to survive after phylloxera had destroyed so many of their vines in the late 1870s. But about 1890 the bottom fell out of the market, for the French vineyards had been restored and an import tariff imposed, while the English demand for currants continued to decline.

By the turn of the century the great emigrations had begun, and by 1914 over a quarter of a million Greeks had gone to America. The islands contributed to this drain, although the exodus was chiefly from the less fertile regions. It has gone on steadily ever since, although the destinations have changed somewhat; today there are more people of Kytheran descent in Australia than on Kythera itself. Only in Corfu did the population not diminish appreciably. Even today it and Levkas are the two most densely populated rural areas in Greece. There was however another cause in the seafaring islands of Ithaca and Cephalonia, for the Greek merchant marine grew dramatically at this period, increasing over a hundredfold in forty years, and the navigational skills of the islanders provided employment for many of them at home and abroad.

The greatest economic change for the Ionians was the advent of tourism. All seven islands had remained virtually untouched by industrialization, and were as essentially agricultural after the Second World War as they had been in Venetian times. When the boom in foreign travel started in the 1950s, and gathered momentum in the 1960s, the Ionians were quite unprepared for it. Even Corfu, which enjoyed an unbroken tradition as one of the top priority attractions for any visitor to Greece, had few hotels and none of the attributes of a sophisticated resort. The resultant mushroom growth in hotel, camping,restaurant, and beach facilities has been a very mixed blessing. Parts of Corfu are permanently scarred by unsightly buildings and injudicious development, mostly thanks to a lack of controlled planning. Even little Paxos, of which Rodwell Wright wrote

> Blest with whate'er a genial clime supplies,
> Remote from human intercourse it lies,

is in danger of being spoiled. The pace of development in the southern islands has been far slower, and now a world recession has shown that tourism is not a bottomless and endlessly expanding goldmine, the hope is they will be changed with more care and foresight.

For agriculture, always in the past the mainstay of the Ionian economy, remains so today. There are nearly five million olive trees in the islands, more than existed under the Republic. Even in Corfu, geared to tourism as it is, the olive crop is still the largest single source of revenue, despite those proprietors who claim it is no longer worthwhile to gather the harvest. Currants have stayed as a major crop in Zante and in the Lixouri peninsula of Cephalonia. Moreover, the Ionians have diversified; tobacco, dairy products, fruit, and vegetables now rank beside the traditional exports of wine, salt, and fish.

Religious life in the islands, like their economies, have changed little in the past century. The sharpest difference lies in the decline of the Roman Catholic Church. Corfu is still the seat of an archbishop, one of only three in Greece, but there are probably 2,500 Catholics plus a mere 200 more so in Cephalonia and Zante, in contrast to the Cyclades where almost all the indigenous population is Catholic. Corpus Christi is now their only major procession in the year. Before the Second World War the community was 8,000 strong, with several schools of its own, none of which exist today. Unfortunately the Roman Church became identified with the Italian occupation and incurred much odium thereby, while the number of descendants of Venetian settlers, or of the Maltese colonists imported by the British, has dwindled.

Another feature of Ionian Society has almost disappeared. The Jewish communities have vanished from all the islands except Corfu, where 150 remain with their synagogue. Yet in 1889, one in every nine townsmen in Corfu was Jewish, and their prosperity was as great as under the Protectorate. Perhaps the German occupation, when stringent anti-Jewish regulations were in force, when all of them had to be registered and observe a curfew from 5 p.m. to 7 a.m. on penalty of death, did the most damage to the communities. Many Jews were deported, and after the establishment of the state of Israel, many more emigrated there.

The Orthodox Church, however, has retained and even increased its hold on Ionian affections. The festivals of the islands' patron saints are celebrated with undiminished zeal, even of the obscurer ones, such as St Charalambos on Paxos. The excitement engendered by St Spyridon's four annual processions is tremendous. Although they have probably increased in size, the striking colours of Venetian days are lacking, except for the splendid vestments of the clergy. The priests are far better educated and as closely associated with their parishioners as ever. The most notable change is in the decay of the monasteries. A few are still occupied, but the majority have been abandoned, or contain just one aged monk, lovingly preserving the buildings and their treasures. Church property has long since been secularized, and the state pays the clergy; yet the Ionian Churches have kept the sumptuous interiors and the hallowed customs of a more pious age.

One of the saddest consequences of the union with Greece was the closure of the Ionian Academy. Its faculties were merged with Athens University, although in 1864 the latter contained only 1,200 students and had indifferent academic standards. Admittedly it had increased eightfold by 1918, but the emphasis was on legal studies, which also produced politicians, bureaucrats, and journalists, while the degree of under-employment for the number of available graduates was comparable to that prevailing under the Protectorate. Ionian frustration was vented in the continuing battle between the 'purist' and 'demotic' forms of Greek, especially as the former became almost synonymous with the centralizing policies of the Athens government.

Solomos' literary traditions were carried on by a host of pupils and admirers. His closest friend and disciple, Iakovos Polylas, the librarian at Corfu, had been a fervent unionist, and later sat in the National Assembly. Primarily a critic and translator, especially of Homer and Shakespeare, he was fluent in six languages and founded *Kodon*—'The Bell'—a satirical newspaper. In *Our Literary Language*, published in 1872, he argued that the demotic offered the only possibility of artistic expression. His Cephalonian contemporary, Gerasimos Markoras, took the same line, and Solomos' influence is apparent in his poems *The Dead Girl's Wish* and *The Oath*.

Other lesser figures who wrote in the demotic included the Zantiote George Tertsetis, who composed lyric and epic poetry; the Cephalonian Julius Typaldos, whose writing was romantic and mystical; the Corfiote Antonios Manousas, whose language was both elegant and erotic; and Stelios Khryssomalis. Distinguished translators abounded in the islands too: George Kalosgouros, who undertook editions of Dante, Tasso, and Foscolo, and Nicholas Koyevinas, who translated Goethe and Schiller. Lavrentios Mavilis, born in Ithaca, composed fifty-five sonnets, and translated many of the great poets, particularly English and German. A fiery patriot and supporter of the demotic, he said in the National Assemly in 1911: 'There is no vulgar tongue, merely vulgar men.' He was killed two years afterwards in the Balkan War.

Constantine Theotokis became the doyen of the Corfiote literati in the late nineteenth century. Having studied at Paris, he returned to his property at Karoussades, where he lived for the rest of his life. A skilled translator, who used the demotic enriched by Corfiote idioms, he was also a marvellous story teller. Realist, moralist, and psychologist too, he described the Ionian mentality in *Corfiote Tales*, and in three major works: *The Value of Money, The Life and Death of Caravellas* and *The Condemned.* Lastly he wrote a novel, *Slaves in their bonds,* which enjoyed a widespread sale throughout Greece.

There was, however, one major writer who stood outside the mainstream of the Ionian School. Aristotelis Valaoritis, born on Levkas, had served in the islands' parliament, but after the union, he retired to his house on Madouri to write. His respect for Solomos was deep and genuine, yet unlike the contemporary romantic poets he looked elsewhere for inspiration. This he found in the patriotic folksongs of his country, whence he derived the vivid adjectives, the evocation of the supernatural, and his rhetorical style. Valaoritis is par excellence the epic poet; his work relates the sufferings and struggles of Greece along the path to independence, and thus he transmitted one aspect of Solomos' creativity to posterity in its purest form.

Levkas produced two more literary figures of distinction. Angelos Sikelianos, born there in 1880, became one of the greatest of modern Greek poets, but always kept a house on his native island. Lefcadio Hearn, the child of a Greek mother and an Irish surgeon in the British army, is still remembered for his travel books and his stories about Japan, where he died in 1904.

Historical writing still flourished in Corfu. The mantle of Moustoxidis, whose great work *Delle Cose Corcirese* traced the island's history from earliest times until Angevin rule, descended on John Romanos, whose study of the local archives and of the Corfiote connection with Epirus remains outstanding. Lavrentios Vrokinis succeeded him in this task, while another Ionian historian, Spyridon Lambros, made a brilliant career on the wider stage of Athens. Not until the First World War did the draw of the capital sap the vitality of the islands' literary renaissance.

The musical traditons, on Corfu especially, dated back to Venetian times. Nicholas Mantzaros studied under the celebrated Zingarelli at the Naples Conservatoire; indeed he was offered the directorship there, but preferred to return to his native island, where he composed fourteen symphonies, and much other music, sacred and secular. In September 1840 the St Spyridon Philharmonic Society was founded, primarily to provide a band for the processions, as the British government had decreed that military bands could not take part in religious ceremonies. Thanks to Mantzaros' tuition, an adequate number of musicians was trained, and various honorary members, like Rossini, were elected. Another well-known Corfiote composer was Spyros Samaros, who composed ten operas and the music for the Olympic hymn. A second Philharmonic Society, named after Mantzaros, was founded in 1890, and the two have trained musicians for orchestras all over Greece. There are several excellent village bands in the islands as well.

Ionian art did not wither away either; indeed it revived in the years following the union. Most of the pupils of Kandounis and Koutouzis had been mediocre, although another Zantiote, Dionysios Tsokos, showed undoubted talent. Best-known as a portrait painter, he also executed a number of icons, and his pictures, if sometimes facile, are always accurate and stylishly composed. He chose many subjects from everyday life, while an ambitious work such as *The Christening of the Captain's Child* displays a rich and varied palette. In the 1870s George Avlichos, a Cephalonian artist, rose to prominence, although his meticulously detailed work expresses a melancholy or even morbid temperament. Charalambos Pachis founded an art school at Corfu, which attracted many local students. He was an excellent draftsman, as well as being a charming and witty character. His compositions were on a national and patriotic theme, or were concerned with the life in his own island, *Mayday in Corfu* being a typical example.

Some artists found it harder to win fame. Nicholas Typaldos-Xydias from Lixouri was a painter of simple tastes, liking village scenes with occasional mythological subjects. Until quite recently his works lingered in junk shops, yet he had studied in Paris and was a friend and imitator of Corot. He used a classic Italian chiaroscuro in his portraits, and his technique is very sensitive. Other painters came from the mainland, like the Athenian John Zacharias, in whom a definite dramatic quality is combined with an artistic self-sufficiency. Unfortunately his highly emotional personality impeded the development of his technical powers, and after illustrating some of Solomos' poems, he died young in the asylum at Corfu.

The past hundred years has seen the growth of Ionian archaeology. The first people to take an interest in the classical heritage of the islands had been the French , under Donzelot's aegis, during their second occupation, but the exigencies of war had prevented any thorough excavation of Palaeopolis. In Cephalonia the British administrator, de Bosset, assembled a fine collection of antiquities and had begun to clear the sites of the ancient Tetrapolis. But, on the whole, the Protectorate had done little to foster archaeology, which Maitland stigmatized as 'fools looking for old stones', and anything done was the achievement of individual enthusiasts.

In the 1860s Heinrich Schliemann visited Ithaca, and inaugurated his astonishing career by digging on what he felt were the likely sites described in the Odyssey. Much of the evidence he uncovered in his excavations on Mount Aëtos and in the southern part of the island was inconclusive or misleading, yet he did valuable groundwork. In Corfu he readily identified the Phaeacian capital on the Palaeopolis peninsula, although later scholarship inclined to Palaeokastritsa. However his pupil, Wilhelm Dörpfeld, was not satisfied with these conclusions. After much fieldwork and patient research, he published his *Alt-Ithaka* in two volumes in 1927, claiming that Levkas was in fact the Homeric Ithaca. Although his theory was painstakingly expounded, the topography just would not fit his arguments, nor did most of his finds there convincingly establish the existence of a late Mycenaean kingdom based on Levkas. He died in his villa near Nyddri in 1940, stubbornly unrepentant of his fantasies.

His attack on the bona fides of the traditional Ithaca provoked more excavations there in the 1930s, mainly under the patronage of the British School of Archaeology at Athens. The digs in the north of the island, supervised by Professor W. A. Heurtley and Miss Sylvia Benton, exposed several possible Homeric sites, including the cave on the Bay of Polis, in which fragments of bronze tripod-cauldrons were discovered. Their conclusions, published in the Annual of the British School, were ably supplemented by Lord Rennell of Rodd's trenchant defence of the Odyssey's topographical accuracy.

Meanwhile much work had been done on Corfu. A British work party under Whitmore's direction had uncovered the site of the temple of Kardaki in 1822, albeit largely by accident. In 1911 the Kaiser financed a dig, which he summoned Dörpfeld to direct, and which found the magnificent Gorgon, forming the west pediment of the Temple of Artemis at Palaeopolis. This now stands, perfectly reconstructed in the Archaeological Musueum. There are many more remains, partly inside the park of the royal residence of Mon Repos, which are still being excavated.

On the other islands, too, a systematic archaeological programme was followed. The remains of the Cyclopean walls and other vestiges of ancient Levkas were uncovered. In Cephalonia the widow of a rich Dutch Homeric enthusiast, A. E. H. Goekoop, sponsored a series of digs, directed by an expert from the island, Professor Marinatos. Although these did not locate the site of Homeric towns or palaces, they clearly revealed the existence of a flourishing community in late Mycenaean times. Since the Second World War, the British School has undertaken the exploration of Minoan sites on Kythera which have yielded much valuable information.

But since the Ionians joined the rest of Greece, there have been far less pleasant disturbances of their native soil than those caused by archaeology. The islands have always lain along two ridges prone to seismic shocks, although Corfu, Paxos, and Kythera seem more or less immune to earthquakes. It is a very different story with the other four islands. Ever since the first travellers' accounts, earthquakes have been mentioned. Zante experienced a terrible one in 1514; Cephalonia another in 1636, and again in 1765. Throughout the eighteenth century and the British Protectorate many of greater or lesser intensity were recorded. In 1866 and 1867 several violent earthquakes shook the islands, especially Cephalonia, where the town of Lixouri was flooded by a tidal wave. It was estimated that 224 persons lay buried in the ruins, that 3,000 houses had been destroyed and an equal number rendered uninhabitable. Further severe shocks followed in 1897-8, in 1903 and 1910.

It seemed unlikely, nevertheless, that an earthquake could do really serious damage to the islands. However in 1948 Levkas was devastated by a disastrous shock. Fortunately only two people were killed, but most of the flimsily constructed houses in the town collapsed immediately. The Civil War was still raging, so the calamity received little publicity. Nature's warning went unheeded, and nothing was done in the other islands to guard against a similar catastrophe. After all, the baroque splendours of Zante and the solid British buildings in Argostoli and Lixouri could hardly be compared to a virtual shanty town, in most people's opinions.

On Sunday 9 August 1953, a stupendous earth-tremor struck the islands of Zante, Cephalonia, and Ithaca at about midday. The churches, houses and colonnades which had earned for Zante the title of 'Venice of the Ionian Sea' were flattened. A fire blazed through the debris of the town, where only three modern buildings, the Church of St. Dionysios, a bank, and a school, survived. It was the same story in Cephalonia, where most of the town buildings were so badly damaged that they had to be dynamited. In Vathy, the ruin was less, but in the mountains of northern Ithaca entire villages disappeared. A provisional casualty list of 500 dead, with many more injured, was drawn up, and soon swelled to 600 dead and 2,300 injured, 800 of them seriously.

The impressions of one visitor, E. J. Simpson, are noteworthy. He wrote that it was fortunate that the towns were laid out on a fairly open plan, unlike the narrow crowded streets of Corfu, as otherwise the damage would have been still worse. For over a week the shocks continued, and 75,000 people were reported homeless. In the countryside the appalling mess could not be cleared up, as the roads were impassable. Israeli, British, and American ships gave unstinted help to the Greek navy, but it was impossible to remedy such a disaster, for over seventy per cent of the buildings on the three islands were beyond all hope of repair.

Gradually the damage has been rectified. Yet the glories have gone, never to return. Zante has been lovingly restored, many of the churches and houses are clever replicas of their predecessors, and the paintings have been pieced together again. The tragedy is that pre-stressed concrete can hardly have the charm of mellowed stone in the arcades along the Platia Rouga. In Cephalonia less effort has been made to recreate the past, and some of the concrete campaniles and rudimentary houses in Argostoli can scarcely be described as attractive. The 1953 earthquake probably set the development of the southern islands back at least a decade. Some comfort can, however, be drawn from the thought that now at least they are able to withstand another such shock.

With the departure of the British, the stream of visitors only dried up temporarily, and Corfu's popularity with foreign travellers remained undiminished. In 1861, the Empress Elizabeth of Austria had stayed with the Lord High Commissioner, and had been entranced by the charms of the island. Twenty-five years later she decided to have a home of her own on Corfu, one, moreover, that would embody her romantic conception of Achilles and his sea-mother Thetis. Eventually a suitable site was found; the Villa Braila above Gastouri was bought, and the site cleared for the erection of a palace in the Greek style, which the Neapolitan architect Cardilo was commissioned to build. 'I want a palace with pillared colonnades and hanging gardens, protected from prying glances—a palace worthy of Achilles, who despised all mortals and did not even fear the gods', wrote the Empress.

The Achilleion was ready in 1892 . But Elizabeth, who was distraught about the sad end of her son Rudolf at Mayerling, was already bored with the idea. She found the building too large, disliked the five styles incorporated by the architect as insufficiently classical, and disdained the modern comforts she had demanded. She led a secluded life in the palace on her infrequent visits there, usually with a hunchback called Christomanos,whose duties were to teach her Greek. Yet she was popular with the local peasantry, with her simple manner and direct approach. Elizabeth paid her last visit to Corfu in 1896, two years before her assassination by an anarchist at Geneva.

Until 1907 the Achilleion stood empty. In that year the Kaiser, whose admiration for Greek civilization was unbounded, bought it. From then until the outbreak of war, he used to come every year for about a month, and the whole court moved with him from Berlin. A landing stage was built down at Benitses, where the imperial family used to disembark from their yacht, *The Hohenzollern.* A fleet of six red Mercedes, the first motor cars seen on the islands, conveyed them up to the house. The Kaiser changed round the furniture, and the statues in the garden. The bust of Heine was expelled from the rotunda, where the Empress had placed it; instead, a characterless bust of Elizabeth was substituted. Near the moving statue of *The Dying Achilles* by Herter, a huge and hideous bronze of the hero was placed. The Kaiser also disapproved of other pieces, like the *Dancing Girl* at the eastern end of the peristyle column, reputedly Pauline Borghese sculpted by Canova, but luckily left them alone. However, he was very fond of Corfu, where he sponsored excavations, and drove around, always in white naval uniform, often stopping at the panoramic view about Pelekas, known today as 'the Kaiser's Throne'.

During the First World War, the Achilleion was confiscated as enemy property. The contents were plundered, and it was converted into a French naval hospital; then after 1918 into a museum. Between 1940 and 1945 it served successively as a Greek, Italian, and German hospital, and was left derelict. In the 1960s a syndicate took it over, and after restoration turned it into a casino, in which capacity it now flourishes. The neo-Pompeian decor is as incongruous as ever, but the Achilleion stands a monument to fin-de-siècle taste which contains many relics of its first owners, although the vaunting inscription the Kaiser put beneath Achilles' bronze, 'To the greatest of the Greeks from the greatest of the Germans', has been removed.

These were not the only royal visitors to the Ionian Islands. Archduke Ludwig Salvator, a member of that branch of the Habsburg family which had ruled the Grand Duchy of Tuscany before the Risorgimento, was a compulsive traveller. In his steam-yacht *Nixe* he cruised around the islands collating a mass of information. He published books on Zante, Levkas and Paxos, which, if not exactly exciting reading, stand as a monument to conscientious scholarship, for they contain every single available fact and statistic about the human and natural aspects of the islands, plus some good illustrations.

Written as they were in the latter years of the nineteenth century, on reading them it is amazing to find how little Ionian life has changed. Like the rest of Greece, the islands have been divided into districts called nomes, since the union. Corfu forms one, of which Paxos and Antipaxos form a sub-district or eparchy; so does Cephalonia, with four eparchies, of which Ithaca and the Echinades Islands are one. Levkas and Zante are nomes without eparchies, the two smallest in the country. Kythera and Antikythera form an eparchy, originally assigned to Zante, then to Corinth. It now belongs to the nome of Attica and is administered from the Piraeus.

Corfu is still situated on the edge of a hostile area. From 1924 to 1961 it was treated as a frontier zone, and traffic movements in the north of the island were restriced. Now anyone is quite free to gaze at Albania, only three miles away across the channel, although attempts to cross the water would be ill-advised as it is supposed to be heavily mined. In 1947, shortly after a Communist government had been established at Tirana, a British destroyer struck a mine in the straits, and the so-called Corfu Channel incident occurred. Two years later a group of thirty-six Albanian agents were smuggled across from Corfu in an Anglo-American intelligence operation, intended to start a rising against the regime. However, the venture had been betrayed in advance by Kim Philby; the party was seized on landing and all were shot. So Albania remains blue, inviting, and mysterious, although older Corfiotes can remember the days between the wars when English sportsmen used to go wildfowling in the marshes round Butrinto.

Otherwise the great days of Corfu as a bastion of Christendom, or as a bone of international contention, are over. It no longer houses a royal residence, since Greece has abolished the monarchy. After the union, King George was presented with the Palace of SS Michael and George and the Villa of Mon Repos, as the houses of the preceding ruler, the Lord High Commissioner. The King and his family used the Palace for official visits until 1913, while the villa was given to his younger son. Wanting a home in the country they took a lease on the imitation fourteenth century Venetian palace, built in 1880 by Count Mimbelli near Dassia Bay, and now the Castello Hotel. Eventually Mon Repos, the birthplace of Prince Philip, passed back into the monarch's hands, and until recently was used as the King's summer home. The Palace, however, which houses a museum, was badly damaged in the Second World War, and seemed fated to be left to rot. Thanks to the initiative of the then British Ambassador to Athens, Sir Charles Peake, a fund was organized for the redecoration of the State Rooms, a task meticulously undertaken and completed in 1954.

The island still has the 'gardeny' atmosphere so well described by Lear. What it has lost is the feeling of unspoiled rustic simplicity which so entranced the Durrells in the 1930s. The four different faces of the campanile of St

Spyridon may all still tell different times, when the hands are blown by the wind, but where now could the visitor find figures like Spiro, the taxi-driver they immortalized with his Brooklyn accent, boastful, warm-hearted, and eccentric, or the Count, who was happiest entertaining his friends with startling if unlikely contentions, such as his theory that Corfu was really the island Shakespeare described in *The Tempest*? On the coast nowadays all is commercialized; in the hills most of the young men prefer to leave their holdings uncultivated and find seasonal work in the soulless new hotels.

A different impression is left by Cephalonia and Zante. Here it seems to be the loss of vanished splendours which saddens the visitor. Even until 1939 the islands had their opera houses, which a touring Italian Company used to visit every year. They were microcosms of the great world outside, proud, self-sufficient, less prosperous than of old, but still imbued with the feeling that their little communities were as civilized as anywhere in Greece. The 1953 earthquake changed all that. Today, although the natural and a few of the artistic beauties remain, they seem shells of their old selves, still searching to recover their lost identity. The indefinably Italianate ethos of Zante persists; the Cephalonians are as independent, not to say truculent, as ever, and yet the spiritual qualities of these islands, which earlier travellers certainly found, are lacking today.

Perhaps the small islands—Ithaca, Paxos and Kythera—are the most satisfying. Each has a beauty of its own, the dense olive groves, indented coastline with little bays, and intimate countryside of Paxos; the magnificent scenery the glorious views, the impression of immemorial antiquity of Ithaca; and Kythera, bare, bleak indeed, more Cycladic than Ionian, but tremendously appealing for its solitude and its tranquillity. Levkas too has a charm which is indefinable. It consists of the mixture of the Turkish, Frankish, and Venetian heritages, of a delightful pastoral land which contains a community that has never aspired to greatness and is content with its lot.

These impressions are subjective, no doubt far too much so. What is fact is that the islands today, with the possible exception of Corfu, are a declining area. In an over-centralized country, where all roads lead to Athens, communications between them are almost non-existent. Very few of the inhabitants of one island have seen another, much less all six of the others. The enjoyment in parodying their neighbours' eccentricities is evident. What is not evident is a feeling of being fellow-Ionians. For the *Heptanesos,* as the Greeks call them,despite their shortcomings, have still a quintessential charm, and a character which is unique. It is to be hoped the future will be kinder to them than the past; and, if Providence smiles, all their inhabitants may again be proud of being Ionians as well as Greeks. It would indeed be tragic to have to echo Byron's words:

The isles of Greece, the isles of Greece!
Where burning Sappho loved and sung,
Where grew the arts of war and peace,
Where Delos rose, and Phoebus sprung!
Eternal summer gilds them yet.
But all, except their sun, is set.

92 The courtyard of the monastery of Panayia Katharon, Ithaca. Samuel, pictured here, is the sole remaining inmate, a sad comment on the decline of monastic life in the islands.

93 *Opposite* — The old Sea Mill at Argostoli, Cephalonia. It was discovered during the British Protectorate that a stream of sea water ran rapidly inland, where the mill wheels now stand, and then seemed to disappear. The mystery was only solved by Austrian scientists a few years ago, who put quantities of yellow dye into the water. This reappeared ten miles away on the other side of the island in Lake Melissani after running underground beneath the main range of mountains.

94 *Above* — Lake Melissani, Cephalonia.

95 View over the salt pans and canal, Levkas.

96 Lakka harbour, Paxos, at dawn.

97 *Opposite, top* — View over Vathy, Ithaca.

98 *Opposite, bottom* — Bridge at Argasi, Zante. The shift of coastline since the 1953 earthquake left it standing in the sea

Η ΒΟΥΛΗ ΤΗΣ ΕΠΤΑΝΗΣΟΥ

ΨΗΦΙΖΕΙ

Αἱ Νῆσοι ΚΕΡΚΥΡΑ ΚΕΦΑΛΛΗΝΙΑ ΖΑΚΥΝΘΟΣ ΛΕΥΚΑΣ ΙΘΑΚΗ ΚΥΘΗΡΑ ΠΑΞΟΙ

ΕΛΛΑΔΟΣ

1863

99 The Declaration of the Union of the Ionian Islands with Greece in the Chronopoulos house at Akrotiri, Zante.

100 Letter written by Ali Pasha, Despot of Epirus from the Palatianos collection.

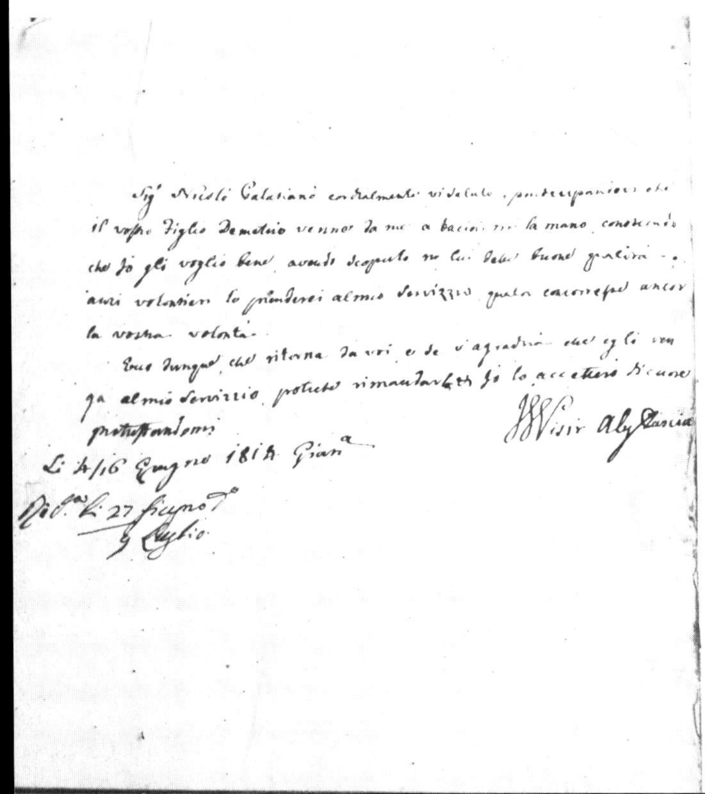

Sig.r Nicolò Palatiano cordialmente vi saluto, partecipandovi che il vostro Figlio Demetrio venne da me a baciarmi la mano, conoscendo che io gli voglio bene, avendo scoperto in lui delle buone qualità - . avrei volentieri lo prenderei al mio servizzio quando concorreva ancor la vostra volontà.

Ecco dunque che ritorna da voi, e se v'agradisce che egli venga al mio servizzio, potrete rimandarlo che io lo accetterò di cuore protestandomi

Visir Aly Bascia

Li 4/16 Giugno 1817 Giannina

Ric.to li 27 Giugno
e Luglio

101 Portrait of Lady Adam, still in the possession of her descendants, the Palatianos family in Corfu. 'The hussar-like moustache' mentioned by Private Wheeler is not so evident here.

102 *Opposite, left*—Corfiote man in traditional dress.

103 *Opposite, right*—Corfiote woman in traditional dress.

104 *Above*—View of Vathy harbour, Ithaca. These paintings were the work of Joseph Cartright, a Devon artist, who in 1815 aged 26 became paymaster to the British forces in the islands. He remained there some ten years and his 'Views in the Ionian Islands' were published in 1821.

8 & 23 Apl. 1862
Jany 28. 3 PM 1864

105 *Opposite, top* — View of Kapsali and the fortress of Kythera.

106 *Opposite, bottom* — At Potamos, Kythera.

107 *Above* — Corfu. These paintings come from Edward Lear's 'Views of the Seven Ionian Islands', published in 1863; this forms only part of his considerable output executed during many visits, mostly to Corfu.

108 *Opposite, top*—A house party of the Kaiser's at the Achilleion, 1913. Among the Kaiser's guests are: King George I of Greece, Crown Princess Sophie, Prince Andrew and Crown Prince Constantine.

109 Sailors from the royal yacht 'Hohenzollern' carrying pieces of the bronze statue of Achilles which the Kaiser erected on the terrace. Cast in Berlin in 1909 it bore the vaunting inscription: 'To the greatest of the Greeks from the greatest of the Germans.'

110 *Above*—Photograph of Empress Elizabeth (wearing mourning for her son Rudolph) taken at the Achilleion.

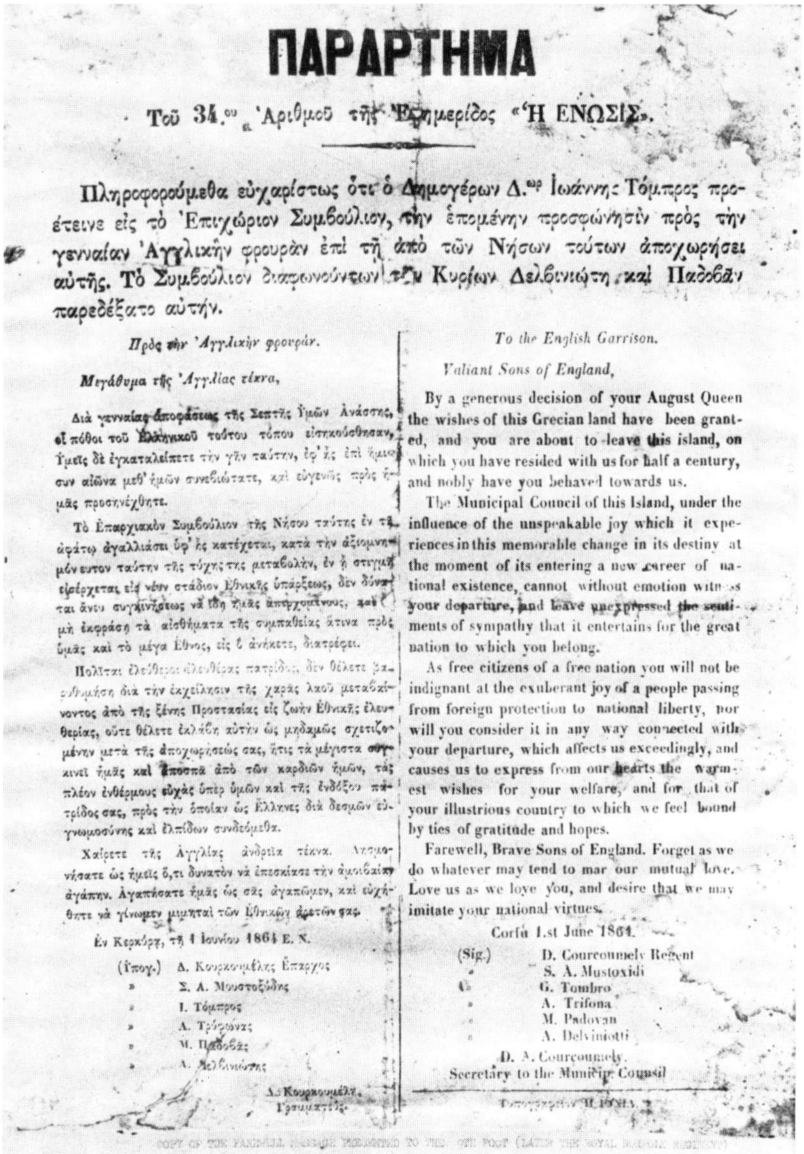

ΠΑΡΑΡΤΗΜΑ

Τοῦ 34.ου Ἀριθμοῦ τῆς Ἐφημερίδος «Ἡ ΕΝΩΣΙΣ».

Πληροφορούμεθα εὐχαρίστως ὅτι ὁ Δημογέρων Δ.ορ Ἰωάννης Τόμπρος προέτεινε εἰς τὸ Ἐπιχώριον Συμβούλιον, τὴν ἑπομένην προσφώνησιν πρὸς τὴν γενναίαν Ἀγγλικὴν φρουρὰν ἐπὶ τῇ ἀπὸ τῶν Νήσων τούτων ἀποχωρήσει αὐτῆς. Τὸ Συμβούλιον διαφωνούντων τῶν Κυρίων Δελβινιώτη, καὶ Παδοβᾶν παρεδέξατο αὐτήν.

Πρὸς τὴν Ἀγγλικὴν φρουράν.

Μεγάθυμα τῆς Ἀγγλίας τέκνα,

Διὰ γενναίας ἀποφάσεως τῆς Σεπτῆς Ὑμῶν Ἀνάσσης, οἱ πόθοι τοῦ Ἑλληνικοῦ τούτου τόπου εἰσηκούσθησαν, Ὑμεῖς δὲ ἐγκαταλείπετε τὴν γῆν ταύτην, ἐφ' ἧς ἐπὶ ἥμισυν αἰῶνα μεθ' ἡμῶν συνεβιώτατε, καὶ εὐγενῶς πρὸς ἡμᾶς προσηνέχθητε.

Τὸ Ἐπαρχιακὸν Συμβούλιον τῆς Νήσου ταύτης ἐν τῇ ἀφάτῳ ἀγαλλιάσει ὑφ' ἧς κατέχεται, κατὰ τὴν ἀξιομνημόνευτον ταύτην τῆς τύχης της μεταβολήν, ἐν ᾗ στιγμῇ εἰσέρχεται εἰς νέον στάδιον Ἐθνικῆς ὑπάρξεως, δὲν δύναται ἄνευ συγκινήσεως νὰ ἴδῃ ἡμᾶς ἀπερχομένους, καὶ μὴ ἐκφράσῃ τὰ αἰσθήματα τῆς συμπαθείας ἅτινα πρὸς ὑμᾶς καὶ τὸ μέγα Ἔθνος, εἰς ὃ ἀνήκετε, διατρέφει.

Πολῖται ἐλεύθεροι ἐλευθέρας πατρίδος, δὲν θέλετε βαρυθυμήσῃ διὰ τὴν ἐκχείλησιν τῆς χαρᾶς λαοῦ μεταβαίνοντος ἀπὸ τῆς ξένης Προστασίας εἰς ζωὴν Ἐθνικῆς ἐλευθερίας, οὔτε θέλετε ἐκλάβῃ αὐτὴν ὡς μηδαμῶς σχετιζομένην μετὰ τῆς ἀποχωρήσεώς σας, ἥτις τὰ μέγιστα συγκινεῖ ἡμᾶς καὶ ἀποσπᾷ ἀπὸ τῶν καρδιῶν ἡμῶν, τὰς πλέον ἐνθέρμους εὐχὰς ὑπὲρ ὑμῶν καὶ τῆς ἐνδόξου πατρίδος σας, πρὸς τὴν ὁποίαν ὡς Ἕλληνες διὰ δεσμῶν εὐγνωμοσύνης καὶ ἐλπίδων συνδεόμεθα.

Χαίρετε τῆς Ἀγγλίας ἀνδρεῖα τέκνα. Λησμονήσατε ὡς ἡμεῖς ὅ,τι δυνατὸν νὰ ἐπισκιάσῃ τὴν ἀμοιβαίαν ἀγάπην. Ἀγαπήσατε ἡμᾶς ὡς σᾶς ἀγαπῶμεν, καὶ εὐχήθητε νὰ γίνωμεν μιμηταὶ τῶν Ἐθνικῶν ἀρετῶν σας.

Ἐν Κερκύρᾳ, τῇ 1 Ἰουνίου 1864 Ε. Ν.

(Ὑπογ.) Δ. Κουρκουμέλης Ἔπαρχος
» Σ. Α. Μουστοξύδης
» Ι. Τόμπρος
» Α. Τρύφωνας
» Μ. Παδοβᾶς
» Α. Δελβινιώτης

Δ. Κουρκουμέλη,
Γραμματεύς.

To the English Garrison.

Valiant Sons of England,

By a generous decision of your August Queen the wishes of this Grecian land have been granted, and you are about to leave this island, on which you have resided with us for half a century, and nobly have you behaved towards us.

The Municipal Council of this Island, under the influence of the unspeakable joy which it experiences in this memorable change in its destiny at the moment of its entering a new career of national existence, cannot without emotion witness your departure, and leave unexpressed the sentiments of sympathy that it entertains for the great nation to which you belong.

As free citizens of a free nation you will not be indignant at the exuberant joy of a people passing from foreign protection to national liberty, nor will you consider it in any way connected with your departure, which affects us exceedingly, and causes us to express from our hearts the warmest wishes for your welfare, and for that of your illustrious country to which we feel bound by ties of gratitude and hopes.

Farewell, Brave Sons of England. Forget as we do whatever may tend to mar our mutual love. Love us as we love you, and desire that we may imitate your national virtues.

Corfu 1.st June 1864.

(Sig.) D. Coureounely Regent
» S. A. Mustoxidi
» G. Tombro
» A. Trifona
» M. Padovan
» A. Delviniotti

D. A. Courçoumely.
Secretary to the Municip Council

Τυπογραφεῖον Η ΙΟΝΙΑ.

111 *Opposite, top* — The British garrison playing cricket on November 29, 1860.

112 *Opposite, bottom* — The British garrison's race-course in Corfu, August 30, 1860.

113 *Above* — Broadsheet in Greek and English, containing the farewell address to the British garrison passed by the Municipality of Corfu with two abstentions in 1864.

114 Landing of French marines in Lassi, Cephalonia, 1916.

115 Greek sailors marching through Argostoli.

116 Argostoli 1953, after the earthquake.

117 British sailors at Argostoli assisting after the 1953 earthquake.

118 Napier Street in Argostoli.

119 Interior of Opera House in 1907, at Argostoli until 1939. Corfu, Cephalonia and Zante all had their own opera houses, which were regularly visited by Italian touring companies.

The serious historian may object to the lack of footnotes in my text. I make no apologies for this, as in my opinion, they detract from the enjoyment of reading a book. Moreover I think that my sources are adequately mentioned and indexed in the bibliography opposite.

Bibliography

The historical period covered by this book begins about 1500 AD. As Chapter 1 is intended solely to illustrate the background to the islands' history from that date it does nothing more than skate over earlier ages. I have therefore omitted the large number of sources consulted for the prehistoric, classical, Byzantine and mediaeval periods, in the hope that I shall be able to deal with them much more thoroughly in a subsequent work. Sources from 1500 to the modern day have been divided into three categories and between those which are primary or secondary material, while there is also a general section.

PRIMARY SOURCES:

The archives at Venice, one of the largest in the world, have still to be sorted and catalogued definitively, so to extract all the relevant material from them would be a lifetime's work. I have thus, inevitably, relied on sources such as Levi and Lunzis, whose books are based directly on them. Similarly the archives in the Ionian Islands, an enormous corpus of records, have yet to be finally organized, although much work has already been done in this respect. The thirty-eight volumes of the Calendar of State Papers Venetian extending from 1500 to 1675 have been invaluably useful in illustrating the Republic's rule in the islands. So have the Livra d'Oros for Corfu, Cephalonia, Zante and Levkas, which throw much light on the composition of Ionian society during these centuries.

SECONDARY SOURCES

A. Venetian Period: c. 1500–1797

ANDRÉADÉS A.—L'Administration financière et economique de Venise dans le Levant (Article in L'Acropole—January 1926)
and review by GUILIO ALESSIO—'Di un opera de M. Andréadés . . .'

BACCHION Eugenio—Il Dominio Veneto su Corfu (1386–1797) (Venice 1956)

BRAUDEL Fernand—Le Monde Méditeranée a l'Epoque de Philip II (2 vols—2nd Edition—Paris 1966)

BROWN Horatio—Studies in the History of Venice (London 1907)

CAWSTON G. & KEANE A. H.—Early Chartered Companies (London 1896)
CHESTERTON G. K.—Stories, Essays and Poems (London 1939)
DAMERINI Gino—Le Isole Ionie nel sistema adriatica dal dominio Veneziano a Buonaparte (Milan 1943)
DARU P.—Histoire de Venise (5 vols—Paris 1821)
DE GUBERNATIS Enrico—Memoire Italiane nelle Isole Ionie (Ravenna 1908)
EPSTEIN M.—The Early History of the Levant Company (London 1908)
GEANOKOPLOS D. J.—Greek Scholars in Venice (Harvard 1962)
GRASSET DE SAINT-SAUVEUR A.—Voyages dans les iles et possessions ci-devant Venitiennes du Levant (Paris 1800)
HANNAY David—The Great Chartered Companies (London 1926)
HAZLITT W.—Venetian Republic (2 vols—London 1900)
HOPF Friedrich—Chroniques Gréco-Romaines (Berlin 1873)
LANE Frederic C.—Venice—A Maritime Republic (Baltimore 1973)
LEVI Cesare—Venezia, Corfu ed il Levante (Venice 1907)
LITHGO W.—The Rare Adventures and Painefull Peregrinations (Glasgow 1906)
LUNZIS Count Ermanno—Della Condizione politica delle Isole Ionie sotto il Dominio Veneto (Venice 1858)
MACNEILL William—Venice, the Hinge of Europe (1081-1797) (Chicago 1974)
MILLER William—Essays on the Latin Orient (London 1921)
MILLER William—The Latins in the Levant (London 1908)
MILLER William—The Ionian Islands under Venice (E.H.R. Vol XVIII 1903)
MILLER William—Three Letters from the Islands (E.H.R. Vol XLIII 1928)
MONNIER H.—L'Administration financière des Venitiens dans les Iles Ioniennes (Paris 1916)
PETRITSOPOULOS Demetrio—Saggio storico sulle prime eta dell'Isola di Leucadia (Florence 1814)
PIGNATORRE Marino e Nicolo—L'Isola de Cefalonia dei tempi Eroici alla Caduta della Repubblica Veneta (Venice 1889)
PULLAN B. S.—Rich and Poor in Renaissance Venice (Oxford 1971)
RUNCIMAN Hon. Sir Steven—The Great Church in Captivity (Cambridge 1968)

SANDYS G.—Travels (7th Edition, London 1673)
TENENTI Alberto—Piracy and the Decline of Venice (London 1967)
WHELER Sir G. & SPON Dr—A Journey into Greece (Amsterdam 1689)
WOOD A.—A History of the Levant Company (London 1952)

B. The Foreign Occupations: 1797–1864

PRIMARY SOURCES:

There are no less than 1427 volumes and boxes of documents in the Colonial Office Records relating to this period, besides various archives in the Foreign Office and the War Office Records. I am greatly indebted to Professor Brian Tumelty's thesis in Cambridge University Library which sifted much of this original material. The Russell, Gladstone and Hudson Lowe papers are also essential sources, while those of Castlereagh, Wellington, Bathurst, Aberdeen and Church are equally important. The Guilford Papers are indispensable to any account of the foundation of the Ionian Academy. Most French and local Greek material is however adequately represented by books already published.

SECONDARY SOURCES:

ANSTED D. T.—The Ionian Islands in the year 1863 (London 1863)
BAGALLY J. W.—Ali Pasha and Great Britain (Oxford 1938)
BOSSET C. P. DE—Proceedings in Parga and the Ionian Islands (London 1821)
BYRON Lord—Letters and Journals Volume VI (London 1901)
DAKIN Douglas—British and American Philhellenes during the Greek War of Independence: 1821–1833 (Thessalonika 1955)
DAKIN Douglas—The Unification of Greece 1770–1923 (London 1972)
DANDOLO Antonio—Des Iles Ioniennes Sous le protection Britannique (Corfu 1851)
DAVY J.—Notes and observations on the Ionian Islands and Malta (London 1842)
DURRELL Lawrence—Lear's Corfu (Corfu 1965)
FREWEN LORD W.—Sir Thomas Maitland (London 1897)
HOLLAND Henry—Travels in the Ionian Islands, Albania et al (London 1815)
JENKINS Romilly—Dionysios Solomos (London 1940)
JERVIS-WHITE-JERVIS Henry—History of the Island of Corfu (London 1852)

KIRKWALL Viscount—Four Years in the Ionian Islands (London 1864)
LANE-POOLE S.—Sir Richard Church (London 1890)
LEAKE W. M.—Travels in Northern Greece (London 1835)
LEAR Edward—Views in the Seven Ionian Islands (London 1863)
LEAR Edward—Correspondence (London 1907)
LUNZIS Count Ermanno—Della Repubblica Settinsulare (Venice 1863)
LUNZIS Count Ermanno—Storia delle Isole Ionie sotto il reggimento dei Repubblicani francesi (Venice 1860)
McLELLAN G. B.—Venice and Buonaparte (Princeton 1931)
MOORE-SMITH G. C.—Lord Seaton (London 1903)
MORLEY Lord—Life of W. E. Gladstone (London 1903)
MÜLLER Christian—Journey through Greece and the seven Ionian Islands (London 1822)
MURRAY John—A Handbook for Travellers in Greece (London 1st Edition 1840; 4th Edition 1872; 7th Edition 1900)
NAPIER C. J.—The Colonies: treating of their value generally and of the Ionian Islands in particular (London 1833)
NAPIER C. J.—Memoir on the Roads of Cephalonia (London 1825)
NAPIER Sir William—Life and Opinions of Charles James Napier (London 1857)
NAPOLEON—Correspondence (Paris—1863 Edition)
NICOLSON Harold—Byron—The Last Journey (London 1924)
NOAKES Vivien—Edward Lear—The Life of a Wanderer (London 1968)
PLOMER William—Ali the Lion (London 1936)
PÜCKLER-MUSKAU Prinz—Südöstlicher Bildersaal (Stuttgart 1840)
REUMONT Alfred von—Sir Frederick Adam (London 1855)
RODOCANACHI—Bonaparte et les Iles Ioniennes (Paris 1899)
RODWELL WRIGHT Waller—Horae Ioniae (London 1809)
SITWELL Sacheverell—Great Palaces of Europe (London 1964)
St. CLAIR William—That Greece might still be free (London 1972)
TRELAWNEY E. J.—Records of Shelley, Byron (London 1858-78)
WHEELER Private—The Letters of Private Wheeler (E. & B. Liddell Hart, London 1952)
WOODHOUSE Hon. C. M.—The Greek War of Independence in its historical Setting (London 1952)
WOODHOUSE Hon. C. M.—Capodistrias (London 1973)
c.f. THE GREEK GAZETTE (London—October 1972 issue) on Andreas Kalvos (Corfu 1851)

C. The Modern Age: 1864–1975

PRIMARY SOURCES:

Here the material is readily accessible in journals, newspapers and personal memoires. The Ionian press, a fruitful source in the British period, proliferated after the union with Greece. *Kathimerinis* is an invaluable source about the Zantiote clergy and the union; so is *Patriotis* for radicalism in the Ionian Islands. In the 1890s a rash of political and satirical magazines appeared: *Nea Politeia, Choron, Phileleuteros, Vourdoulio, Astir* and *Neon Syntagma.* The pity is that they have no successors today, which is a sad testimony to the impoverishment of intellectual life in the islands.

SECONDARY SOURCES:

AVOURIS, Spyros — Brève histoire de l'Eglise des Iles Ioniennes (Athens 1956)

AVOURIS, Spyros — Tome Commémoratif à l'occasion du centennaire de l'union de l'Heptanese (Athens 1964)

COMMERCIAL BANK OF GREECE — Greek Painters of the 19th Century (Athens 1957)

DINOS Kenomos — The Ionian Islands during the Italian Occupation (Athens 1954)

GARDINER Leslie — The Eagle Spreads his Claws (Edinburgh 1966)

GOLDING Louis — Goodbye to Ithaca (London 1955)

HASLIP Joan — The Lonely Empress: Elizabeth of Austria (London 1965)

LASTUREL Louis — L'affaire gréco-italienne (Paris 1925)

LINARDOS G. — Chronicles of The Town of Corfu (Athens 1937)

LUDWIG-SALVATOR Archduke — Anmerkungen über Levkas (Prague 1908);

Paxos und Antipaxos (Würzburg 1889);

Zante (Prague 1904);

Sommertage auf Ithaka (Prague 1903);

Wintertage auf Ithaka (Prague 1905)

MILLER William — Modern Greece (London 1928)

NICOGLOU St Ph. — L'affaire de Corfou et la Societé des Nations (Dijon 1925)

RODD Sir Rennell — Customs and Lore of Modern Greece (London 1965)

ROMAS Count Dionysios — Zante before and after The Union (Athens 1965)

SERGEANT Lewis — Greece in the Nineteenth Century (London 1897)

SIMPSON E. J. — Time after Earthquake (London 1954)

STRUPP E. — L'Incident de Ioannina (Paris 1924)
WARE T. — The Orthodox Church (London 1963)
ZORAS G. — Alexander Manzoni and The Intellectuals of the Heptanesos (London 1911)

D. General

There are a number of books which do not deal with specific periods in Ionian history, but which are necessary reading for a detailed knowledge of the islands, including the general guide books and the Durells' works which immortalized inter-war Corfu.

ASPIOTI Marie — The Enchanted Isle of Corfu (Corfu 1964)
DENHAM H. M. — The Ionian Islands to Rhodes; A Sea Guide (London 1972)
DURRELL Gerald — My Family and other Animals (London 1956)
DURRELL Lawrence — Prospero's Cell (London 1945)
FORTE John — Venus of the Isles (Fifth Edition Corfu 1971)
MARINATOS S. — Cephalonia (Argostoli 1962)
MATTON Raymond — Corfou (Athens 1960)
POLITIS Jacques — Corfou et les Iles Ioniennes (Paris 1964)
STAMATOPOULOS Nondas — A brief Account of Corfu (Athens 1970)
TSITSELIS E. — Mèlanges Cephaloniens (Athens 1960)

A complete bibliography covering all aspects of Ionian history and culture is unfortunately lacking, but the Bibliographie Ionienne (2 volumes — Paris 1810) by E. S. Legrand, completed by H. Pernod and divided between 1494-1854 and 1855-1900 contains a fairly comprehensive list.

Index

PEOPLE

PLACES

R. Beratino
R. Boiussa
Otranto
C. di Leuca
Koridjen
Presba
Monastir
Berat
Koryitza
Avlona
Dukatis
Argyro
Libokovo
Delvino
Ianina
Pop. 28,000
Butrinto
Philates
Paramithia
Parga
Arta
CORFU
Paxo
Previsa
Arta Gulf
Sta Maura
Kefalonia
Argostoli
Ithaca
Zante
Strophadia
Kastoria
Kailari
Veria
Vodina
Moglena
L. Tokina
Demirhissar
Seres
Pop. 25,000
Orfano
Saloniki
Pop. 70,000
Galatz
M. Santo
R. Karasou
Katrin
Servia
Tricala
Turnobe
Zagora
Larissa
Velestino
Volo
Saloniki G.
Lemnos
Karpenisi
Rendina
Zeitoun
Skopelo
Skyro
GREECE
NEGROPONT
Egripo
Talanta
Lepanto
Salona
Livadia
Thebes
Lepanto G.
Patras
Gastouni
Corinth
Napoli
Pop. 10,000
Lala
Tripolitza
Pop. 20,000
ATHENS
C. Doro
Aegina
MOREA
Arkadia
Kalamata
Zonkhio
Navarino
Erikos
Mistra
Spezzia
Hydra
Zea
Thermia
Syra
Serpho
Paros
Siphanto
Milo
C. Gallo
Koron Bay
Monembasia
Cape Matapan
Kolokythi B.
C. Malea
Kerigo
Santorin
Kerigotto
Grabusa
C. Spada
Khania
Pop. 6000
Suda B.
Retimo
Dia I.
C. Krio
Lutro
Sphakie
Gortyna
C. Matala
Fair Havens
Arvi
CRETE OR CA
MEDITE